The Soul of the Greeks

The Soul
of the Greeks

An Inquiry

MICHAEL DAVIS

The University of Chicago Press   Chicago and London

The University of Chicago Press, Chicago 60637
The University of Chicago Press, Ltd., London
© 2011 by The University of Chicago
All rights reserved. Published 2011.
Paperback edition 2012
Printed and bound by CPI Group (UK) Ltd, Croydon, CR0 4YY

21 20 19 18 17 16 15 14 13 12   2 3 4 5 6

ISBN-13: 978-0-226-13796-4 (cloth)
ISBN-13: 978-0-226-00449-5 (paper)

Library of Congress Cataloging-in-Publication Data
Davis, Michael, 1947–
The soul of the Greeks : an inquiry / Michael Davis.
    p.   cm.
Includes index.
ISBN-13: 978-0-226-13796-4 (cloth: alk. paper)
ISBN-10: 0-226-13796-1 (cloth: alk. paper)
1. Soul. 2. Philosophy, Ancient. 3. Greek literature—
History and criticism. 4. Soul in literature. I. Title.
B187.S6D38 2011
128'.10938—dc22   2010024178

Ode to Plato

The query rooted
assuredly in us—
whether we are still
born in a static world
or moved
to fend off
the crush of chaos—
yet sounds comical
to the human ear.

Were we born still
we were still to be born,
and the time would be
perilous little
which we,
in our infinite leisure,
might selflessly spend
on this serious riddle.

Still, we are
equally lost
when thrust
into war
against chaos,
for what one
is occupied with
at all cost
will occupy one
at the cost
of all else.

The curiosity of this perplexity is
that we find ourselves in it.

GRACIE TAPLO

Contents

Acknowledgments

I am grateful to my friends Robert Berman, Ronna Burger, and Richard Velkley, whose writings and conversations over the years have helped me to understand the enormous complexity of the problem of soul. Gwen Grewal read and studied with me many of the texts treated here and has been an invaluable interlocutor. Susan Davis has been, as always, my most honest critic. I want to thank the Earhart Foundation and Sarah Lawrence College, both of which once again have supported my work with grants. I owe thanks as well to John Tryneski and two anonymous readers for the University of Chicago Press, all of whom gently, but firmly, urged me to make the shape of the whole of *The Soul of the Greeks* clearer—I hope with some success.

Several of the book's chapters have been published in somewhat different forms. Parts of chapters 2 and 3 are altered versions of "Father of the *Logos*: The Question of the Soul in Aristotle's *Nicomachean Ethics*," *Epoché*, vol. 7, no. 2 (Spring 2003): 169–87. Versions of chapter 6 appeared as "The Fake That Launched a Thousand Ships: The Question of Identity in Euripides' *Helen*," chapter 12 of *Logos and Mythos*, edited by William Wians (Albany, NY: SUNY Press, 2009); of chapter 7 as "Euripides among the Athenians," *St. John's Review*, vol. 44, no. 2 (1998): 61–81; of chapter 8 as "The Tragedy of Law: Gyges in Herodotus and Plato," *Review of Metaphysics*, vol. 53, no. 3 (March 2000): 635–55; of chapter 9 as "On the Intention of Plato's *Cleitophon*," *Metis: Revue d'anthropologie du monde grec ancien*, vol. 13 (1998): 271–85; of chapter 10 as "Making Something from Nothing: On Plato's *Hipparchus*," *Review of Politics*, vol. 68, no. 4 (Fall 2006): 547–63; and of chapter 12 as "The Grammar of the Soul: On Plato's *Euthyphro*," in *Logos and Eros*, edited by Nalin Ranasinghe (South Bend, IN: St. Augustine's Press, 2006), 57–71.

Finally, I want to indicate my indebtedness to the late Seth Benardete—the soul was in a way his life's work. Every page of this study bears Benardete's imprint. I can only hope that the mark is true.

The Soul of Achilles

The Soul of the Greeks—the very title puts us on slippery ground. Soul? Greeks? If what follows here is meant as another historical inquiry into the difference between Greek soul and soul as it manifests itself in other cultures, is it really necessary? Haven't the Greeks been "done"? And anyway, given our postmodern sophistication, is such a comparison even possible? And if what is intended is not a historical analysis but a philosophical inquiry into the nature of soul using the Greeks as a guide, why "privilege" the Greeks? Moreover, doesn't the whole project already beg a much more fundamental question: Is there even such a thing as the soul?[1]

The question of soul in the West has been shaped by Christianity. While the Christian soul in its various incarnations clearly has great bearing on our lives, its origin in ordinary experience is less clear. As this soul is thought to be what gives us our identity over time, it is in some way not itself temporal. Nor is it bodily, for our bodies undergo constant change. Although everything around us seems enmeshed in a causal network, this soul, while itself a cause, is nevertheless not caused. It is splendidly, if mysteriously, free.

---

1 · One might wonder whether this is really a question. Consider that Aristotle's *De Anima* (in Greek, *Peri Psuchēs*, or Concerning Soul), which seems to be an attempt at a comprehensive account of soul and to be the first book devoted exclusively to soul, nowhere raises the question of the soul's existence. Aristotle looks at the world and notices two powerful distinctions among beings. Some are alive, and some are not; some are aware, and some are not. Now, even should one or both of these distinctions prove illusory—so that, for example, life can be explained completely in terms of nonliving elements—still, the appearance of a distinction so powerful must have a cause. One can say with some confidence that soul is this cause without making assumptions about what soul is. Whatever this soul is, it cannot not exist. We know this as surely as we know "the capability of being awake and receiving" when we "look into the eyes of very small children" (Jacob Klein, "Aristotle: An Introduction," in *Ancients and Moderns: Essays on the Tradition of Political Philosophy in Honor of Leo Strauss*, ed. Joseph Cropsey [New York: Basic Books, 1964], 62).

As what initiates, it is what makes us morally responsible agents, and so worthy of punishment and reward. These, in turn, are such serious matters because an immaterial, atemporal, and free soul may be understood to be immortal and so ultimately concerned not with the ephemeral needs and pleasures that we encounter in this vale of tears but with things more final and substantial. The soul with which we are familiar is serious business. There are, of course, reasons for this understanding of soul, and, while it is perhaps most available to us as the soul of Christianity, it is not so very different from what we sometimes seem to encounter elsewhere—say, in Plato's *Phaedo*. Still, it is not obvious that it reflects how we first encounter, and so first come to speak of, soul. It is not obviously the soul of everyday life. Was soul music designed to appeal to a detached, nonbodily, immortal being?[2] Might there be a more natural way to begin thinking about soul that is obscured by the tradition of soul made dominant by Christianity? While such a beginning need not be the truth of the being of soul, it might be the truth of how soul first appears. And even if first impressions prove subsequently problematic, it is always worth reflecting on why things initially appear as they appear. To ask about the soul of the Greeks, then, may provide us with a more natural beginning than is now immediately available to us. To think about anything means to begin with its appearance, to begin with certain preformed opinions about it—prejudices. If thinking moves from what only seems to be to what is, thinking must naturally begin in error, with what is not. But we come by some of these prejudices more unreflectively—in a way, more naturally—than others, which may be the result of subsequent and elaborate variations on our more immediate beginnings. An archaeology of soul might help us recover these more natural beginnings so that we may think more seriously about what it means that we take soul so seriously. If all human thought begins with opinion, with what seems, and if, as Plato suggests, to be human means to inhabit a cave and be cut off from the light of the sun, it is our current situation to be in "a cave beneath a cave."[3] The Greeks may prove useful in digging ourselves out, for the importance of soul for them is clear from the very first sentence of their first and most famous poem.

But what would such an archaeology of soul look like? It is no accident that, although we may still say things in contemporary English like "not a

---

2 · Those inclined to doubt this sort of argument—that is, to doubt the relation between the way things show up in ordinary life and their deeper reality, or between the surface and the depth—might consider the remarkable overlap between the subject of the indisputably "deep" *Oedipus tyrannus* and the most insulting of street epithets.

3 · See *Republic* 514a–518d, and Leo Strauss, *Persecution and the Art of Writing* (Glencoe, IL: Free Press, 1952), 155–57.

soul was present," such expressions strike us as a little dated (we find them reminiscent of the manner in which Russian landowners under the czar once measured the size of their estates in numbers of souls). Our language no longer seems to contain a word that comfortably covers the range that once belonged to soul. Talk of "self," while common enough, always has the flavor of reflexivity; it is always a little selfish. Whatever we mean when we talk about soul music wouldn't really be captured by "self music," and "beautiful self" lacks the grandeur of "beautiful soul." In religious contexts, we still speak of souls and mean something quite grand, but we are usually referring to the fate of our "immortal souls" and take for granted their responsibilities and attendant rewards and punishments. Does this moral soul have room in it for what we sometimes call personality? Is an idiosyncratic fondness for coffee ice cream an attribute of soul in the grand tradition? In our clinical moments, we frequently resort to "psyche," but psyches are objects of analysis; they no longer soar. That we are so interested in knowing what makes a psyche tick may suggest that psyche is too much like a clock to be a soul. If this fragmentation of meaning is an indication of the necessarily illusive character of soul, our difficulty in grasping its nature would not be accidental. Any adequate account of soul would have the seemingly oxymoronic, and hence perhaps poetic, task of articulating the principle and structure of its unity while at the same time preserving its nature as fundamentally illusive.

An example of the necessity of this illusiveness may clarify our perplexity. *The Soul of the Greeks* will return again and again to the nature of soul as alienated—as essentially apart from and at a distance from the world— but when Aristotle says, "Soul is somehow all beings" (*De Anima* 431b21), doesn't this suggest precisely the opposite of alienation—a fundamental connectedness to the world? And even if soul, as only "somehow" all things, is not fully at home, wouldn't this very disconnectedness still imply a more fundamental connectedness? Soul would have to be somehow in the world in order to feel at odds with the world. What precludes this happier version of soul as essentially at home? Why dwell in its alienation?

Soul is alienated because its deepest longing—to be one with the world— is at odds with its nature as necessarily detached from the world. Apollinian self-affirmation wars with Dionysian self-cancellation. At the same time, it is true that soul can feel detached only because it is immersed in the world. Admittedly at odds with itself, soul can be said to admit of harmony (being one with itself and unalienated) only because it *is* at odds with itself. However, this peculiar connectedness emerges only in self-conscious alienation (Socratic knowledge of ignorance is a version of this problem). *The Soul of the Greeks* thus does indeed mean to articulate soul's deep connectedness to the world—a connectedness understood in the end as philosophy—but to acknowledge too directly the power of philosophy risks so idealizing soul's position in the world that this position may seem simply desirable. Soul would be utterly at home with itself, save that no longer feeling itself problematic, it would no longer exist. It may be the case that philosophy, properly understood, fulfills our deepest longings—that it is the highest of lives; but highlighting this height makes possible a pursuit of philosophy because it is "highest" that is at odds with the pursuit of wisdom that constitutes the philosophical life as what it is. You no longer philosophize because you are moved by a question that troubles you; you rather ride in like a knight on horseback "philosophizing" because it is the most noble thing to do. Philosophy, now an object of ambition, is politicized, externalized, and transformed into something of a piece with the goals of men like Achilles and Alcibiades whose understanding of life proves tragic. Soul must have an edginess to it. Making it too neat a package, by engendering complacency with alienation, fundamentally misrepresents what it is. Edginess loses its edge when embraced with open arms. While idealizing soul is one way of fixing its structure—we put it at rest so as to make possible its comprehensive description—as soul cannot be at rest, fully to describe it, to turn it into an object, is to kill it.

There is a tension between the structure of soul and the nature of soul. On the one hand, we seek a fully discursive theory of soul—something to be kept in our back pocket or, perhaps because it is so complex, on a shelf in our library. On the other hand, shelving soul in this way saps it of the spontaneity without which it is not really soul. While it would be a mistake to let this tension between structure and nature serve as an all-purpose excuse for saying less than might be said (*The Soul of the Greeks* is, after all, a book that will be shelved), at the most fundamental level, to reveal the soul, one cannot simply speak of it. In any description of itself, soul simultaneously puts itself on display (the only question is how revealingly). Absent the display, the explanation proves hollow and lifeless. This has something to do both with the character of the argument of *The Soul of the Greeks* and with the choice of the books it discusses, for the thinkers treated here all understand that the nature of soul does not admit of being spelled out directly, that it cannot have an altogether determinate structure—whether id, ego, and superego or desiring, spirited, and rational. If it did, its actions would be perfectly intelligible and predictable, and it would cease to be soul. These thinkers nevertheless also understand that soul is something that we can come to know. We differentiate among kinds of souls; it makes sense, for example, to say that someone has a certain character even though this does not (and cannot) mean his actions are altogether predictable. Aristotle will call this a *hexis*—deriving from the verb *echein*—which means both "to have" and "to be able."[4] A soul has a certain disposition; it is something like an actualized potentiality—we have a certain ability.[5] At the same time, it also makes sense that we are so disposed because we are rooted in a particular tradition. There is thus a political aspect to soul. The tension between its fixed structure and its nature is in a way the defining feature of soul. We are Egyptians or Scythians when our behavior conforms to the customs of Egypt or of the Scythians, but Egyptians and Scythians are never perfectly Egyptian or Scythian. However much formed in determinate ways, human beings are always capable of crimes. Yet even this truth about the soul is delicate, for articulated too straightforwardly, it becomes so structural as to dissolve.

The necessary indirectness of talk about the soul has governed the selection of texts treated in *The Soul of the Greeks* as well as their order of treatment. Whether nominally history, poetry, or philosophy, these texts are all in a profound sense both poetic and philosophic. Herodotus, Plato, and Aristotle, no less than Euripides, may be said to practice the art of the muses; they "know how to speak many lies like the truth."[6] Even Aristotle (who, of the authors under consideration, no doubt seems least obviously poetic) regularly employs hyperbole (for example, his distinction between active and passive mind), coins crucial terms (for example, *eidēsis*), and writes in such a way that what is under discussion is made self-reflexively manifest in the manner of its discussion (for example, his unrelentingly dualistic treatment of various psychic dualisms at the beginning of *De Anima*).[7] Ludwig Wittgenstein once remarked that "if a man could write a book on ethics that was really a book on ethics, this book would with an explosion destroy all of the other books in the world."[8] A philosophical text on ethics— after all, Wittgenstein made this remark in his "Lecture on Ethics"—to be philosophical, would therefore have to treat its subject in an indirect and delicate manner. If, in writing about ethics, Aristotle finds it necessary to praise first greatness of soul, then justice, then prudence, and then friendship as though each were the very peak of moral virtue, this may be less owing to his confusion on the question than to his awareness that the peak of morality will look different depending on where one stands. Standing in various places, Aristotle reports the view. If his exaggerated praises are lies, they are certainly lies like the truth, "for the precise is not to be sought

4 · *Nicomachean Ethics* 1105b–1106a.
5 · *De Anima* 412a27–28.
6 · Hesiod *Theogony* 27.
7 · See chapter 1 below.
8 · Ludwig Wittgenstein, "Lecture on Ethics," *Philosophical Review* 74, no. 1 (Jan. 1965): 7.

similarly in all speeches."⁹ What Wittgenstein says of ethics may also be said of soul. Accordingly, it is not surprising that an author attempting to make the being of soul manifest might self-consciously avoid the use of the term *soul* altogether (for example, Plato in the *Euthyphro*) or perhaps mention it only once and so highlight its absence elsewhere (for example, Herodotus 2.123.2) and by so doing call attention to the fact that at the heart of the being of soul is a resistance to being named—objectified. Sometimes a presence is made most fully manifest by way of an obtrusive absence, and with regard to the discussion of certain phenomena, the poetic way is sometimes the most philosophic way. In thinking about soul, we discover more than anywhere else that thinking itself is something more fundamental than the conventional distinctions among the poetic, the philosophical, and the historical to which we have grown so accustomed.

Homer, Aristotle, Herodotus, Euripides, and Plato are all thinkers of this order. This list is not exhaustive—there is, for example, no reason in principle why *The Soul of the Greeks* could not include chapters on Hesiod, Pindar, and Sappho; on Aeschylus, Sophocles, and Aristophanes; on Parmenides and Heracleitus; on Xenophon or on Thucydides. There is also no reason in principle for the exclusion of other texts by the authors who are included—the *Odyssey*, the *Rhetoric*, the *Bacchae*, and the *Phaedo*, for example, come immediately to mind. But *The Soul of the Greeks* is not meant to be a comprehensive survey on what the Greeks thought about soul; it is rather an attempt to recover a problem by way of thinking through in whole or in part twelve texts that are especially complementary in their understandings of this problem.

In the introduction, we begin at the beginning, with Homer, because in the *Iliad*, what proves to be the central problem of soul first comes to light—its nature as longing for, but necessarily falling short of, perfection. Before tragedy, the soul of Achilles was tragic. We then turn in part 1 to Aristotle. It is useful to begin with *De Anima*, for, while it may be the last written of the texts considered, it is the first to raise the question of soul in a direct and nonancillary way. Because it explicitly raises a series of problems that would need to be addressed in any discussion of soul, it helps us to see how the tentacles of necessary imperfection might reach into every aspect of soul as ordinarily experienced—whether as living, sensing, thinking, or moral. With this map in hand of the range of what is at stake, we turn to two thinkers, Herodotus (part 2) and Euripides (part 3), in whom soul as an issue is understated or not stated at all but who nevertheless are much concerned with issues at the heart of the imperfection of soul—rest and motion, identity and change. In thinking deeply about the human things,

9 · Aristotle *Nicomachean Ethics* 1094b14.

Herodotus and Euripides are psychologists in the original sense. We see in Herodotus and Euripides the continuation of a theme that begins to emerge in Aristotle's *Nicomachean Ethics*—the manner in which soul is formed by *nomoi*, customs or laws. Euripides and Herodotus are particularly well paired, for the *Helen* is Euripides' gloss on book 2 of Herodotus (he sees the relation between the longing for stability that characterizes Herodotus's Egypt and the longing for fixed personal identity that is the focus of the *Helen*), and the *Iphigeneia* is Euripides' gloss on book 4 (at the heart of both is the question of the human longing for freedom and its connection to our necessarily poetic self-understanding). Finally, in part 4, we turn to Plato—first to his appropriation of Herodotus's Gyges story in the *Republic* and its weaving together of the questions of law and of *erōs* (one a principle of stability, the other of change); then to a pair of dialogues, *Cleitophon* and *Hipparchus* (one exploring the consequences for soul of a world in which justice was completely objective, the other the consequences for soul of a world in which the good was completely subjective); then to the *Phaedrus* (for Plato's account of *erōs* as the structure of the soul's self-movement); and finally to the *Euthyphro* (which teaches us that soul is not a combination of active and passive principles but must be understood as a more fundamental unity that grounds this distinction).

The Soul of the Greeks concludes with Plato, for in Plato the various manifestations of the imperfection of soul ultimately all point to the activity of philosophy—what happens when soul, always at odds with itself, thinks through what it means that it is necessarily at odds with itself. *The Soul of the Greeks* is an ambiguous title. Does the book it names mean to address the Greek understanding of soul, or is its subject the soul as it becomes manifest among the Greeks—the soul specific to Greek "culture"? But are these two finally distinct? Philosophy can be always somehow about itself because "the soul is somehow all beings." Plato understood that any inquiry into soul is finally not separable from an inquiry into the world. In the end, to study the soul of the Greeks is to study what studies the soul. Plato's *Symposium*, to which we turn briefly in the conclusion, provides us a final glimpse of this soul by way of Acibiades' profound misunderstanding of the soul of Socrates. We discover what it means for Socrates to replace Achilles as the paradigm of soul. This movement from Achilles to Socrates reveals what is in a way the deepest level of the question of soul. But we are getting ahead of ourselves. Let us return to the beginning, the soul of Achilles.

The first word of the first extant work of Greek literature is *mēnis*, "wrath" or "anger." *Mēnis* occurs twelve times in the *Iliad*—four times describing

Achilles (1.1, 1.517, 19.35, 19.75) and everywhere else describing a god. Accordingly, it seems worth asking what Achilles, and Achilles alone, might share with the gods. The *Iliad* is the story of a choice. Achilles seems to know before he comes to Troy that he will either return home to Phthia and live a long life without glory or remain with the army and gain immortal glory but at the cost of his own death (9.410–20). While Achilles does not so much choose death as the manner of his death, our first impression is still that in choosing glory, *kleos*, he thinks himself to choose a kind of immortality. Achilles longs to overcome death. Homer thus uses him as a paradigm for what moves he-men (*andres*) generally. Their longing for glory sets them apart from ordinary human beings (*anthropoi*) and signals their wish to live as gods. The tension between god and he-man is echoed by the distinction between he-man and human being, which, in turn, points to a tension within human beings as such. As an exemplar of this human quality, Achilles is in some way essentially human. And yet, as an exemplar, he is also in some way qualitatively different from what he exemplifies. Achilles, as the man who wished to transcend his humanity, is exemplary of humanity. The *Iliad* is the story of man's striving for what seems highest, for an immortality that preserves one's greatness as a person. It is the story of a man's attempt to become a god—a perfect soul—which, by virtue of being perfect, will no longer be human.

Given this aspiration, it is curious that nowhere in the *Iliad* or the *Odyssey* or, for that matter, in any text extant in all of Greek literature prior to the dialogues of Plato is a god ever said to have a soul. And even in Plato, the attribution is rare and arguably ironical.[10] In the first sentence of the *Iliad*, Homer urges an unnamed goddess to sing of the *mēnis* of Achilles, a wrath that sent many worthy souls—*psuchai*—to Hades.[11] Perhaps *psuchē* here is not yet quite "soul"; it is frequently thought rather to mean something like

---

10 · See *Euthydemus* 302d1–302e3, *Symposium* 195e4–7, and *Timaeus* 29d7–30c1 and 40b8–41a6. See also *Phaedrus* 245c, where Socrates speaks of the "nature of the soul concerning both the divine and the human," and 246a, where he introduces an image for soul (two horses and a charioteer) and then speaks of the horses of the gods. Immediately thereafter (247b), Socrates first speaks of the "toil and struggle" set before the soul and then goes on to speak of "those called immortal" who stand on the back of heaven. It is of note that he does not name them as souls. He goes on to juxtapose the "thinking of god by mind" with that of every soul (247d) and the "life of the gods" with "other souls" (248a).

11 · At 2.484–93, with respect to the catalog of ships, Homer comments on the difference between what he reports and what the Muses report. The Muses know all; Homer's knowledge (and presumably ours as well) depends on *kleos*—that is, on what is said, or rumor, but also fame. Homer's account, the poetic account, proves to aggrandize the role of leaders as agents.

"the breath of life." Homer does use a collection of words to refer to what one might call our inner life—*thumos, phrēn, ētor, noos, kardiē, kradiē*, and *kēr*; depending on the context, they may mean "spirit," "breast," "mind," "heart," or "the seat of our life"—what animates us. Still, by the time of the classic age of Greek literature in the fifth century, *psuchē* has become the most important of these words by far. And it has a splendid future, for it is the word that Christianity will adopt in the New Testament.[12] It is thus of some interest that of the thirty-three times *psuchē* appears in the *Iliad*, thirty have to do directly with dying or avoiding death.[13] Of the remaining three instances, one is Hector asking Achilles to swear by his *psuchē* that he will return Hector's corpse to the Trojans when he dies (Achilles refuses), one is Achilles claiming that a man's *psuchē* cannot be brought back after it passes the wall of his teeth, and one is an account of Andromache's *psuchē* departing when she faints after she has seen the corpse of her husband. So, in a way, all thirty-three occurrences have to do with death or the appearance of death. From the very beginning, then, *psuchē* is connected to human mortality and, insofar as we seek to avoid and overcome death, therewith to incompleteness and imperfection. Insofar as soul makes an appearance in the *Iliad*, it seems to mean imperfect soul.

The plot of the *Iliad* divides in three.[14] The Greeks go to war against the Trojans for the sake of Helen. Whether understood in terms of *erōs* (of Paris, of Helen, of Menelaus, or of some combination) or in terms of justice (that is, of retribution for the violation of the law of *xenia*—guest-friendship), the initial cause of the war is grounded in the particulars of a specific situation and demands a specific resolution. The first three books of the *Iliad* display the gradual erosion of this framework. Helen belongs to Menelaus as a matter of conventional right, but the poem begins with a challenge to conventional right as Achilles' quarrel with Agamemnon sets at odds conventional rank and natural superiority. In book 3, the story of the *monomachia* between Paris and Menelaus, this tension comes to a head, for as soon as Menelaus agrees to settle the question of Helen by personal combat with Paris, he relinquishes any claim to her that is grounded in right. That he proves to be Paris's superior in combat does not mean Mene-

---

12 · *Psuchē* occurs 105 times in the New Testament. It is not always translated as "soul," but generally there is no other word in the text translated by "soul." See E. W. Bullinger, ed., *The Companion Bible* (Grand Rapids, MI: Kregel Publications, 1993), appendix 110.

13 · 1.3, 5.296, 5.654, 5.696, 7.330, 8.123, 8.315, 9.322, 9.401, 9.408, 11.333, 11.445, 13.763, 14.518, 16.453, 16.505, 16.625, 16.856, 21.569, 22.161, 22.257, 22.325, 22.338, 22.362, 22.467, 23.54, 23.72, 23.100, 23.104, 23.106, 23.221, 24.168, and 24.754.

14 · For this division, see Seth Benardete, *Achilles and Hector: The Homeric Hero* (South Bend, IN: St. Augustine's Press, 2005), 85–90.

laus has a legal right to Helen. If the war is about Helen in particular, then settling the question of Helen should end the war. The ground rules set for the contest between Paris and Menelaus confirm this (3.67–110). Whoever wins will get Helen and her possessions; Trojans and Greeks will then become friends. But Homer shows us that, while Helen may have launched the war, once launched, this war, and perhaps all war, acquires a life of its own, for after the failure of the *monomachia* (Aphrodite spirits Paris away), another principle is at work in the conflict, the paradigm for which is the second *monomachia* in book 7, where Hector and Ajax fight solely for the sake of glory—*kleos*. In the second stage of the poem, men fight not only to be "best and preeminent among men" but also to make their preeminence known. They fight for immortal glory. Of this sort of war, there is in principle no end, for the question of justice, the answer to which might settle things, has disappeared. After they fight, Ajax and Hector can exchange gifts to indicate their mutual esteem. They do not hate each other; they even recognize that, in a way, they are alike in their deepest longing.

After Hector and Ajax fight, the transition begins to the final stage of the poem, where the war changes its character once more. When Achilles returns to avenge the death of Patroclus, a return foretold by Zeus to Hera at the end of book 8 (473–77), the war once again has a particular goal and so a potential end. As Seth Benardete puts it,

> The love for Helen turns into the love for fame, which in turn becomes Achilles' love for Patroclus. From *erōs* to *erōs kleous* ("love of fame") to *erōs* is the cycle of the *Iliad*; but how Achilles' *erōs* unites the other two will be our final problem.[15]

The movement of the poem first traces the origin of heroic longing as love of *kleos* and then reveals the tragedy of this longing in the tragedy of Achilles. One can begin to see the root of this tragedy by reflecting on the transformation in the *mēnis* of Achilles. He is not initially angry at the Trojans—his putative enemies; they are for him just the opportunity to display his virtue. The anger of the poem's first line is directed at Agamemnon, who claims precedence over an obviously superior Achilles. Achilles resents his dependence on conventional men and conventional distinctions. He therefore withdraws, for he is bigger than the battle that surrounds him. When Patroclus is killed, Achilles' anger is redirected at Hector and the Trojans. But Patroclus dies because he seeks to save the Greeks from the catastrophe Achilles has brought upon them. Achilles is in an awkward position. The Greeks are losing badly, and it seems to be his fault. If things continue as they are going at the end of book 15, Achilles' immortal glory will give way

15 · Benardete, *Achilles and Hector*, 90.

to ignominy. And yet he cannot return to the battle without acknowledging Agamemnon as his lord and so losing face. Patroclus is for him the perfect solution, for when he begs for Achilles' armor so that he may pretend to be Achilles, it becomes possible for Achilles to remain apart from the battle while "Achilles" returns to save the day. If even a simulacrum of Achilles is sufficient to rout the Trojans, what must this mean about the virtue of the real Achilles? Achilles thus accepts Patroclus's proposal. The problem, however, is that by accepting, he places Patroclus's life in jeopardy and knows that he does so.[16]

> May the gods not bring to pass evil troubles for my spirit, as my mother once made clear to me and told me that while I yet lived, the best of the Myrmidons would leave the light of the sun at the hands of the Trojans. (18.8–11)

Moreover, Achilles lies to himself about what he has done, for, while he claims to have warned Patroclus not to fight with Hector (18.13–14), in fact he said nothing about Hector at all (16.80–96). And when Patroclus asks him whether he has some prophecy that makes him reluctant to lend his armor (16.36–39), Achilles flatly denies having any such knowledge (16.49–51). When Patroclus dies, then, at whom is Achilles really angry? When Achilles takes revenge by killing Hector, we are told that he knew precisely where to strike because he knew the weakness of his own armor, the armor Hector wears because he has stripped it from the body of the dead Patroclus (22.320–27). We also know that the armor of the time hides the man beneath it, for the Trojans initially believed Patroclus to be Achilles.[17] Accordingly, when Achilles confronts Hector, what he really confronts is himself insofar as he is revealed by his armor. He confronts "Achilles." The *Iliad* thus marks Achilles' gradual discovery that a self-idealized version of himself is the true object of his *mēnis*.

This tragedy begins first, however, with the problematic status of love of fame as a means to immortality. At the beginning of book 6, it is the Trojans who are in trouble—they have just suffered the *aristeia* of Diomedes in book 5, and now fifteen of them die in quick succession. Hector is far and away the most able of their warriors, and yet on the advice of Helenos, the seer, he returns to Troy.[18] After first arranging for the women to

16 · Ibid., 106–9, 111–15.

17 · It will prove important that Astynax, Hector's infant son, is frightened by Hector in his armor and wearing a helmet. He does not recognize his father and cries (6.467–73).

18 · That Hector should become a messenger in the middle of a desperate battle seems a strange use of resources—unless perhaps he who is best in deeds is thought also to best describe deeds. I owe this observation to Charlie Gustafson-Barrett.

prepare a sacrifice to Athena, Hector has a conversation with his brother, Paris, in which it becomes clear how little the charms of Helen affect him (6.359–68)—Helen is no longer the issue; she has become a mere spectator of the unfolding events (6.323–24). Hector is hot to return to the battle, but in a famous scene, before leaving the city, he spends a moment with his wife, Andromache, and his infant son, Astynax (6.390–502). We are meant to see how fond he is of his son, for whom he even has a pet name; while all others call him Astynax, Hector calls him Skamandrios. Weeping out of fear for Hector's life, Andromache begs him to remain in the city. Achilles already has slain her father and her seven brothers, and Artemis has struck down her mother. Hector, she says, is now her whole family—he is father, mother, brother, and husband to her. With shocking candor, Hector admits that he will not save Troy—that his mother, father, and brothers will perish, and Andromache will be carried off (he does not mention the fate of his son and a few lines later even expresses his hope that Astynax will surpass him as a leader of the Trojans). Nevertheless, Hector does not waver in his intent to reenter the battle. As solace to Andromache, he announces that "sometime someone will say, seeing your tears pour down, 'This is the wife of Hector, who was the best in fighting of the Trojans, breakers of horses, when they fought about Ilion'" (6.459–61). Unlike Helen and Paris, Hector is not erotic. Nor is he particularly moved by the fate of his family or his city. "For I know this well in my mind and in my heart; there will be a day when sacred Ilion will perish . . ." (6.447–48). For Hector, there remains but one thing—immortal glory. The true Hector—the potentially immortal, and so permanent, Hector—is Hector armed for battle. Yet when this Hector reaches out to take his son in his arms, Astynax wails and withdraws from the frightening figure of his father's plumed helmet. Hector in armor is somehow not real; he is only "Hector." Permanence, apparently, will come at a cost.

Book 7 contains the second great *monomachia* of the *Iliad*, the battle between Hector and Ajax. It is not insignificant that in proposing it, Hector refers to himself in the third person. Standing outside himself as though to contemplate himself, he challenges the Greeks to choose someone to fight "brilliant Hector" (7.75) in one-on-one combat. This is not the *monomachia* of book 3.[19] Here there is no talk of ending the war. The ground rules too are different: whoever wins will strip the armor from the other but return his corpse for burning or burial. Hector glosses this by saying that should he win, the following will happen when the Greeks bury Ajax in a tomb or mound (a *sēma*, or sign):

19 · Benardete, *Achilles and Hector*, 88–89.

And at a future time, one of those human beings seeing [the *sēma*], one sailing in his many-benched ship on the wine-dark sea, will say, "This is the *sēma* of a man who died long ago. Shining Hector killed him who was once one of the best." Thus will someone at some time speak, and my *kleos* will never perish. (7.89–91)

In order that Hector's *kleos* not perish, there will be two signs: the funeral mound of his opponent and the armor that Hector will strip from him and hang in front of the temple of Apollo (7.83). Hector thus acknowledges that his immortality depends on, or even consists in, signs. Not he but a *sēma* will last forever; not Hector but his name will "live" on.

At the end of book 7, Poseidon complains to Zeus that in the guise of a funeral mound, the Greeks have built a wall around their camp that threatens to rival the wall he and Apollo previously built around Troy. Furthermore, these clever Greeks have artfully used the truce declared to bury the dead to enhance their defenses. A sign of human mortality has been turned into a display of defiance. This undermines the respect owed to the gods. Zeus replies to his brother that he need not worry, for human *kleos* is ephemeral, while his will last as long as there is a dawn. The wall of the Greeks will be worn away by the sea (as in fact will Poseidon's wall as well). But the sea, of which Poseidon is the lord, will last forever.[20] Accordingly, Hector's claim to immortality earlier in the book represents an enormous exaggeration. Signs do not have such power. Now, on the one hand, this means that no physical monument can grant immortality. On the other hand, we are meant to be reminded of book 6. Even if Helen is right when she claims that she and Paris will "hereafter be sung of by human beings in the future" (6.357–58), only their names will live on. They will not. There is something hollow in the immortality of immortal fame. Immortality in speech by way of a sign preserves the shell of a man—his helm—but not his person. It preserves "Hector" but not Hector. Minus a name, a monument does not preserve a memory. Without explanation—words—mounds (*semata*) do not memorialize. They are not signs at all but only piles of dirt. Even if poetry, the *Iliad*, is the true monument, this means that Hector depends on a poet for his immortality; he is not preserved as "best and preeminent among men" but as the creature of a wordsmith. What about the wordsmith, then? Since the poet is responsible for the preservation of his own deed, his poem, doesn't the *Iliad* immortalize Homer? One is at first tempted to say yes but then reminded of the old joke that the poem was written not by Homer but by another poet of the same name. The person Homer is not immortalized in the name Homer. The attempt to become

20 · Ibid., 89.

immortal in one's particularity seems willy-nilly to lead to something like generic immortality. The Caesar who first ruled the world "lives on" not as a soul but only as a name, which, in turn, displays its curious reality by giving way to various caesars, czars, and Kaisers.

The problem deepens as the *Iliad* takes us still one step further. The truce in book 7 is for the purpose of honoring the individual dead. On the advice of Nestor, however, the Greeks construct a mass grave that serves also as a defensive wall. This mound is at best a generic honor, and so, if the enemy here is death, it is not clear that their defense works. We are reminded of Zeus's remark to Poseidon. If the sea is the model for immortality, then what becomes of the gods as individuals, as persons? In book 5, Diomedes wounds Aphrodite, who, depending on how one translates *ambroton haima*, bleeds either "immortal blood" or "bloodless blood" (5.339); she is characterized by an oxymoron.[21] Diomedes then proceeds to wound Ares, whom Homer addresses at the beginning of book 5 as "Ares Ares" (5.31). A repetition of a vocative occurs only twice in Homer—both times of Ares and both times in book 5.[22] It is as though we are meant to take the first "Ares" as a proper name and the second as generic, as "war." We are witness to Aphrodite being forced to withdraw from battle as a person and to Ares becoming generic. Neither of the two ever return to battle human beings in the *Iliad*.[23] In book 7, Zeus thunders for the first time in the poem (7.479); his thunder will be far more prominent in book 8. Thus, as the *Iliad* moves away from gods as persons toward gods as cosmic principles, it echoes on the level of the gods the problem of immortality on the level of human beings. That Hector seems to disappear in "Hector" suggests that immortality is incompatible with life—with soul. But then what would it mean for the gods to be immortal? And if not immortal, how would they be gods? If the imperishability of his *kleos* depends on being identified with the sea, Poseidon may have more to worry about than Zeus acknowledges. Human beings (*anthrōpoi*) long for immortality, and some of them (*andres*) try to do something about their longing. The model at which they aim is the gods. The *Iliad*, behind its own back (because it needs them for the unraveling of its story), brings the very possibility of the existence of the gods into question.

In the final stage of the *Iliad*, we witness Achilles' tragic attempt to reconcile a splendid but lifeless and only nominal immortality with the humanity signified by the particularity of his love of Patroclus. When Patroclus enters the battle wearing Achilles' armor in book 16, he kills more Trojans

21 · Seth Benardete, "The Aristeia of Diomedes," in *The Argument of the Action* (Chicago and London: University of Chicago Press, 2000), 56.

22 · See also 5.455 as well as G. S. Kirk, *The Iliad: A Commentary*, vol. 2, *Books 5–8* (Cambridge, UK: Cambridge University Press, 1990), 56.

23 · Benardete, "Aristeia of Diomedes," 48.

(fifty-two) faster than occurs in any other *aristeia* of the *Iliad*. This is all the more surprising because there is no hint before this that he possesses such prowess. We have seen him previously as a domestic partner, as one who prepares Achilles' food and drink (9.199–211) and does his bidding by fetching Briseis when she must be returned to Agamemnon (1.335–50). As soon as Apollo strips him of Achilles' armor (16.793–805), however, Patroclus is killed easily and without much opposition. Book 16 is thus an *aristeia* not of Patroclus but of Achilles' armor. It is a testimony to the power of Achilles' reputation—his *doxa*, or seeming. The greatness of Achilles, however, brings with it the problem of Achilles: how can a great man show himself as great once he is thought already to be great? Once Achilles becomes the measure of praise, it is almost impossible for him to do anything that will be praised. His virtue becomes his nature.

Zeus's great concern for Achilles conceals, even to himself, a profoundly selfish motive, for at the bottom of this concern lies the problem of his own existence. Achilles is a test case for Zeus's own possibility. The poem reveals in various ways two sources of "action." On the one hand, natural forces like the sea simply behave in a certain way owing to their natures; they are what they are. They are governed rather by necessity than by intention. On the other hand, there is choice—persons as causes. Initially, gods seem to be the combination of these two—they are perfect beings with fixed natures who nevertheless have souls and make choices. The last part of the *Iliad* is concerned with the extent to which these two can really be combined. Achilles, as both the standard against which all heroes are measured and a hero himself, is the battleground on which the possibility of this combination is tested. Achilles' reputation, what he seems to be, is so powerful as to be in no way lacking. His armor, his exterior shell, terrifies his enemies. However, this means that he need no longer do anything at all; his success is altogether mechanical—soulless. There is therefore no place for him in battle. Prior to the death of Patroclus, then, Achilles has become like a force of nature. He is all outside and no inside. It is Zeus's plan to use the death of Patroclus to restore Achilles' soul and therewith demonstrate his own possibility.

This is the meaning of the structure of the *Iliad*. The principle of books 1–3 is *erōs*. Helen is the purpose, the external goal, of the war; here Menelaus is prominent. From book 4 to book 15, there is no external goal to action. The principle of the war is *kleos*. Helen disappears after book 6, and, with one interesting exception (13.581–642), Menelaus recedes from view. The fighting has no goal but to show one's splendor—to live up to one's epithet, one's armor, and become like a force of nature. In books 16–24, Achilles seeks to show his fixed nature, not for its own sake but out of love of Patroclus. He thus tries to synthesize principles of the first two stages of the poem. This synthesis is not easy to understand; the Trojans, for example, mistaking Patroclus for Achilles, think that Achilles has "put aside anger and chosen love" (16.282). They do not realize that Achilles will put aside anger for love only out of anger. Achilles cannot enter the battle without armor, his external shell. It will be fashioned by the defective god, Hephaestus, who forges an image on the shield in which he likens himself to a mortal, Daedalus (18.590–605, 18.378, and 18.479). Achilles' new armor is meant to represent the new object of his longing—perfect humanity, the idealizing of the defective. Hephaestus is now the paradigmatic god.

In his lament, Achilles remembers Patroclus as serving him food (19.315–18). Just prior to this, Odysseus unsuccessfully urges Achilles to eat, remarking that men need food if they are to fight (19.162–63). Patroclus makes Achilles human; he attaches him to his humanity. Agamemnon is *the* conventional ruler, Hector *the* enemy, Briseis *the* object of love (19.282), but Patroclus is a particular that cannot be subsumed under a class. This is what it means to love another.[24] In feeding Achilles, Patroclus makes him real. When Patroclus dies, however, with what is Achilles in love? The difficult-to-describe attachment to a person is transformed into an attachment to the idea of a person. Once humanized by love of a human being, Achilles rages on behalf of a lost love. It is no longer a particular, incomplete, and contingent being who moves him; he is now moved by the idea of particularity, incompleteness, and contingency. For Achilles, the heroic life once meant becoming like a god; now it means the redemption of the human by avenging the loss of the human. Achilles' ideal has now become "attachment to humanity" and shows itself in his insatiable grief for Patroclus.

In this final version of his *mēnis*, Achilles the exemplar of heroic action gives way to Achilles the exemplar of human mourning. If really to love another means to love another as a soul—a person—loving the dead proves problematic. And if loving the dead is problematic, to seek to overcome death by way of immortal glory is a fool's errand. In the last two books of the *Iliad*, we discover the tragedy of human mourning, for it does not seem possible really to mourn a person. The act of mourning turns the object of sorrow into just that, an object. What was previously a soul becomes a sign or a tomb—a *sēma*.[25] Perhaps we find it so difficult to speak our sorrow because to speak of a soul necessarily involves leaving out what is most important about it. This is the necessary sadness of our humanity that the longing for immortality seeks to overcome but tragically simply re-creates.

24 · If the mother points to the attachment to one's own because it is one's own—Antigone and Clytemnestra come to mind—then it is important that Achilles' mother is a god. There will be a problem with turning particular attachment into a principle.
25 · See Plato *Gorgias* 493a–e.

If we wish to be gods, the sadness of death is like Achilles' inability to cease punishing Hector. It is without limit, for, absent the soul, there is no punishing a body. Achilles' anger requires that he invent a proper object for it. To do this, he must make the body (*sōma*) a sign (*sēma*) of the person. To make what he hates visible to himself, he thus turns it into something undeserving of hatred. Something similar happens with his love. When Patroclus dies, Achilles discovers Hades, where Patroclus longs to be allowed to go. But when a soul passes into Hades, it becomes an *eidōlon*—an image. Like a character on a movie screen, it has a semblance of life but lacks what is the most distinctive feature of life—the hope characteristic of an open future. Its story is complete—written. Achilles would perhaps change nothing of what he does that leads to his own death; nevertheless, the *eidōlon* of Achilles in *Odyssey* 11 would rather be a day laborer than king of all those in Hades. This is simply a version of the issue that winds like a thread through the entire *Iliad*—the oxymoronic character of the gods. The *Iliad* is the tragedy of heroic virtue. Like Oedipus, who, having recognized that he overreached in his attempt to control his own life, proceeds to seek to take control of his own punishment, Achilles comes to recognize the hollowness of the immortality of godlike *kleos* only to reproduce it in his celebration of the human. Achilles struggles with human imperfection; he attempts to perfect it. Zeus looks on with great interest because the gods are nothing but the perfection of the human. Achilles must fail, and so Homer creates a poem in which Zeus comes to recognize his own impossibility; this amounts to the discovery of the human soul.

PART ONE

ARISTOTLE

As we have seen, the Greek poets were preoccupied with soul from the very beginning. *Psuchē* is conspicuous in the first lines of both the *Iliad* and the *Odyssey*.[1] Soul proves equally important for the philosophers[2]—although even in Plato, where it looms especially large, soul is always treated as instrumental to an inquiry into something else. Soul comes to be thematic in the *Republic*, but for the purpose of addressing the question "What is justice?" Similarly, in the *Phaedrus* and the *Phaedo*, the discussions of soul are used to further the accounts of love and of the fear of death. Not until Aristotle's *De Anima* is the question of soul broached directly. By itself and apart from all else, soul is addressed for its own sake and in its own right. Accordingly, it will be useful to begin our inquiry into soul with Aristotle.

Isolating soul as Aristotle does proves not so straightforward, for soul is a strange sort of being—at once embedded in the world and connected

1 · Achilles sends many souls to Hades; Odysseus seeks to save his own soul. There is considerable disagreement about what Homer means by *psuchē* and about how self-conscious he is in using the term. See, for example, Seth Benardete, *The Bow and the Lyre* (Lanham, MD: Rowman & Littlefield, 1997), 1–6; Erwin Rohde, *Psyche* (Eugene, OR: Wipf and Stock, 2006), 1:1–10, 1:28–32, and 2:362–67; and Bruno Snell, *The Discovery of the Mind* (New York: Harper, 1960), 9–17 and 311n8. Hesiod is a more difficult case. The word *psuchē* does not occur in the *Theogony* and occurs only once in the *Works and Days* (686), where because it is coupled with mortality, it seems to mean "life." It is a serious question for both Hesiod and Homer whether the gods can be said to have souls.

2 · At the beginning of *De Anima* (I.2–5), Aristotle discusses the views of his predecessors on soul and includes Democritus, Leucippus, the Pythagoreans, Empedocles, Anaxagoras, and Plato. Parmenides does not use the term *psuchē* in the fragments we have, but that he is concerned with soul in some sense was clear to Plato, who made the proem of Parmenides' poem the model for his image of the soul in the *Phaedrus*. Heracleitus explicitly mentions *psuchē* in seven fragments (Hermann Diels, *Fragmente der Vorsokratiker* [University of Michigan Library, 1903], fragments 12, 36, 77, 98, and 136, but especially 45 and 115).

to things and at the same time sufficiently detached so as to be able both to take things in or apprehend them (whether by way of sensation or by way of cognition) and affect them or move them without thereby being affected by them. Soul is characterized by a double detachment; at once theoretical and practical, it is responsible for two apparently different sorts of things—thoughts and actions—and it is far from obvious how these two fit together. As we shall see, this problem is central not only to Aristotle's *De Anima* but also to his *Nicomachean Ethics*.

· CHAPTER I ·

The Doubleness of Soul

The problem of the dual function of soul is the soul of *De Anima*. Roughly speaking, Aristotle understands *psuchē* as a principle of life or motion and a principle of awareness. Awareness, in turn, is double, dividing into the sensing of changing things and the cognition of unchanging things. The unity of the soul as aware is thus no less problematic than the unity of the soul as a whole. Sensation, in turn, is not unproblematically one. To be at all, it must first be unified in the common sense, for without a sense to unite the other senses, we would see red, touch softness, and smell sweetness but have no sensation of a flower as being something red, soft, and sweet-smelling. Now, if there were a separate organ of sensation for the common sense, it would have to sense the various acts of sensing it unifies—for example, sight seeing and touch feeling. The senses always have objects, and every act of sensing is defined by the object sensed. The common sense would thus both sense the act of seeing and in doing so also sense what the act of seeing sees—color. And yet if it, as a kind of sense, can have this double power, why isn't this possible for the various particular senses themselves? If there is a sense that can sense seeing, why cannot this sense be the sense of sight? Why needlessly complicate things? Yet, if the common sense does not have this double power, then another sense will be required to unify what it senses. This sense, in turn, would be subject to the same difficulty, and we would have begun an infinite regress. All of this suggests what Aristotle says quite explicitly at the very beginning of his account of the common sense—that is, that each of the senses both senses its object and senses itself sensing (425b12–20). In other words, sensation is itself fundamentally double in its nature. Aristotle, it seems, is reflecting on the status of the "I" in the following conversation: "Do you see the bird?" "No, but I'm looking. Oh, now I see it."[1] We are aware of seeing through its successful taking in of an object—here, the bird. But we are also aware of it as an operation, as a

---

1 · I owe this observation to Seth Benardete.

verb. "I'm looking for x" does not mean "I see x." Sensation is thus double. At the same time, it is one, for the "I" must be the same not only of "I am looking" and of "I see" but also of "I hear," "I touch," and so forth. Aristotle wishes to give a coherent account of soul by itself. To do so, he articulates the unity of its two functions—as a principle both of life and of awareness. But this unity requires that he first unify each of these parts in turn. The unity of life requires the unification of nutrition and local motion—plant life and animal life. The unity of awareness requires the unification of the two parts of awareness—sensation and cognition. This, in turn, requires the unification of sensation by way of the common sense, which proves to be possible only by way of an analysis of sensation as fundamentally dual in its own right. And, as we will see, the other part of awareness, cognition, is intelligible only as itself embodying the fundamental dualism—passive mind and active mind. It begins to look as though in *De Anima* the sought-for unity of soul shows itself only as the repeated unfolding of the problem of the unity of soul.

To understand soul, then, would require that we understand the principle that fuels this ongoing dualism. As a start, one might observe that life or motion seems to involve a particular and interested engagement with the world. Roughly speaking, the principle governing a being that needs nourishment is its good. On the other hand, awareness requires a certain neutrality to things that will not get in the way of their showing themselves as they are. But how is it possible for a being with a particular disposition or bent to be so self-effacing as to be "somehow all beings"?[2] Won't the good proper to my nature interfere with the truth of my awareness? Put differently, how is it possible for awareness to be "mine" and still true? What sort of being is it that in order to be what it is—that is, something that takes things in—cannot be anything in particular? Can something that is potentially everything actually be anything? Or, if soul somehow becomes whatever it is aware of, what is it when it is not aware of anything in particular?

There is yet another way of getting at this tension within soul. It makes a certain sense that the principle of soul should be self-motion. Ensouled beings are alive—animated; they grow or have local motion or sense or think or combine these features in some way. They are in this way unlike things that are not alive, which seem to move or change only when they are affected from without by other things. Now, in order to understand this movement—to make it intelligible—we characteristically engage in some version of psychology. We give a *logos*, or account, of *psuchē*; ordinarily, it takes the form of an analysis of soul in terms of its structure. The terms of the analysis vary, but whether we have in mind Freud's id, ego, and superego

2 · See *De Anima* 431b20–21.

or the black horse, white horse, and charioteer in Socrates' famous image of the soul in the *Phaedrus*, once divided into its parts, one part of the soul is understood to be the cause of the motion of the whole. But if the black horse or the id is the principle of the soul's motion in the sense that the other parts simply regulate this more fundamental drive, we still do not know what moves the black horse. We are once more at the beginning of an infinite regress. In giving our account of the structure of soul, we have destroyed the principle of the soul as self-moving, for either the soul is not the soul—so, for example, the black horse is really the soul—or the soul is moved by something other than itself, and so is not the principle of its own motion, and so is not the soul.

One might put this in more contemporary terms. When we say that our libido or our DNA is responsible for what we do, part of what we generally mean is that *we* are not responsible. To give an explanation—a *logos*—of the behavior of soul turns out to be at odds with the soul's being a soul. There thus looks to be a necessary tension between the structure of soul (what would make it intelligible) and the principle of soul (what makes it soul).[3] What sort of account might then be given of this remarkable being that can at once place it in a context (this is, after all, what we do when we explain things) and at the same time preserve its nature as the being in the world the being of which is to be detached from the world? If, in Aristotle's famous sentence, "the soul is somehow all beings," then the nature and possibility of psychology lie in the meaning of this "somehow."

The first sentence of *De Anima* already reveals the dualisms that make soul a problem.

> Supposing *eidēsis* to be one of the beautiful and honored things, one more than another either on account of precision or by belonging to either the better or more wondrous, on account of both of these, the inquiry about soul would with good reason be put among the first.

De Anima is not an obviously beautiful piece of writing. It is an ugly book that literally begins with the word *beautiful*.[4] By praising the inquiry in the way that he does, Aristotle offers us an inducement to think about soul. The inquiry does not simply happen by itself; we must be moved to think. Our own activity is in its way an example of the problem we are about to address—soul as being a principle at once of motion and of awareness. Ac-

3 · The tension between structure and principle is Seth Benardete's formulation.
4 · See Michael Golluber, "On the Primary Place of Touch in Aristotle's Primary Inquiry into Soul: An Interpretation of Aristotle's *De Anima*" (PhD diss., Tulane University, 1998), 29–36; and Patrick Goodin, "Towards an Understanding of Aristotle's Definition of Soul in *De Anima*, Book 2, Chapter 1" (PhD diss., Graduate Faculty, New School for Social Research, 1996), 7–8.

cordingly, when Aristotle homes in on the object of inquiry in *De Anima*, he says first that it is "one of the most difficult things to grasp with any confidence" (402a10–11) and directly after that what is sought is "the seeking about substance and the 'what is?'" (402a12–13). What Aristotle seeks in *De Anima* seems to be not so much a being as a way of seeking—an activity. It is no wonder, then, that the book should be self-reflexive. The soul is apparently to be discovered in our attempt to discover soul.

Aristotle begins by calling psychology an *eidēsis*. The word appears nowhere else in *De Anima*—indeed, nowhere else in Aristotle. Nor does it occur in any extant text prior to Aristotle. For several centuries after its debut in *De Anima*, *eidēsis* is rare.[5] Aristotle thus begins with a claim about the precision of knowledge of soul, but this knowledge is designated by a term that is absolutely unique and therefore so precise as to be too precise. It conveys nothing determinate. But perhaps this is too extreme; we can construct a meaning for *eidēsis* on the basis of its etymology and its similarity to other words. Its root is a verb *eidō*—"to see"—that is not extant in the present tense but in the perfect tense means "to know" in the sense of being in a state of having seen and in the aorist means that one saw. So the noun we are interested in derives from a verb that shows up either when reflecting back on what was done or as some sort of continuing completed state. And it has to do with seeing. The cognitive status of *eidēsis* is clear from its connection to *eidos*—"idea" or "form" in Plato and "species" in Aristotle. As deriving from the perfect, the least temporal and so least verbal of the tenses, and the aorist, the tense expressing action at a moment, *eidēsis* seems to involve looking but with a certain atemporality. It involves what is taken in at a moment and is thus appropriate to the way in which *De Anima* presents soul in terms of an isolated slice of awareness without before or after.

Eidēsis is formed similarly to a number of other words in Greek. For example, *mimēsis* and *poiēsis* derive from the verbs "to mimic" (or "imitate") and "to do" (or "make"), respectively. Both nouns initially retain a verbal sense, so that *mimēsis* designates the process or act of imitating and *poiēsis* the process or act of making. But then, as is the way with language, their meaning spreads and slides into a noun that is more nounlike; they come to be regularly interchanged with *mimēma* and *poiēma*—"an imitation" and "a thing made"—and so can also stand for the end result of the process for which they stand. If *eidēsis* is understood to have been formed in the same

5 · Eventually, *eidēsis* acquires two sets of uses—one having to do with medicine, the other with the gods. It is used in reference to soothsaying and also comes to be especially common in Christian theology—for example, in Eusebius and Gregory of Nyssa.

way, then it would initially mean the act of knowing or having seen and subsequently the product of that act, knowledge.

According to the first sentence of *De Anima*, one *eidēsis* is more beautiful either because it is more precise or because it is both better (or of better things) and more wondrous (or of more wondrous things), and/or it is more honored for the same reasons. And on account of both (what *both* refers to here is hard to make out), the inquiry (*historia*) into soul is with good reason placed among the first. (What does *first* refer to here? Its gender—either masculine or neuter—does not match either *eidēsis* or *historia*, both of which are feminine.) We are confronted with an unusually complex series of distinctions and a consequent density of ambiguity that does not relent until the end of the first chapter.

Among *eidēseis*, psychology is distinct as either more beautiful or more honored or both. It is either something loved or something respected or both. Its beauty would belong to it in itself; honor depends on being honored. The distinctness of psychology thus has an ambiguous ground; it depends either on what it is as an object or on how it is received, its way. Furthermore, an *eidēsis* is either (A) more beautiful, (B) more honored, or (C) both, if either (1) it is more precise (this seems to have to do with its character as a way of knowing) or (2) either both (a) as an object (i) it is either itself better (as a way of knowing) or (ii) it is concerned with objects that are better (that is, as a way, it is better because of what it is a way to) and (b) either (i) as an object, it is itself more wondrous (that is, as a way) or (ii) it is concerned with what is more wondrous (that is, it is more wondrous as a way because it is concerned with more wondrous objects).

The inquiry into soul is characterized both by a certain way and by a certain sort of object. *De Anima* reflects this ambiguity in the regressively dyadic structure of its beginning, as the way and the object of inquiry repeatedly fold into each other. It is initially not clear whether the inquiry into soul has any distinctive character apart from the object with which it is concerned. At first, we think it is distinctive in its way, which is characterized by a word, *eidēsis*, that is altogether unique and seems to point to an atemporal kind of knowing. But by the end of the first sentence, *eidēsis* has been replaced by *historia*, an inquiry that essentially chronicles what happens to happen.[6] In addition, *historia*, like *eidēsis*, has a double sense: it can refer both to the act of inquiring and to the product of the inquiry. The inquiry into soul therefore has a thoroughgoing doubleness. It is precise—there is no mistaking what it is about; on the other hand, what it is about, as well as it itself, is perplexing and inspires wonder. Soul seems to be precisely

6 · See Aristotle *On Poetics* 1451a–b.

what must always inspire wonder. Because it is so distinctive—there is nothing else like soul in the world—knowledge of it will be precise; because it is "somehow all beings," knowledge of soul will be absolutely comprehensive.

In the sequel, Aristotle redoubles his account of the doubleness of soul. He introduces two new terms for the knowledge he is seeking. He says that "*gnōsis* [or recognition] of it contributes greatly [or great things] toward all truth and especially toward nature [or the truth of nature]" (402a4–6). Then he says we seek "to contemplate [*theōrēsai*] and recognize [*gnōnai*] its nature, *ousia*, and however many attributes there are concerning it" (402a7–8). He thus announces a double way (recognition and contemplation) of approaching a double object (nature, a principle of growth and so change, and *ousia*, a principle of stability). He then re-redoubles his account by distinguishing nature and *ousia*, now taken as one, from attributes or accidents as what attach to something not of necessity or essentially but accidentally. And then within these attributes, now called *pathē*, Aristotle distinguishes between those proper to soul by itself and those existing in living things on account of soul but nevertheless inseparable from body.

One might say provisionally that for Aristotle there are three theoretical pursuits.[7] Physics deals with nature, or *phusis*. Metaphysics deals with substance, or *ousia*. Psychology deals with what unites these two realms—the changing and the permanent. Soul as the principle of this unification reflects within itself the tension between the two aspects of the whole—change and permanence. It is not an accident that personal identity—how a person can remain one and the same even while growing and changing—is such a prominent problem for psychology.

We need to revisit one more time the first sentence of *De Anima*.

> Supposing *eidēsis* to be one of the beautiful and honored things, one more than another either on account of precision or by belonging to either the better or more wondrous, on account of both of these, the inquiry about soul would with good reason be put among the first.

The natural reading of this sentence is, as we have indicated above, thoroughly ambiguous. There is another reading that, while less natural, is nevertheless instructive, given that we do not really know what Aristotle means by *eidēsis*. Aristotle never says that *eidēsis* is of the soul; he says only that it is one of the beautiful and honored things. Suppose, then, that the inquiry into soul is among the first things because it is an inquiry into *eidēsis*. This

---

7 · I owe this formulation to Seth Benardete. It is a provisional formulation because change makes itself felt in any inquiry into permanence (it is not possible to inquire into being without speaking of beings) as permanence makes itself felt in any inquiry into change (the *phusis* of something may be understood as its fixed nature).

would, in turn, be true because *eidēsis* has a double nature. It is, on the one hand, connected to the precise and more wondrous—that is, to the true; it is, on the other hand, connected to what is better—that is, to the good. Whatever *eidēsis* means, it is a mark of how we are simultaneously connected to the world in terms of what is true (awareness, sense, cognition) and in terms of what is good (life, motion toward). Aristotle would then mean to indicate that *eidēsis* is one thing that shows up in two ways. *De Anima* is not, therefore, an attempt to put these two features of soul together but rather an attempt to tease out how they are already necessarily together, albeit in a way that is admittedly obscure. The recognition of it—that is, of *eidēsis*—contributes to all truth and to nature because it (again, *eidēsis*) is a principle of living things (402a6–7). *Eidēsis* understood in this way is an *archē*—a principle or origin—of both truth and life.

One might put the problem that unifies soul in this way. We are directed to the good, and we are directed to the true. What the two share seems to be this: unlike the beautiful, which remains beautiful even if we know it to be illusory, to be good, the good must be real.[8] Aristotle seems to coin the word *eidēsis* to capture the unifying feature of soul as the being in the world the being of which is its encounter with the real. Because it is so difficult to grasp, this registering of reality has no name, and yet it is the common root of thinking, knowing, and seeing (**eidō*) on the one hand and eating or devouring (*edō*) on the other. This problematic unity is the underlying theme of *De Anima* and points the way toward an understanding of soul that perhaps first shows itself in Homer but is powerfully present as well in thinkers as different as Herodotus, Euripides, and Plato and deserves to be understood as the soul of the Greeks.

8 · See Plato *Republic* 505d.

CHAPTER 2

Out of Itself for the Sake of Itself

I. Nutritive Soul

The Greek title of *De Anima* is *Peri Psuchēs*, About Soul, but upon turning to Aristotle's book, we are immediately puzzled, for it seems to omit almost everything that compels our interest about soul. There are no soulful looks here. Although it treats the passions (notably, anger) as examples, it does so very cursorily. Love, and erotic love in particular, is obtrusively absent. *De Anima* mentions virtue only once, in connection with the health of the body. There are no accounts of habits, of dispositions, or of character. Aristotle concentrates on what connects the soul to the world of objects, whether conceived of as objects of sense or as objects of thought. He seems altogether unconcerned with what connects soul to other souls—to other subjects in the world. This soul, which is "somehow all beings," nevertheless exists in a state of curious isolation. It is a consumer of, not a participant in, the world. No one would think of saying of it that without friends it "would not choose to live, even having all the remaining good things."[1]

De Anima furthermore has nothing to say of memory and little of experience. It contains an account of thinking but not really of the process of working through a problem in order to put things together. To a remarkable extent, then, Aristotle's *De Anima* treats the soul as though it were altogether apart from time or any awareness of time (although see *De Anima* 3.11).[2] Accordingly, it takes no account of wonder or even of the disposition of all human beings by nature to desire to be in a state of knowing.[3]

But perhaps we have been unfair. Aristotle's title promises us an account of soul, not of human soul. Accordingly, after dispensing with the views of his predecessors, he turns to three progressively more complex versions of soul, each incorporating what comes before it. He first treats soul as nutri-

---

1 · See *Nicomachean Ethics* 1155a1.
2 · For a remarkable reflection on the significance of these questions, see Seth Benardete, "Aristotle, *De Anima* III.3–5," *Review of Metaphysics* 28, no. 4 (June 1975).
3 · See *Metaphysics* 980a21.

tive—plant soul, then as perceptive—animal soul, and finally as cognitive—human soul. While we are left to puzzle out for ourselves what it is the three have in common that justifies calling them all soul, at least we know where to start. All soul contains nutritive soul. What most distinguishes him both from those who come before him and from those who come after is the attention Aristotle pays to plants.[4] Plant soul is for Aristotle the principle of nutrition and reproduction, which, curiously enough, he says are the same process. He does not make the nature of this sameness explicit, but when we chew on the problem a bit, we discover that nutrition occurs in a being that takes what is other than and apart from itself and transforms it into what is the same as itself. Reproduction, Aristotle tells us, is the creation of *heteron hoion auto*—"another like itself" or "an other like same" (415a28).[5] Reproduction is a sign of a feature present in all soul—a desire to participate in the divine and eternal. And since it is the same as nutrition, this must be true as well of nutrition. Ensouled beings eat to maintain themselves / the same (in the context, *auto* could mean either) as themselves / the same by incorporating what is other; they reproduce to maintain themselves / the same by making another that is like themselves / the same. These two processes are the same insofar as they involve a being that is defined in relation to and by negation of what is other; one could say that only ensouled beings have an inside because only for ensouled beings is there an outside. A soul can be *somehow* all things—things can be *in* it—because it is fundamentally apart from everything else. Now, in working to preserve itself in its distinctness from what is other, every soul places itself on a collision course with time, for it is the condition of time that beings in it become other than themselves or move out of themselves. Nutrition and reproduction represent the essential, albeit necessarily incompletely successful, tendency of soul to resist time in time.

Initially, it comes as something of a surprise when Aristotle claims that what is most natural for living things is "making another like itself / same . . . in order that they may participate to the extent possible in that which is always and divine, for all [*panta*] desire that / the former [*ekeinou*] and for the sake of it do whatever they do by nature" (415a28–b2). What is puzzling is first that, in the context, Aristotle must mean that all living things—plants and animals—desire (*oregetai*), but this must surely mean that they have the faculty of *orexis*. Previously, *orexis* had been said to depend on the presence of sensation, which presence is one of the distinguishing features of animal

<hr />

4 · The one exception to this claim might be Rousseau, perhaps most in *Les rêveries du promeneur solitaire*, and especially in the *septième promenade*.
5 · Compare *Nicomachean Ethics* 1166a30 with 1170b7 and Plato's *Lysis* 211d8 with 212a5.

over and against plant soul (414b2). The first puzzle, then, is that Aristotle
seems here to indicate that plant soul is not so distinct from animal soul—
both somehow have desire. The second puzzle is Aristotle's use of *ekeinos*. If
taken to mean "that," it would simply point to what "all" desire, but, in the
context, it is equally natural for it to mean "the former" and so to single out
"what is always" as what all desire. But this would make the introduction of
the divine here strange and a little gratuitous.[6]

In the sequel, "always and divine" will be coupled again when Aristotle
indicates that it is not really possible for a living being to share in them since
nothing capable of destruction allows of remaining "the same and one in
number" (415b4–5). The suggestion seems to be that the desire of all soul
to be always is a desire to differentiate itself from everything else. To do so,
a temporal being would need to work at preventing itself from becoming
other. One mode of this work is nourishment or eating, but it is a losing
battle. Living beings grow old and die. Another mode is reproduction. This
proves successful in an inverse proportion to how individuated a soul really
is. Insofar as one plant is just like another of the same species, reproduction
is relatively successful. Insofar as the ensouled being is of the sort that is
individual enough to get a name—say, a dog rather than a begonia—the
longing for what is always is less fulfilled. In either case, however, the desire
for the always has a similar problematic structure. The self, what remains
the same, the inside, defines itself as distinct from and in opposition to what
is other than itself—what is outside. Its unity, and so its being, is therefore
dependent upon what is outside, what is other. Yet it can be what it is only
by virtue of a constant distancing of itself from what is other. The soul in
its very being is always involved in a complex dance with the other according to which it must simultaneously put it at a distance and appropriate
it. The soul is what goes out of itself for the sake of remaining itself; nourishment and reproduction, but also all desire, share this structure. When
Aristotle says "all *desire* what is always and divine," he temporarily collapses
the distinction between plant soul and animal soul in order to indicate the
fundamental feature of all soul. When he says first "all desire what is always
and *divine*" and then adds that they do so for the sake of the former, he

---

6 · Aristotle goes on in the immediate sequel to distinguish two meanings of the word
heneka—"for the sake of." On the one hand, it may refer to that "of which" something
is—what belongs to it (the case here is genitive); on the other hand, it may refer to
that to which or for which something is (the case here is dative). Here one might
say that the goal of a desire may be understood as either the object of longing or the
subject who is longing. *Something* will fulfill me, or something will fulfill *me*. In one
instance, the emphasis is on what is other than me; in the other instance, it is on what
is the same as me. I long either to preserve myself always or to be something (a god?)
that is always.

means to point to the problematic status of this longing. All soul desires to make itself permanent in its distinctness, but its permanence (the always) is at odds with its being as a distinct individual (the divine). This tension is constitutive of all soul, but in plant soul the emphasis is on permanence and in animal soul on individuation. The two taken together point to the divide within each taken separately. Zeus apparently had good reason to wonder about his own possibility.

Soul is what goes out of itself for the sake of remaining in itself. Aristotle sees that this, the distinctive feature of every living being, can be understood to characterize not only nutritive soul but both appetitive and cognitive soul as well. Just prior to his account of soul as nutritive, Aristotle pauses for a methodological comment on the nature of understanding. We move, he says, from what is most apparent but still unclear to what is clearer and more knowable according to reason. Thinking thus has the character of transforming appearances, what seem external, into something *kata ton logon*—in accord with reason—something much more like thinking itself. The process is not altogether unlike digestion. Insofar as appearances too are food for thought, cognitive soul may be said to go out of itself in order to affirm itself as itself. By treating the parts of soul separately, Aristotle's *De Anima* maintains an artificial clarity, but to grasp soul means also to grasp nutritive, perceptive/appetitive, and rational soul in their necessary togetherness.

II. Sensing Soul: Vision

The initial terms of Aristotle's account of sensitive or perceptive soul are remarkably similar to those of his account of nutritive soul.

> The sensing thing is in potency such as the thing sensed is already in actuality, as has been said. On the one hand, then, it undergoes when it is not like, but, on the other hand, having undergone, it has been made like and is such as that. (418a3–6)

Nutritive soul has as its end to generate one such as / like (*hoion*) itself/same (*auto*). Sensing soul has as its end to undergo or experience what is *hoion ekeino*—like or such as what is apart from it. The one makes another like itself; the other makes itself like the other. Both—the one as agent, the other as patient—involve spanning the gap between same and other. It is not strange that, in this context, Aristotle should once again raise the issue of whether sensation involves like acting on like or opposite acting on opposite (416b32–417a9). On the one hand, sensing soul cannot be simply like what it senses, for were this so, being most like itself, it would sense itself. The act of sensing is what distinguishes it from what it senses. Sensation is a power, a *dunamis*, that can be actualized only by encountering something other than itself. On the other hand, were soul altogether different from what it senses, how could its sensations ever be true? Once again we have encountered a certain doubleness within the soul (417a9–20). The model for sensation in general seems to be a process in which the object of sensation, which is necessarily other or unlike, is acted upon by perceptive soul so as to make it the same or like, and thus capable of being taken in. As in the case of nutritive soul, sensing soul is once again both the same as and other than what is apart from it.

What it means for sensing soul to be of necessity simultaneously apart from its object and identical with its object becomes especially clear in Aristotle's account of sight. To know any faculty, any potency, is to know its object—what it is a potency for. The object of the faculty of sight is the visible. What is in its very nature visible is a surface, and it is characteristic of a surface to be colored (418a26–30). So, initially, we are told that color is the proper object of sight. But Aristotle quickly adds something else—a co-object—"what is possible to say in *logos* but happens to be without a name." What Aristotle means becomes clear through the sequel when he says that "every color is the setting in motion of the transparent [*diaphanes*] in its activity, and this is its nature" (417a31–b2). So the object of sight is in a way color, but color now understood as what makes the transparency of what is between us and the object manifest. You look at a chair and notice that it is blue. The less obvious, but in a way more important, point is that this experience somehow makes manifest that through (*dia*) which the chair becomes apparent (*phaneron*). It is color that makes visible to us the *diaphanes* in its in-betweenness. This is in a way the general form of all sensation—applying not only to sound and smell but also, contrary to our initial expectation, to touch and taste as well (419a25–b3). What is between, the *metaxu* (419a20), is the necessary condition for all sensing, which, in making this medium manifest, makes the "out-thereness" of its object manifest, an out-thereness that thus becomes the co-object of all sensation—but not only sensation, for Aristotle in quick succession in the sequel twice reminds us that his most recent moves in the argument are apparent/*phaneron* (419a8, 419a12). The out-thereness of things comes to be visible in sight as that through which we must look to see surfaces as colored. Sight thus gives us a sensation of space as the condition for the outsideness of things.

There is a further step in the account. Color may be the agent that brings transparency into action, but there is something else that makes what is potentially transparent really transparent—light (*phōs*). The transparent is apparently first made active or brought into *energeia* by light and then again activated in a more determinate way by color. That we do not see in the dark means that we do not have any awareness of spatial betweenness, but light makes possible a second actualizing of this betweenness only insofar as we look through it until our vision stops at a colored surface. The transparent is thus being given a double actuality or *energeia*. This leads Aristotle to conclude that light is the color of the transparent and moves him to find so interesting sources of light that are themselves visible—for example, phosphorescence and fire.

That the transparent can be energized by light so as somehow to take on the color of the surfaces seen through it is of interest in yet another, more playful, way. It seems to mimic on the level of sight the manner in which soul will be said later to be somehow all the beings (431b21) and reminds us of Aristotle's complicated argument at the beginning of book 2 to show that "the soul is a first entelechy of a natural organized body" (412a27–28)—not so much the actualized sensing or thinking but the potency for sensing or thought that is the consequence of body that has been actualized in a certain way.[7] Now, with a slight change of accent—from a circumflex to an acute (and these, of course, would not have been written in the Greek of Aristotle's time)—*phōs* becomes not "light" but "man" or "mortal." Aristotle thus seems to present us with a playful analogy between light as what makes things visible and man, and so perhaps cognitive soul. If light is the first entelechy of sight in its actualizing of the transparent, then it is analogous to the living body actualized by soul. This is, in turn, connected to the way in which *logos* gets brought into the light by soul, as is suggested by Aristotle's use of *phaneron* (at 419a8 and 419a12) to reflect on the progressive clarity of his own argument. A sign becomes apparent as a sign—it comes into the light—by virtue of the thinking of it. This act is what makes a thinking being visible. It is further suggested (and complicated) by Aristotle's language at 418b24, where he says that "this [the movement of light] is both opposed to the brightness/being in the light [*enargeian*] of *logos* and opposed to appearances." This is the only use of the word *enargeia* in all of Aristotle's extant writings. It seems plausible that it is meant here as a pun on *energeia*—actuality. In making betweenness manifest, every act of sight has a particular object, but ultimately, its purpose is to make manifest the between. Sight is in this regard paradigmatic of all sensation, for every sensing is also a sensing of sensing. Aristotle's playfulness suggests that this

---

7 · Thus, for example, one might say a harp when strung and tuned is in a state of first entelechy—a certain potential has been realized—but the state it is in prepares it for another sort of realization, a second entelechy when the harp is actually played. The first entelechy is thus from one point of view a realized state and from another point of view a potency. It is an actualized potentiality. In this regard, it is like Aristotle's treatment of *hexis*, as a state of character, in the *Nicomachean Ethics* (see especially book 2.5).

reflexivity may be characteristic of soul as soul and consequently as true of thought as it is of sensation.

III. Thinking Soul

A. Sensation and Imagination

The word *soul*—*psuchē*—appears over 140 times in the first ten chapters of Aristotle's *De Anima* (book 1–book 2, chapter 5). It then disappears for the next eight chapters (book 2, chapter 6–book 3, chapter 2), reappearing only at the beginning of the account of imagination in book 3. In the eleven chapters that follow, *psuchē* appears, but somewhat less frequently than in the first section—about 20 times. Soul is thus obtrusively absent in Aristotle's account of the five senses and of the common sense—an account that occupies a full third of *De Anima*.

Before this hiatus, Aristotle treats nutrition, a process in which a certain kind of body is separated off from the rest of body so that to continue to be what it is, it must transform what is outside of itself into itself. In this way, plants are ensouled because they are constituted by the boundary between inside and outside. Still, when plants incorporate what is outside, they do so in such a way that it ceases to be outside. There is thus no awareness in plants of the outside *as* outside. They manifest what it means to have a boundary and yet are not aware of the boundary as a boundary.

After the account of sensation, Aristotle treats mind and thought, and so awareness and self-awareness. Now, thinking is understood to be the same as what it thinks (430a2–3), and, unlike an object of sense, its object is altogether in the soul itself—it is form without matter (417b23–24). Accordingly, in mind, the discrepancy between thinker and thought, soul and object, inside and outside, would ultimately vanish. Thinking soul would then seem to appropriate its objects effortlessly and without resistance. But would such a soul be self-aware?

If nutritive soul lacks awareness of what it does when it brings the outside inside, and the object of thinking soul is altogether inside and its process of appropriation frictionless, it seems possible that soul as somehow self-aware—that is, genuine soul—really shows itself only in sensing soul. Accordingly, soul must be prominently mentioned in the accounts of nutrition and thinking because otherwise it would not be manifest. It needn't be mentioned in the account of sensation because it is only there that it is manifest as mediating between simple nutrition (which may not really be possible) and simple cognition (which may not really be possible). Put differently, even nutritive soul somehow desires, and even thinking soul somehow takes in what is outside. Genuine soul shows itself only when it is divided against itself—when, as at once reflecting the now of the object it appropriates and the now of the act of appropriation, it is both one and two (426b24–427a16). Because this dividedness within unity is its defining feature, soul becomes especially manifest in an act of erring. This centrality of error is connected to the importance of imagination—*phantasia*—in Aristotle's account of thinking.

Aristotle begins his account of cognitive soul by returning to the common understanding of the double function of soul—on the one hand, as a principle of awareness; on the other hand, as a principle of motion (427a17–b8). This reminder calls attention to the tension within soul; how can what gives us a motive to act at the same time allow us passively to render what is as it is?[8] The purity of mind seems to be at odds with the movement of mind. In the sequel, Aristotle criticizes those who say thinking is like sensation because they do not see that were this so, there would be no way to account for error. The two points are connected. There can be no misperception unless one thing is said to belong to another. Otherwise, we simply see or know a thing or do not—it either gets inside or it doesn't. Accordingly, if sensation and thinking are the same, then either all appearances (*phainomena*) are true, or, if there is error, it must be a sensation of something that is itself already not true. So either everything that appears is as it appears, or a nonbeing has to appear. These alternatives prepare the discussion of *phantasia*, for an image appears and is always real—that is, it is a real image—but this reality consists in its not being what it appears to be. Insofar as thinking requires the possibility of error, it will require something like *phantasia*, which, in turn, will require sensation, which, in turn, requires body. Even though Aristotle certainly sometimes seems to argue that mind cannot be mixed with body (for example, 429a24–26), it will prove a difficult claim to sustain.

It is apparent (*phaneron*, which is etymologically related to *phantasia* by

8 · It is in this context that Aristotle for the only time in *De Anima* uses the word *mētis* to refer to mind (he is quoting Empedocles— 427a23). This occurs just prior to a citation from Homer. Aristotle seems to wish to remind us of perhaps the most famous pun in Homer. In *Odyssey*, book 9, Odysseus tells the cyclops, Polyphemus, that his name is *outis*, "no one." When Odysseus blinds Polyphemus, he cries out, and when the other cyclopes come to ask him what has happened, he replies that no one has blinded him. They provide him no help, "for surely no one is trying to kill you" (*Odyssey* 9.405–6). In their reply, however, they use another word for "no one" in Greek, *mētis*; it differs only in accent from the word for mind. Homer's pun means to call attention to the connection between the operation of mind and being no one—that is, having no perspective, no motive. This is precisely the problem that will preoccupy Aristotle in *De Anima* 3. It seems to culminate in the tension between mind as active and mind as passive.

way of *phōs*), Aristotle tells us, that sensing is not the same as thinking. All animals sense; only some think. Sensing, then, can exist apart from thinking and so cannot be the same as thinking. Now, to argue in this way, we have to make thinking appear (*phainesthai*) before us as not sensing together with sensing. We bring both faculties into our presence at will in order to compare them. But making them appear at will is possible only because of the faculty of *phantasia*, and this has made it *phaneron* that the two are not the same. *Phantasia* is exactly what those who equate sensation and thinking have left out of their account, for thinking means making things present to oneself that are not in fact present. To think about fear, for example, we put a frame around it and isolate it; this allows us to "experience" it without really experiencing it. Only in this way could we possibly put something together with something else with which it is not initially experienced as together—that is, think. This process involves a detachment of experience from time, which is the characteristic feature of *phantasia*.[9] That we are able to imagine something whenever we wish means that we are not committed to the reality of it whenever it appears. Without this possibility of detachment from reality, neither *logos* (thinking in the declarative form of S is P) nor *hupolēpsis* (supposing or assuming—a conditional mode of thinking) is possible (427b11–16). *Phantasia* needs sensation for its content, and thinking things through (*dianoia*) needs *phantasia*. *Phantasia* brings with it the possibility of error even though it itself does not err, but by detaching images from experiences, it makes it possible to combine them in such a way as to claim they go together. *Phantasia* itself makes no claims about reality so as to make it possible to make claims about reality.[10]

   Phantasia makes something interesting possible. The first stage of awareness is sense. With sensation, we are already at an end; the object of sensation is ours—we get it or we do not. When we get it, we are committed to its reality. The final stage of awareness is intellection—*noein*. Here too we are already at an end with respect to the object of thought—we either get it or we do not, and, getting it, again we are committed to its reality. Between these two stages are several steps. First there is a severing of sense from the real; this makes possible a reconstruction of what was once sense. Accordingly, about the reality of this object, we can suspend belief. The image is true—that is, true as what it is—but it also makes possible thinking as

9 · See Benardete, "Aristotle, *De Anima* III.3–5," 611.

10 · Aristotle's language in this section is revealing. The discussion of error brings with it a new verb: *dianoeisthai*—literally, "to think through." There is no error without this "through." Or, insofar as the activity of mind (*noein*) is like sight, it would never err. Two nouns also enter with the discussion of error—*dianoia* (thought as thinking through) and *aisthēsis* (sensation). Nouns involve a framing, a detaching of an activity from what it leads to. This is of course possible only by virtue of *phantasia*.

dianoia, a putting together that is on the way to a conclusion but not at an end. *Phantasia* thus makes possible a negating of reality that is a necessary prelude to the reconstituting of reality that we call thinking.

Phantasia is "that according to which we say a *phantasma* comes to be in/for us" (428a1–2). Aristotle quickly adds that he does not mean when we are speaking metaphorically, for, however poetic and so in some way concealed, we use metaphor to make truth claims about the reality of the world. But is *phantasia* a single faculty, or is it a disposition of another faculty? Aristotle first distinguishes it from sensation, for we imagine when we are not sensing—for example, when we are dreaming. Second, while sense seems always to be present, *phantasia* is turned on and off. Third, while sense is the defining feature of animal soul, it is not clear that all animals imagine. And finally, while sense is always true (we always see what we see), *phantasia* is often false (there is nothing there to see). Ordinary speech bears out the distinction between imagination and sense. Of an object of sense, we do not say, "This appears to be a man" but rather "This is a man." Only when unsure do we say, "It appears . . . ," and so we suspend the truth of the matter. As we do this, we vanish as agents in the report of what we see; the report goes into the third person—*dokei* / "it seems" or *phainetai* / "it appears"—and we get pulled into what we are reporting. The object of sight is somehow present to us but does not reflect us. The object of imagination, the *phantasma*, thus has an uncertainty built into it that reminds us that we are inspecting the object. Or the *phantasma*, unlike the object of sense, brings along with it the perspectival character of experience. And so, by casting doubt on the reality of its object, *phantasia* suggests a reality that is more real than what appears, even though it cannot tell us anything about it. As sending us beyond what it presents us with, it initiates a motion.[11] This is what most differentiates *phantasia* from sensation or sense.

Aristotle quickly distinguishes *phantasia* from knowledge (*epistēmē*) and mind (*nous*), for both of these can never be false (mind and sense seem to share in common a certain one-dimensionality). He then turns to what remains—*doxa*, opinion or seeming. Now, *phantasia* cannot be a form of *doxa* because *doxa* involves belief or trust that cannot be suspended. Opinion never knows itself to be opinion; it always understands itself to be true. To say "It's only my opinion" therefore means that it is not really your opinion, for how something seems (*dokei*) to you is how it is for you. *Doxa* thus lacks the double vision that is necessary for *phantasia*. Nor can it be *doxa* plus sensation; you do not get double vision by adding together two single visions. What would this addition amount to? Opinion tells us the sun is big, and sensation tells us it is little. Saying both at the same time does not

11 ·Benardete, "Aristotle, *De Anima* III.3–5," 613–14.

reveal to us the principle of the togetherness of the two claims in one experience. For the same reason, it cannot be opinion through sensation or opinion woven together with sensation. None of these explains the doubleness that is proper to *phantasia*.

What, then, is *phantasia*? In a rather dense account (428b10–429a1), Aristotle indicates that it is nothing but the coincidence of three layers of sensation.[12] Sensation is always first of the objects of the individual senses. Here we cannot err—sight is never deceived in seeing white. But along with this first-order sensation, we also sense that white is being predicated or attributed to a subject. Here we may err, for we may mistake "this" of "This is white." Finally, we sense "the common things" that follow upon the things predicated to which particular features attach—things like motion and size. So we never err that we are seeing white; we may err about what is white; and we are most of all liable to err when it comes to what the common sense tells us belongs to the shared "this" of "This is white" and "This is hard." Aristotle suggests here that were this coming together of these three layers of sensation final and settled, doubt would not enter in so easily. *Phainetai* ("it appears"), and so *phantasia*, is therefore bound up with a "metaphysical urge"—a movement to thought, which, as grounded in an awareness of the synthetic nature of sensation, is aware of the fragility of the final product. *Phantasia* thus seems to be a movement that has its origin in the *energeia*, the activity, of sensing. This does not mean that every sensing being will have the faculty of imagination but rather that *phantasia* will somehow be the natural fulfillment of a tendency built into sensation. Accordingly, Aristotle's etymological remark of *De Anima* 3.3 is more important than it at first seems. We have already seen that the precondition for sight, which Aristotle singles out here as most especially sensation, is light (*phaos* or *phōs*). *Phantasia* is said here (429a3) to take its name from light, even though, unlike sight, it does not require light. *Phantasia* should therefore designate the self-evident—what brings light to itself. In a way, this is exactly what it does. The light of *phantasia*, as no longer the connection between the object seen and the eye, allows the imagination to become something into which we put both ourselves as sensing and the things sensed. *We* imagine when *we* wish, and so the dependency of sensation on an object external to us (the dependency that shows itself once we come to see that sense always senses its object at a distance—that is, sense is always not only of the object but also of "the between") is severed. This allows *phantasia* to give us in one experience a togetherness of the soul and sensible being. However, as *phantasia* always also involves an awareness of the fragile and uncertain synthesis that its object represents, the experience is always of this togetherness as problematic.

12 · For the following account, see Benardete, "Aristotle, *De Anima* III.3–5," 614–15.

One might say that we experience the necessary togetherness of soul and world most when we make mistakes about the world. Otherwise, we either lose the experience of the "we" or lose the experience of the world. But this is precisely the experience of *phainetai*, where "it appears to be" implies "but maybe not," and because of this duality, "being shows itself."

B. Passive and Active Mind

Early in book 3 (429a24), Aristotle reminds us that mind (*nous*) is somehow apart from body.[13] Unlike the senses, thinking seems to have no organ. But, contrary to first appearances, even the role of the organ in sensing proves problematic. The senses sense by way of an appropriate object, but, as they also are said to sense themselves sensing, do they use the same organ for both activities? Aristotle makes clear that among the senses, touch has a special status (425a11–20). We never turn it off, and it is somehow connected with, or doubles up with, each of the other four senses. But does it have an organ? Aristotle seems to refer to it only as "within" (423b22–23). And what about the common sense? Were it to have a specific organ apart from those of the particular senses, there would be need of yet another sense to unify it with the original five senses. And *phantasia*? While functioning differently from both sensation and thought, it is ultimately understood as a modification of sense. *De Anima*, then, seems on the one hand to be an attempt to understand soul in terms of its constituent "parts"—that is, the various things it does.[14] On the other hand, it must also understand these heterogeneous functions as constituting a whole so as to make possible one experience. While this is true even of plants, which undergo what they undergo as unified beings, as soon as sensation enters—that is, as soon as we consider animal soul—the registering of this unified undergoing as one becomes necessary to experience. Even when it undergoes diverse things, the soul must not change and must be aware of its constancy, so that, in sensing many things, the soul necessarily also senses itself as one. Now, this experience could never be accounted for by positing an additional function—something like a unifying function—that uses an additional organ. One might say, then, that the assumption at the beginning of book 3 that mind is "nonbodily" has in a certain way been present from the outset and must apply not just to mind but to soul as such. We will need to see why it is made explicit only with regard to mind.

Aristotle begins his account of the "part of the soul by which the soul

13 · Aristotle has made this point previously; see, for example, at 411b16–19 and 413b24–27.
14 · See 429a10–13.

recognizes and thinks" (429a10–11) by acknowledging that mind may be separable from soul not in fact but only in *logos*, which is to say it may be a "part" demanded by thinking itself in order to make sense of thinking but may not exist in space—that is, have any magnitude. Aristotle is puzzled that what cannot be understood as in space and time nevertheless has an effect that shows itself at least temporally. He also wonders why something that is eternal would give rise to an activity that is not. That is, why does thinking come to be when it comes to be? Why here? Why now?

Now, if thinking is like sensing, it will be a being affected by what is other than it. Sight is affected by what is visible—thinking presumably by what is thinkable. The faculty or potency for thinking must then be in a state of not already having been affected, for, otherwise, it would not be wholly receptive to whatever can affect it. "To be unaffected [*apathēs*] means not to be in the state of having been put in any state permanently."[15] This condition has enormous consequences, for it means that the faculty cannot be bodily. This is true in part even of the individual senses. The eye is made of "water," but its *energeia*, its actualization, is to be transparent. Still, vision can be linked to an organ because, while the organ must be potentially transparent, it does not have to be completely indeterminate. It can, for example, be specified in its nature with regard to other senses—it may be hard, warm, and so forth. But since thinking has as its object, in principle, everything, it would have to be altogether "transparent," and so neither visible nor tangible, and so on. It must be *apathes*—without affect. Mind, then, in order to be what it is—that is, open to everything—must have nothing that singles it out. As the potentiality to be anything, it must have as its nature nothing in particular (429a21–22). Its potentiality (*dunamis*) is its power (*dunamis*). Accordingly, if thinking is what Aristotle claims, the nonbodily character of mind is absolutely necessary.

Mind also cannot be in time. That is, since it vanishes when it is not at work (429a22–24), it does not persist through time. Or, before it shows its power by becoming any of the particular beings, it is nothing. So, in order to be able to take on any form, mind must be pure potential. And yet, because mind is not in time—that is, it is sometimes engaged and sometimes not—there must be something that turns it on and off. If it is in its very being a pure receptor and so purely *passive*, what *activates* it? What is it about what must be essentially nothing that causes it to move?[16] Aristotle must somehow account for the willfulness of mind, for mind "comes to

---

15 · See Benardete, "Aristotle, *De Anima* III.3–5," 403.

16 · Aristotle indicates that he has this problem in mind in the following sentence: "It is by the perceptive that [he? it? one?—Aristotle leaves the subject of the sentence indeterminate] judges heat and cold and the things of which flesh is a *logos*" (429b14–16).

be each thing," and "this occurs when it is able to activate through itself" (429b5–7). This tension between the activity of mind and its essential passivity points to an even deeper problem. On the one hand, mind (*nous*) must be *apathēs*—without affect—if it is to be able to take on or receive all possible affects. On the other hand, since thinking (*noein*) is an affect, an experience, it must be possible for mind to take up thinking as an object. Accordingly, mind must be both able and unable to think itself. This is in a way simply the split between the noun, *nous*, and the verb, *noein*. Aristotle transforms this split into the distinction between active and passive mind, so that mind stands to thinking as doing, making, or producing (*poiein*) stands to undergoing, experiencing, or suffering (*paschein*). Active mind (*nous poiētikos*) is like the "I" of "I think," whereas passive mind (*nous pathetikos*) is the "thinking" of "There is thinking going on." No thought is possible without passive mind, but there seems to be no possibility of describing it without undermining the purity of thought, for to do so is to give it conditions and thereby undermine its contingency. To describe mind as purely passive or receptive is to say that it is everything; it is a many but without a principle of unity. To describe mind as active or productive is to make it responsible for what it thinks. Bringing it to the forefront makes the objects of mind in the decisive sense the same or one. In a way, it doesn't matter what it thinks; mind is simply this unity. The difficulty, of course, is that mind cannot be mind without being both of these things—active and passive. And yet the two seem necessarily at odds.

Like anything else in nature, mind has a potentiality, its own matter, and something that brings this potentiality to fruition, an agent that imposes a form on this matter. Insofar as this applies to soul (Aristotle does not say mind here, 430a14), its matter is the potentiality to become all things, but what makes it become anything in particular? What is the "I" of the "I think"? Insofar as this agent is mind, mind would make all the objects of thought in the same way light makes color by actualizing the transparent. Active mind—*nous poiētikos*—would thus be what binds together thought and the objects of thought. It would be what causes thinking to be the thinking of something in particular. Now, this mind would have to be separate from what is thought, for, otherwise, it would always be in operation, and, as the cause and caused would not be distinct, there could be no experience of the form "I think." Active mind would also have to be by itself without affect—*apathēs*—since it is what determines what will affect us. It would have to be unmixed since it is the principle of all mixing. As active, it is in its being not a *dunamis*, a potentiality, but an *energeia*, an actuality or a "being at work." Yet were it really always "at work," it would always be thinking. And were it always doing so perfectly, it would be simply identical to what it thinks. "I think" would be nothing other than "knowledge" without an agent, and the being (*on*) that is thought would become something that is, insofar as it is a being for me, a *pragma*. Active mind thus has a double character. It first seems to grant a certain distance of the "I" from the "think," but then it collapses the two back into each other. Active mind is, on the one hand, constantly engaged in knowing and, on the other hand, exclusively what it is as separated from what it knows. As the latter, it is deathless, eternal, and, unlike passive mind, incorruptible. And yet, as constantly being exactly what it thinks, it cannot preserve any memory of what it was, and therefore, in the very perfection of its own activity, it too marks the loss of the "I" of the "I think."

What is at issue here is the unity of the soul in the face of the heterogeneity of experience. There is a parallel to this problem of soul on the side of being. To explain how we can grasp the heterogeneous and changing things in the world around us, we are moved to say that they are ordered on the basis of certain fixed and unchanging principles. That there are trees depends on the existence of "tree itself." Yet, having once made this supposition in order to ground the limited intelligibility that we know to exist in the world, we are no longer able to explain why the eternal and unchanging principles should operate only incompletely and intermittently. We are unable to understand how things can be partly intelligible. In the case of soul, we introduce mind to account for how we take in what is stable and does not change. This, however, leads to an instability within mind itself. Passive mind, as a perfect representation of the forms of its objects, has no being apart from the sequence of their presence. This disunity requires that there be something within mind itself that accounts for what it is pointed toward—that is, that accounts for the way mind focuses. This is what Aristotle calls *nous poiētikos*. But because active mind has its sole being in this activity of focusing, it has no principle within it to keep it from being totally at work at every moment and so completely submerging itself in what it is thinking. In tracing this problem, Aristotle seems to be articulating a fundamental pattern within mind (and within soul) whereby it alternately (although not really temporally) establishes and closes the distance between itself and its objects. Perfect mind would have these two features perfectly; it would simultaneously perfectly absorb the world and be perfectly aware of this absorption. The problem is that this idealized mind proves unstable. There is no such thing as perfect thought. To understand mind, then, means to understand how it is possible for it to put these two moments of thought, distancing and the identity of thinker and thought, together imperfectly. This proves possible only if the distance is understood as virtual—that is, as imagined. Aristotle's presentation of active and passive mind, which appears at first to be the peak of the argument of *De Anima*, is really instrumental to establishing the importance and necessity of *phantasia* for thought.

For thinking to be possible, false thinking must be possible; both involve putting together things not obviously together. The separate existence of the diagonal and the incommensurable make it possible to say the diagonal of a square is incommensurable with the sides (430a30–31). Aristotle's example is telling, for the proof of this incommensurability requires a construction of another square with the diagonal of the first as its side.[17] This construction in itself has nothing whatsoever to do with the diagonal of the initial square, but we use it to make manifest to ourselves the relation between the diagonal and the side. That is, what was not available to us by way of intellectual inspection (*noein*) comes to be available to us by way of a making (*poiein*) of something altogether unrelated that nevertheless proves to facilitate a thinking through (*dianoein*) of our initial problem. We have to step back from what we are inspecting in order to see what it is. How do we gain this distance? We say to ourselves, "Imagine a square with the diagonal as its side."

Having presented us with "perfect thinking," presumably without *phantasia*, Aristotle thus now brings us back to the necessary role that *phantasia* plays in all actual thought. Moreover, he does so in a way that points to what his own argument has been doing. In his own geometrical example, construction proves necessary to create a context within which a truth comes to be visible. Here Aristotle has found it necessary to construct active mind so as to make visible the reality of *phantasia*.

C. Imagination and Thought

De Anima seems to reach its high point in Aristotle's account of mind as separate and eternal (3.5). However, the account proves to be of a mind so pure that the argument turns into a reductio ad absurdum. In their purity, passive mind is nothing but the disconnected series of its objects, and active mind, altogether distanced from its objects, allows for no multiplicity and hence no objects. Perfect mind is the sum of the two; it would therefore combine perfect absorption (that is, no distance) with perfect awareness (that is, complete detachment). As this combination is impossible, perfect mind is impossible. Yet we come to understand the necessary imperfection of mind only by first constructing mind in its perfection and subsequently seeing how this construction fails. This process—the construction of a one that is not really a one in order to see that and how it is not a one—seems to be the true structure of thinking. *Phantasia* is required for its operation. This seems to be what Aristotle means by saying that *phantasia* is necessary

17 · See Plato *Meno* 82b–85b with my *Ancient Tragedy and the Origins of Modern Science* (Carbondale: Southern Illinois University Press, 1988), 126–27.

for thought. It requires, in turn, thinking through the role of falsehood in thought—that is, representing things as they are not. Thus, Aristotle had to turn to the question of falsehood after his account of mind. It is no accident that *phantasia* and *falsehood* reenter the argument with a quotation from Empedocles that suggests that things in the world are made one by *philia*—love or friendship (430a29–31). An appetite—that is, a principle of goodness—is introduced to account for how things are made whole. In the remainder of *De Anima*, Aristotle thinks through the relation between soul as the location of a passive taking in of things and soul as initiating motion. The link between the two objects of soul—the true and the good—will be *phantasia*.

Aristotle begins this new discussion of *phantasia* with an interesting shift in language. "Knowledge," he says, "with respect to its activity [*energeia*] is the same as its object [*pragma*]" (431a1–2). "Mind" has become its product, "knowledge," and the being mind takes up has become a *pragma*—a thing insofar as it exists for us. From the sides of both agent and object, knowing is being understood from the perspective of the completed act of knowing. Aristotle then draws a parallel to sensation and its objects and concludes that in both sensing and thinking, the faculty is not so much altered or moved as realized or actualized. By themselves, then, when they become aware of simple objects, the receptive faculties of soul are not understood to undergo motion or change. So far we have only passive mind and its analogues in sense. This "motion" is not change but presentation; something is made to appear alone (although this is complicated by the fact that the verb in question, *phanai*, means both "to make to appear" and "to declare" or "to assert"—its two meanings suggest the relation between "Yes" and "Yes!").[18] The "motion" of thought, as well as of sensation, is thus first presented as an altogether other form (*allo eidos*, 431a7) of motion or change (it is an *energeia* of something complete), although he immediately backtracks somewhat and calls it "relatively other" (*hetera*, 431a7).

Aristotle's separation of thinking from motion undergoes further revision with the introduction of pleasure and pain (431a9–14). When what is presented in sensation is pleasant or painful, the soul does not simply receive it neutrally but either affirms it or denies it. This amounts to an experience of the object of sensation as good or bad, which, in turn, inclines us to pursue or flee the object in question. Sensation is thus necessarily linked with appetite (*orexis*) and flight. Yet, while appetite and sensation are not different (*heteron*) with respect to their faculties, they are other (*allo*) with

18 · This was suggested to me by Seth Benardete. *Phanai* is the infinitive of *phēmi* (to say or affirm) and the aorist infinitive of *phainō* (to bring to light or cause to appear).

respect to their being. Aristotle seems to mean by this that, while thinking and sensing cannot have organs or faculties that are different from those of appetite (since they can exist only in relation to each other), still they must be understood and thought of as other. The sign of this is the structure of *De Anima* itself—that is, its movement from soul as aware to soul as moving. Thus far the necessity of a connection between appetite and thinking has been suggested only on the basis of an analogy between sensation and thought. The connection is made firm when Aristotle makes clear first that, like objects of sense, images too bring with them the good and the bad, and then that "the soul never thinks without an image" (431a14–16). These images differ as objects of sense differ, but they are necessarily unified just as objects of sense are unified by the common sense. Like sensation, the imagination experiences one object with many modes. So, for example, that the soul discriminates between sweet and hot means that there is "in" soul a "place" capable of discerning both sweet and hot. This is what Aristotle names the common sense. Now sweet stands to hot (or white) as taste stands to touch (or sight), and so sweet will stand to taste as white stands to sight. But taste and sight must go together in one aware being. Accordingly, this must be true as well of what they are aware of; sweet and white will therefore be modes of one being. Soul, then, as aware, is necessarily aware of unities—of ones. This is as true of thinking as it is of sensing, and so the imagination is as subject to a "common sense" as is sensation. The faculty of thinking thinks forms by means of images, and as is the case in sensation, these images carry with them the good and the bad, and so are affirmed or denied, pursued or avoided. Thinking is inseparable from appetite.

Aristotle's general point seems to be that whether in sensing or in thinking, what we take in is always a unified object. These objects are not just syntheses of the several senses; they are already objects of pursuit or avoidance. The objects of sensation and thought are never simple and neutral but rather always already dual—composed of their being and of their being good or bad. We sense not just a yellowish red, moving, crackling, smoky thing but a fire, or even a beacon fire. We perceive an object as potentially painful—as something to be avoided. There is, then, a difference between the true and false and the good and bad, but "without action, the true and the false are in the same genus as the good and the bad, but they differ in [being present] simply or to someone" (431b10–12). We have the ability to abstract the true and false from the good and bad just as we can speak of snubness apart from snub nose and make it the same as concavity, but while these differ genuinely in their being, they are not different in fact. They do not exist apart from each other. That this is somehow the case—that the theoretical is never simply separable from the practical—seems clear from the first sentence of Aristotle's *De Anima* and from *eidēsis* as the taking in of the real in its goodness.[19] Every object of soul is at once an object of desire and of awareness. To understand how this is the case would mean to understand the unity of soul as simultaneously a principle of awareness and of motion.

Aristotle begins *De Anima*, chapter 8, with the following famous claim:

> But now, bringing together the things said about soul under one head, let us say again that soul is somehow all the beings. (431b20–21)

Before launching into his account of soul as motive, Aristotle summarizes—he unifies his account of soul as "that which unifies." He does it with a view to providing the best possible foundation for the remainder of the argument of *De Anima*—that is, he does it with a good or end in view.

Soul is somehow all beings. There are sensible beings and thinkable beings (the assumption is that these are exhaustive of what is). Soul takes both in and is somehow both. But what is the meaning of this "somehow"? Soul has the potential to actualize all things, whether sensible or thinkable, but it does not simply reproduce them. Rather, soul takes in their forms—their *eidē*. But what does this mean? Aristotle gives us only an analogy, an image of what he has in mind: "The soul is like the hand, a tool of tools, and the mind is a form of forms [*eidos eidōn*] and sensation a form of sensibles" (432a1–3). The hand is a tool of tools in fitting itself to special tools, each of which is designed to do one job. By itself, the hand cannot do what a screwdriver, a keyboard, or a toothbrush does. It supplies the general force that activates the potentiality specific to each tool. The mind (notably not the soul here) is thus like an empty hand. It cannot do anything without the *eidē* as instruments (one of which seems to be the *eidos* of the sensibles, which seems to be the same as the form of bodies once body has been left behind). Now, if the function of *eidē* generally is the division of the unlimited continuum of being into different kinds of beings, then the mind would use them for this purpose. Still, as itself an *eidos*, it would have to be a principle of division, of distinctness. The mind is what divides, and so makes ones, in general. In specific, it is what provides the general force that allows the specific *eidē* to do their jobs. To know mind in its specific character thus means to know it as not thinking anything in particular; it is to know it as identical to the "it" that it happens to be thinking. Yet, if the mind, like the hand, is a tool of tools, and if this means using an *eidos* to turn one's attention to something, then what is it that turns mind on? What *moves* us to attend to one thing rather than another?

Aristotle's move from soul to mind at 432a1 suggests an answer. As the

19 · See chapter 1 above.

form of forms, soul is necessarily like what it orders—it is a more general tool than the specific tools it uses. This connects soul as form of forms to mind, which seems objective—neutral. However, as what calls our attention *to*, soul as form of forms is necessarily unlike what it orders. It is not simply used—it uses. Insofar as soul is like what it knows, it is one with itself; it is a knower of knowable things and is itself a knowable thing. Insofar as soul is unlike what it knows, it is apart from itself; it is an unknown knower of the knowable. Now, that soul is somehow *all* things means that both must be true. Soul could not be what it is unless both were true.

To explain how soul is somehow all things, Aristotle must rely on an image—an image connecting soul with touch insofar as the activity of knowing is likened to grasping. Aristotle had claimed that "all beings" were exhausted in the combination of thinkable and sensible (431b21–24). This is, of course, true only if we include the imageable in the thinkable.

> And on account of this, one not sensing anything could neither learn nor understand anything, and when he contemplates, it is necessary at the same time to contemplate some image. For images are just like sensibles, except without matter. And imagination is different [*heteron*] from affirmation and denial since the true or the false is a weaving together of intelligibles. The first intelligibles, in what way will they differ from being images? Or are these not images, but not without images? (432a7–13)

Imagination is sensation without matter, and, while thinking is not imagining, thought is impossible without images. Aristotle has set the stage for another account of *phantasia*. As necessary for both thinking and, by way of sensation, movement, it will be the principle of the problematic unity of the soul.

To make imagination central means to make central the nature of appearance as appearance, and not as reality. It is to make what we would call subjectivity central—the fact that I sense something rather than the something I sense. This makes possible a bond between what thinks from its own perspective and what acts for its own good. With *phantasia*, the "ownness" of soul emerges—that is, its experience of its own ownness.[20] This is why the unity of soul emerges only in the context of the possibility of error. The argument of *De Anima* itself illustrates a certain motion within thinking. Soul as the *eidos* of *eidē* wants to become what it is by becoming what it isn't. Or, soul senses some connection between itself as everything and itself as

20 · Consider with this Martin Heidegger, *Nietzsche*, Erster Band (Pfullingen, Germany: Verlag Neske, 1961), s.358–59.

itself. But the one is no more possible than the other. Now, the *eidos* of *eidē* ought to be the being of the beings, and yet this is not what soul is. Rather, it is the awareness of the being of the beings. This awareness, however, shows up only as an awareness of the differences among beings—that is, the particular *eidē* in their differences make manifest the disparity among beings. The soul thus shows up as an awareness of partiality.[21] But a conscious lack is a desire. Thus, in its being as the *eidos* of *eidē*, soul is already desiring soul. Desire is built into soul as aware.

What, then, does it mean that soul initiates movement? First we must ask whether all soul initiates movement or only a part. And before this we must ask what the parts of soul are. Now, Aristotle says in one sense they are unlimited—that is, soul is somehow all beings. And insofar as it has parts, there are various candidates (432a25–b3). Some divide the soul into calculating, spirited, and desiring parts—Aristotle clearly has *Republic*, book 4, in mind. Others—namely, Aristotle himself in *Nicomachean Ethics*, books 1 and 6—divide the soul into rational and irrational parts. For still others, like Aristotle in *De Anima*, the soul divides into nutritive, sensitive, and the imagination (notice that mind has been absorbed into the imagination). The division one opts for seems to depend on what one plans to do with it. The division of the soul by thought into parts that are one seems like a mathematical construction; it is for the sake of making something manifest. The division is therefore governed by its end—the good at which it aims. This seems to be Aristotle's point when he says the following:

> This tearing apart is surely absurd [*atopon*]. For wishing comes to be in the calculating [part], and desire and spirit in the irrational. But if the soul is three, appetite will be in each. (432b4–7)

Appetite in some way governs thought.

Aristotle first eliminates nutritive soul as a source of motion. Motion, as always for the sake of some end, requires both appetite and imagination, for it must be possible to make present what is not present as not present if it is to be aimed at. Nor is sensing soul a possibility since many animals lacking movement nevertheless have sensation. "So-called mind" (432b26) or the calculative part (*logismos*) cannot initiate motion since mind thinks things without the attraction or repulsion that attends them. Not even appetite by itself is sufficient since it is possible to resist it. What appears (*phainetai*, 433a9) to initiate motion is appetite in conjunction with mind. But mind proves to qualify only insofar as we consider *phantasia* a species of

21 · See my *Autobiography of Philosophy* (Lanham, MD: Rowman & Littlefield, 1999), 51–65.

thinking—that is, thinking in connection with a representation of something particular. And appetite has just been denied to be a separate faculty of soul.

Appetite provokes, and practical mind (this seems to be the thinking that is connected to imagining) follows. That is, appetite posits the end, and practical mind calculates the means to that end and therefore identifies the first step to be taken. At 433a18, Aristotle replaces appetite (*orexis*) with the object of appetite (*to orekton*), which now becomes the origin or *archē* not for mind but for thinking through (*dianoia*). However we are to understand the two parts of motion, Aristotle now combines them into one since the agent of movement must be one *eidos*. He calls the unified cause of motion wish (*boulēsis*), and the object of appetite now becomes "the good" or "the apparent good." Aristotle therefore seems determined to hedge. The origin of motion must be one because if it were two, there would be no motion of *this* soul. Yet the origin of motion must be two because the object of longing must be simultaneously present and absent to soul for motion to be initiated. It is this double demand that forces Aristotle to introduce time into the argument. Only a being with a sense of time could perceive appetites as at odds, but this means a being able to step out of time and compare the two appetites. Were this not possible, the appetites would be like vectors resolved in the direction and strength that their combination dictated. They would never be perceived as distinct. Mind thus tells us to "hold back because of what will come in the future," while appetite tells us that "what is in the present is good." We must be able to step back and compare the two times. At the same time, it is also true that a sense of time is necessary for a soul to initiate any movement across space. It must be necessary to make present what is absent as present. This cannot mean simply being immersed in the flow of time. The initiation of motion therefore requires *phantasia* both as a species of thinking and as inseparable from appetite.

Movement has three elements: what originates movement, that by which it does so, and what is moved. The first is double; it involves an unmoved mover, the object of appetite or the good, and a moved mover, the faculty of appetite. The final element, what is moved, is the animal. What about the second element, that by which the first moves the third? This is a gap that Aristotle does not, and somehow cannot, fill. It would require a bodily account that he cannot give. Still, he wants to say it is the meeting point of the other two elements—what is unmoved but moves and what moves.[22]

---

22 · The example Aristotle uses to illustrate this combination, the concave and the convex, seems designed to remind us of the relation between the two parts of the soul, rational and irrational, in *Nicomachean Ethics* 1.13.

Aristotle admits that soul must be simultaneously at rest and in motion. On the one hand, this is perplexing; on the other, he means us to see that the soul could not be understood to be in motion (in time) *unless* it were at the same time understood to be at rest.

At the end of *De Anima*, Aristotle seems to return to the view he rejected at the beginning. Book 1, chapters 2–5, is an extended argument to show that soul should not be understood as a principle of motion and awareness. Aristotle argues that his predecessors erred by placing soul in space and time. Accordingly, in book 2, chapter 1, he defines soul as a first entelechy of natural body with a potency for life. This proves to mean that his predecessors did not think sufficiently about plants. What, then, are we to make of Aristotle's claim late in *De Anima* (432a15–17) that the soul of animals is defined by two potencies—the first discriminating, which is the work of thinking through and of sensation, and the second moving, with respect to local motion? And what are we to make of the enhanced role of touch as that by which every ensouled body senses (435a13–14)? In the end, Aristotle seems to restore the conventional view of soul, and as a consequence, plants seem to disappear as ensouled beings. Put somewhat differently, the reemphasis on soul as principle of both motion and awareness somehow seems to require the revision of Aristotle's account of sensation so that touch becomes the paradigmatic sense. Why?

Aristotle restores the ordinary view he had rejected, because having shown that appearances, *ta phainomena*, are not what we thought they were, he is now prepared to give an account that preserves appearances. On the level of the argument of *De Anima*, then, Aristotle first explodes the apparent, then gives an alternate account that is not apparent and requires him to introduce considerable technical language, and finally returns to give an account of the apparent. *De Anima* is thus an account of the being of seeming—that is, of something that, because it has as its being to somehow be something else, is essentially incomplete in its own being.

The end of *De Anima* also emphasizes teleology in a way hitherto unprecedented in the book (for example, at 434a30–32). This is connected to Aristotle's attempt to think together motion (active soul) and awareness (passive soul). On the one hand, to register the world means in some way to be immersed in it. On the other hand, self-movement—initiating a causal chain—means to be outside the world. The question is how both are possible. If an intention amounts to an idea of what is good, then motive soul would be somehow rooted in cognitive soul. Teleology seems to be a view of the world according to which what is necessary for understanding is also necessary for action. A teleological account would thus put together the pieces of the rational animal. The problem, however, is that perfect teleology—entelechy, where a being is at its end—is rather like the behavior of a plant, where there is no possibility of deviation and therefore no awareness of alternatives.[23] Genuine teleology may prove to require incompleteness (433b31). Soul would then be most fully revealed neither by plants nor by mind but by animals. Only with the incomplete does *phantasia* enter; it is characteristic of animals and the crucial feature of soul as imperfect. One might say, with all the appropriate qualifications, that because soul is what becomes more perfect (more an entelechy) when it is less perfect, for Aristotle, only animals have souls. Soul is a first entelechy as a kind of potency or possibility, but in plants this is always operating. Because they have no off/on switches, in them entelechy is a kind of mechanism. *De Anima* as a whole is the progressive story of the demechanizing of soul, making it more perfect as it becomes less perfect.

Aristotle's account makes appetite ultimately responsible for motion; it provokes motion by identifying an end. Thereafter, mind specifies the means to this end, and appetite is transferred from the end in question to the means that will bring it about. This process requires that the object of appetite—whether ultimate or immediate—be at once present to us and absent, and this, in turn, requires *phantasia*. While this may seem at least in part adequate as an account of how the human soul initiates movement, what about animal souls of the sort that lack practical mind? The question must be broached, for at least on one level, Aristotle seems concerned with animals in only a minimal sense—that is, with incomplete beings, beings not at entelechy (433b31–434a5). To explain the movement of such beings, Aristotle must introduce alternative versions of desire and *phantasia*, which are now said to be present indeterminately (*aoristōs*). We are able to understand this only as a construct, for the desire and imagination under consideration are certainly not ours (434a6–10). It is necessary to have some way to render conflicting impulses one so as to make movement possible. Appetite can conflict with deliberation, as it frequently does in human beings, but it can also conflict with appetite. How exactly then is it possible that an animal is torn between conflicting alternatives? Aristotle proceeds to discuss the faculty of knowing and says that it is not moved (434a16). That is, knowing sets up the possibility for a certain kind of motion, but only appetite flips the switch. Still, in the unmoved thinking faculty, one part— concerned with the particular and not the general—is more responsible for initiating motion (334a17–21). Of course this means that in some measure both parts have this responsibility. The question of what causes motion then

---

23 · See my *Politics of Philosophy: A Commentary on Aristotle's Politics* (Lanham, MD: Rowman & Littlefield, 1996), 15–26.

seems irreducibly double. First we are told that appetite and mind together
are the source of motion. Then we are told that appetite actually initiates
motion—mind merely makes it a possibility. Yet appetite divides into deliberative and nondeliberative. In the former, responsibility is once again split
into a cognitive part (*phantasia*) and a noncognitive part (desire); in the
latter, this split is duplicated, but because nondeliberative appetite presumably lacks a deliberative or cognitive component, here imagination and desire are said to be "indeterminate." On the other side of the divide—the part
that does not throw the switch—mind nevertheless splits into a part more
mind-like and a part more appetite-like. The first deals with the general and
does not initiate motion; the second with the particular and initiates motion more although doesn't do so really. The one constant in this account of
the motive power of soul is the persistence of both parts of soul in each part
even after our divisions have supposedly separated the two. Aristotle seems
to have reproduced the "indeterminate dyad" he elsewhere assigns to Plato
as a fundamental principle.[24]

That soul is an indeterminate dyad is connected to Aristotle's rethinking
of touch at the end of *De Anima*. Local motion requires sensation, for, once
an ensouled being is uprooted, in order to get nourishment, it must be able
to locate something apart from itself that will provide it. Depending on
its location, a plant will either get nourishment or not, but a being able to
change location can seek nutrition and therefore needs to be able to "know"
to stop when it finds it. Thus, in animals, at least, nutrition requires sensation. And we have already seen that thinking requires imagination, which,
in turn, requires sensation (427b14–16, 431a16–17). But there is no sensation without touch (435a14–20). Touch is therefore at once the condition
for motion and for thought. Touch is somehow the principle of the unity
of soul as responsible for both motion and awareness. We have already seen
that *phantasia* binds together the two parts of soul that are aware. It unifies
sensing and knowing, but it does so in a way that undermines the purity of
both. That there is no thinking without images means that desire always
permeates thought. That sensing is always of objects means that thought
always permeates sensation. The question that looms large at the end of *De
Anima* is the relation of these two unifiers—*phantasia* and touch.

Touch is special because all sensation in a way reduces to it. With the
exception of taste, the other senses simply "touch" indirectly by way of an
in-between medium. Touch, on the other hand, seems to put us in direct
contact with its object (435a17–20). Touch (*haphē*) derives from the verb
haptō, which means "to fasten on" or "to grasp." More than any other sense,

24 · See *Metaphysics* 987b20–26, 1081a–b, and 1088a–b.

then, touch seems to place us directly in the world. We are not detached from it, and, as our taking in of it is a part of it, the act of taking it in alters it and alters us. We feel pleasures and pains because of these alterations, and so our thinking and sensing are colored by the goods we apprehend. Unlike the other senses, we cannot turn touch on and off. It is intimately connected to our survival. What we touch and eat affects our whole being. Excessive light may destroy the eyes, but excessive touch leads to death, so that when touch is altogether gone, so are we. Touch, then, more than any of the other faculties of soul, is somehow what it means to be alive.

Now, while all of this has a plausible ring, we ought not to forget what Aristotle says in his earlier account of touch (423b1–8, 423b22–23). Touch and taste are in fact not in direct contact with their objects. The truth of the matter seems to be that touch is the illusory overcoming of the distinction between inside and outside. While we seem to grasp things themselves with no distance between us and them, touch is the actual manifestation of the character of the distance between us and them. It establishes distance as decisive for soul, but a distance that comes to be aware of itself as distance only in its attempt to close the gap between itself and the world. Touch shows that it is soul's nature to want to close this gap. This distance is the "somehow" of "Soul is somehow all beings." It is the character of soul as soul. To be soul is to be alienated.

This is connected as well to the imagination. On the one hand, touch seems to overcome the split between inside and outside by putting us in direct contact with what is outside. It seems to bring us outside. The most extreme version of this would be plants—a sort of limit case of soul where soul finally disappears. On the other hand, *phantasia* seems to overcome the split between inside and outside by bringing the outside altogether inside. The most extreme version of this would be pure mind—a sort of limit case of soul where soul finally disappears. But the closing of the gap between inside and outside effected by *phantasia* is also illusory, for *phantasia* is not possible without sensation, which always brings with it a necessary trace of the outside as outside. Both touch and *phantasia* may be said to unify the soul because superficially they collapse the distinction between inside and outside. But that there are two versions of this unification suggests that neither is altogether successful. On reflection—that is, at a distance—both touch and *phantasia* prove to be affirmations of the very distance they appear to overcome. And both of them do this both on the level of unmoving awareness and on the level of appetite and motion. Two things thus point to the being of soul as something that shows its unity in its ongoing attempt to overcome its multiplicity. This potency (*dunamis*) of soul is somehow its actuality (*energeia*).

Aristotle's own account of soul in *De Anima* begins with plants. Plant soul is peculiarly like the soul of a god in its lack of motion. Aristotle "ends" his account with pure mind. It too seems peculiarly like the soul of a god. Together these two point to the problem of unity, which is somehow what constitutes soul as soul. Aristotle explores another version of this problem in his *Nicomachean Ethics*.

CHAPTER 3

The Soul as Self and Self-Aware

I. "The Father of the *Logos*"

The *Nicomachean Ethics* speaks to us about what is most important to us in what proves a deceptively straightforward way. Everything human beings do is goal-directed; it aims at some good, whether real or apparent. Every good, in turn, must be either an instrument for the sake of some further good or final and for the sake of itself. Now, if all goods were instrumental, their goodness would always be defined by another good, the goodness of which would, in turn, be derived from some still further good. As there would be in principle no end of such goods, they could also in principle have no beginning. Everything would be good for nothing, and so nothing would be good. And yet since we do experience things as good, must there not be a good that is final and for the sake of itself? Human beings demonstrate their belief that there is such a good by agreeing on its name— happiness—while nevertheless disagreeing on what happiness is. The most important question for us, then, is What is human happiness? To raise it in a serious way, we must first ask what human beings are, and this requires that we ask after the function, task, or deed (*ergon*) that is specifically human. Now, human beings are distinct not insofar as we are ensouled (we share this with plants and animals), or insofar as we desire and move ourselves in accordance with our desires (this we share with animals), but rather insofar as we have *logos*—speech or reason. It stands to reason, then, that a distinctly human happiness would consist in the exercise of what most truly distinguishes us in a way that allows its unimpeded activity. Accordingly, Aristotle defines human happiness, that good which is for its own sake and not for the sake of anything else, as activity of soul in accordance with the virtue that is distinctively human—that is, rational activity. Rational activity, however, takes two forms. On the one hand, reason may govern our desires or appetites; on the other, it is directed at its own ends. It is practical, and it is theoretical. Accordingly, there are two forms of virtue indispensable for human happiness—moral virtue and intellectual virtue.

Now, the foregoing is a summary (far too simple) of the argument of book 1 of the *Nicomachean Ethics*. It prepares the way first for an account of moral virtue in general (books 2–3.5), and then an account of the specific moral virtues (books 3.6–5), followed by an account of intellectual virtue (book 6). Thereafter, things seem to get a little more complicated. Aristotle first finds it necessary to make a second beginning in book 7, then turns to the question of friendship in books 8–9, and concludes by examining the life of contemplation in book 10. Still, complexities notwithstanding, one thing should be clear: the question of the human soul is the heart of Aristotle's account of the human good. What, then, is this soul?

At the end of book 1, Aristotle gives an account of the structure of the human soul in what seems at first a fairly straightforward manner, as is apparent from the following passages (excerpted, but in their original order):

> Some things are said sufficiently about [the soul] in everyday speech [literally, "external speeches"—*exōterikoi logoi*], and we must use them—for example, on the one hand, for there to be a nonrational [*alogon*] [part] of it and, on the other, a [part] having reason [*logon echon*]. (1102a28–30)

> Of the nonrational, the one seems common to plants—I mean the cause of being nourished and of growth. (1102a34–b1)

> But there seems to be another nature of nonrational soul, participating, however, in some way in *logos*. For we praise the *logos*, and that in the soul that has *logos*, of those who are continent and of those incontinent.... (1102b13–16)

> The nonrational indeed also appears double—the plantlike in no way sharing *logos*, while the desiring and generally appetitive somehow does participate, as it heeds and obeys it (thus we also say [to heed and obey] a father or friends is "to have *logos*" but not in the way we [heed or obey] mathematicians). (1102b29–34)

> And if one must say this too to have *logos*, having *logos* will also be double—on the one hand, sovereignly and in itself and, on the other hand, as ready to hear a father. (1103a2–4)

This soul contains the elements present in *De Anima* but differs in its explicitly progressively dyadic structure. It first divides into a rational part and a nonrational part. The nonrational part then also divides in two—the nutritive, vegetative, or plantlike and the desiring or appetitive. The latter is capable of listening to reason, which suggests that there must be a part of the rational soul that speaks to it. Accordingly, the rational part of soul also divides in two—that is, into a practical part and a purely theoretical part. This seems to be the structure of soul. But is it?

Aristotle himself raises our suspicions when he remarks first of the difference between rational and nonrational soul that

> whether these divide as do the proper parts of the body and all that is divisible into parts or, although two in *logos*, are inseparable by nature (like the convex and the concave in a curve) makes no difference for the present. (1102a30–34)

And later, of the opposition manifest in acts of continence and incontinence within the soul itself, he says that

> perhaps also in the soul something must be held to exist contrary to *logos*, in opposition to and standing against it (how it is other makes no difference). (1102b24–26)

These parts of the soul may therefore not be proper parts at all but only different for the purposes of the argument—different in *logos*. To this must be added a queer fact. Aristotle nowhere in book 1 quite specifies, and indeed seems to go out of his way not to specify, that part of the rational soul giving commands to the appetites.[1] Instead, he always refers to that part of the soul "having *logos*" in the sense of a rule of conduct imposed from without. As this would be the very part of the soul in which we would expect moral virtue as rational *activity* to be located, its omission is a serious matter.

The problem may be seen most starkly when one considers the image used to shed light on the nature of this part of rational soul. Soul has reason in a double sense—"on the one hand sovereignly and in itself and on the other hand as ready to hear a father." Rational soul is two. In the only description Aristotle gives of this division, one part is said to be sovereign, the other like a child. The subsequent division of virtue into two kinds is based on this split in the soul. The sovereign rational soul is the home of intellectual virtue, the childlike rational soul of moral virtue. But, as Aristotle himself says, just as we cannot properly speak of the happiness of a cow

---

1 · This needs to be compared to book 6 (1139a5–9), where Aristotle specifies that the soul has a rational and a nonrational part and then of the former says, "Now let two [parts] having *logos* be assumed, one in which we contemplate [*theōroumen*] the sort of beings of which the principles do not allow of being otherwise and one in which [we contemplate] those things that do allow [of being otherwise]." While the argument of book 6 requires a more rigid distinction, it is not simply to be taken at face value; indeed, even in book 6, Aristotle introduces the parts of rational soul as existing by hypothesis and not necessarily in reality. Once again, they are for the sake of the *logos*.

or a horse, "no child is happy, for not yet is it able to perform such deeds [noble deeds] on account of its age" (1100a2–3). How, then, is it possible for moral virtue to make us happy? The whole project of the *Nicomachean Ethics* seems to depend on a "part" of the soul that never really makes an appearance. Where is the father of the *logos*?

There are various ways in which this question can be pursued. The simplest perhaps is that the father of the *logos* is a father, or a mother. Initially, at least, someone else's reason, usually a parent's, governs our appetites. Accordingly, at the very beginning of book 2, Aristotle points to the etymological connection between character (*ēthos*) and habit (*ethos*). The image is striking; just as a short vowel gets progressively lengthened until finally an altogether different sound and word emerges, so also habitual behavior is ultimately transformed into character. In neither case, however, is it clear exactly how this happens. As far as it goes, book 2 gives a plausible etymology—a genealogy—of the morally responsible agent. From the beginning, pleasure and pain govern us. Through some agency external to us—the "father"—we are habituated by means of pleasure and pain to resist pleasure and pain. These rewards and spankings engender a split in the soul that makes it possible for us to take pleasure in our very resistance to pleasure and pain while at the same time making self-awareness possible. Long before Freud, then, Aristotle gives an account of how external authority is internalized. However, he is unwilling to leave matters at the level of a descriptive psychology, for this would amount to an account of moral agency as illusory, however pleasant the illusion. Accordingly, in book 3, Aristotle will turn to the last of the issues preliminary to an account of the moral virtues severally—the voluntary in its connection to intentional action—for we still do not know how what comes to be from training or habit (*ethos*) is transformed into a responsible agent, character (*ēthos*). How is it possible for something essentially formed by its context to lift itself outside of that context so as to move from having been a part of the world determined by its antecedents to become something separate and apart from the world? Or, what does it mean for the part of soul that has *logos* in the sense of having an externally imposed structure or pattern of behavior to come to have *logos* in the sense of a power to impose such a structure? How does *logos*, the noun without a subject, become *legein*, a verb requiring a subject? A version of this difficulty emerges in book 2, when Aristotle twice articulates a duality within virtue. Virtue is on the one hand a mean between two extremes of irrationality (1107a2) and on the other an art of aiming at the mean (1106b16). In the first case, we "have *logos*" in the sense of embodying rational activity so perfectly that it would be as natural to us as digestion and hence scarcely involve choice at all. In the second case, we "have *logos*" in the sense of having a power to choose that suggests a certain detachment from what it is that we are choosing.[2]

The same duality recurs in book 3, where the most striking feature of the account of choice is the way Aristotle keeps returning to the question of whether all action might be involuntary. Since action always occurs within a context that is not itself chosen, no action is voluntary simply or in itself. Aristotle himself acknowledges that saving one's life in a storm at sea by jettisoning cargo is at the very least a mixture of the voluntary and the involuntary. One chooses from among the limited options available in the situation but would never choose the situation itself. Now, given that pleasure and pain as accompanying all action constitute each situation, and given that we do not choose what pleases and pains us, how can any of our actions be understood to be voluntary? Put in the most radical way, how can any being with a nature be understood to be responsible for its own behavior? The "I" of "I will" seems as problematic as the "I" of "I think."

Aristotle twice (1110b10–18, 1114b20–25) responds to this radical argument with the threat that if it were true, we would have to forgo not only blame but praise as well. At first, this seems hardly decisive; we could simply accept the loss of praise as the price for avoiding blame. But Aristotle has shrewdly seen that the issue of the voluntary comes up at all only because we want to escape feeling responsible for our actions, and yet only one who already feels responsible wants to escape responsibility. It may be true that "if one should say the pleasant and beautiful things to be by force (for, being external, they necessitate), then everything would be by force" (1110b9–11), but no one can really affirm the protasis of this conditional. To say things are pleasant and beautiful is to have identified them as desirable and so to have longed for them already in one's thoughts. One cannot identify the beautiful without imagining oneself in pursuit of it. Aristotle thus means to point to the fact that to have wondered about morality is already to consider oneself moral, and so to have thought of oneself as a responsible agent. It is for this reason that he makes a point of saying that although one can be ignorant of some of the facets of one's action so as to make it nonvoluntary, one can never not know that one is the agent of one's own action. "For how," says Aristotle, "would anyone be ignorant of himself?" (1111a8).

The rational part of the soul that commands the appetites is the crucial part of the soul, for it alone bridges the gap between our nature as animal and our nature as rational; it alone makes us whole. This part that disappeared at the end of book 1 reappears in book 3 as what we cannot be igno-

---

2 · Compare this to the tension between intelligibility and intelligence discussed in part 4, chapter 12, in connection to Plato's *Euthyphro*.

rant of, for our very attempt to find it makes it manifest. But while Aristotle has apparently shown us ourselves in the search for our selves, perhaps we have not been sufficiently scrupulous in following the *logos* in which we reveal ourselves to ourselves. We seem only to know *that* this is the case and not precisely *how* it is the case. We have the argument without having argued it.

Now that we know that we are in search of the soul, we must make a fresh beginning and turn to the opening sentences of book 1.

> Every art [*technē*] and every inquiry [*methodos*], and similarly every action [*praxis*] and intention [*proairesis*], seems to aim at some good. Therefore, they have beautifully/nobly [*kalōs*] asserted the good [to be] what all things aim at. But a difference appears among ends [*telē*]. For some are activities [*energeiai*], but some are certain products [*erga*] apart from them [the activities]. And of those, where certain ends are apart from the actions [*praxeis*], among these the products [*erga*] are better by nature than the activities [*energeiai*]. (1094a1–7)

Aristotle begins with a list of things that human beings do; they all seem to aim at goods, although we do not yet know whether they seem to do so to those who do them or to observers of them or to both. Then Aristotle draws the quite extravagant conclusion that all things (now neuter, so he seems really to mean all things) aim (they do not just seem to aim) at *the* good. This extravagance is attributed to others, who are said to commit it *kalōs*— beautifully (we wonder in passing what beauty has to do with extravagance). In the next two sentences, Aristotle first divides ends in two: *energeiai*— activities; and *erga*—products, works, or deeds apart from "them," namely, apart from *energeiai*. Aristotle thus looks at the world and sees two sorts of things we do: we dance and we make shoes. Then he adds that some ends are apart from actions—*praxeis*; these ends are called *erga* (the action leading to them goes unnamed). Some actions do not have ends apart from them; these are called *energeiai* (the etymology of *energeia* helps him here, since it suggests something that has its *ergon* within—*en*). Then, however, Aristotle adds that in actions (*praxeis*) with ends that are apart, the *erga* are better by nature than the *energeiai*. Now, here *energeia* clearly must refer to an action apart from its *ergon*—its work understood as its end. But this is not what it meant at the start. Notice what has happened. *Energeia* initially refers to an action like dancing that is understood as complete because done for its own sake and so not instrumental to some end outside itself. It comes to be understood as incomplete when it is characterized as a *praxis* that leads to some end, some *ergon*. In the space of two sentences, *energeia* has been emptied of its *ergon* and more or less treated as a synonym of *praxis*. Aristotle thus reproduces a motion in which activities originally understood as for their own sakes are subsequently understood as instrumental. This proves to be exactly what happens in the opening argument of the *Nicomachean Ethics*. Having begun with a crucial distinction between art or craft (*technē*) and inquiry on the one hand and action and intention on the other, Aristotle proceeds to argue for the existence of something good in itself on the basis of an analogy to the hierarchy among the arts alone, even saying, "It makes no difference whether the *energeiai* themselves are the ends of the actions or something else apart from them" (1094a16–18).

Aristotle begins with an observation about particular things—they each aim at what seems good. He then identifies the generalization that all things aim at *the* good with the *kalon*—the beautiful. This *kalon* generalization about the good leads us to conclude that the apparent goods at which our original empirically observed instances aim cannot simply be good. That is, the *kalon* generalization has the effect of transforming all goods experienced by us, even those originally experienced as good in themselves or *energeiai*, into instrumental goods. Dancing first seems to be an example of something good in itself, but when placed in relation to what is good simply—say, happiness—dancing looks to be instrumental. What was first an *energeia* in the sense of having an end within itself comes to be understood as an *energeia* with an end apart from it. This transformation is the effect on the good of attempting to know the good. That the movement of the initial sentences of the *Nicomachean Ethics* is not accidental seems clear when we remember that later in book 1, Aristotle articulates the human good by way of the *ergon* (here apparently to be understood as function) of human beings. And this *ergon* of human beings is the "*energeia* of the soul according to *logos* or not without *logos*" (1098a7–8). In the very act of spelling out the fact that the human good cannot be understood as an object, it is turned into an object. This seems to be a necessity of thought, which understands what is within by rendering it as external.[3]

Let us take another look at the opening sentence:

> Every art [*technē*] and every inquiry [*methodos*], and similarly every action [*praxis*] and intention [*proairesis*], seems to aim at some good.

Four things are coupled in two ways. The first split is between theoretical and practical—art and inquiry being relatively more theoretical than action and intention. In the second, less obvious than the first, art and action belong together over and against inquiry and intention, for the first pair is connected to a visible and external result, while inquiry and intention both seem invisible apart from what they lead to. They are both incomplete in

---

3 · See Seth Benardete, "Aristotle, *De Anima* III.3–5," *Review of Metaphysics* 28, no. 4 (June 1975): 611.

their natures and essentially internal. The principle at work in this second way of pairing the things that seem to aim at some good is the split between inside and outside.

Aristotle's second sentence points to something peculiar about the first:

> Therefore, they have beautifully/nobly [*kalōs*] asserted the good [to be] what all things aim at.

It is not human beings that are said to have aimed at the good, but the various things we do. Aristotle has taken the realm of intention (something essentially internal in the sense that it can never be fully revealed by anything we can see) and treated it as though it were an external phenomenon. The remainder of the chapter confirms this movement outside. First inquiry and intention drop out of the argument altogether and are replaced by knowledge or science—*epistēmē* (1094a7–8) (perhaps because Aristotle needs activities with obvious ends, and inquiry and intention are rather too indeterminate for his purposes). Within ten lines, by using art or *technē* as a model for everything we do, Aristotle implicitly folds action into *technē* and explicitly collapses *technē* and *epistēmē*, with the result that the model for all human behavior has become that sort of activity which always has an end apart from itself, an end that can be understood as external and visible.

Having made *technē* the paradigm for what aims at the good, Aristotle then argues for a hierarchy among goods based on a hierarchy among the arts: the art of bridle making is for the sake of the art of horsemanship, which is, in turn, for the sake of generalship, and so on. The argument is problematic in several ways. It does not account for the sort of activity in which the end is unknown or only dimly known. One could not, for example, subordinate one inquiry to another in this way unless one always knew in advance where the inquiry would end, and then, of course, it would not be an inquiry. One also wonders about those arts that are instrumental to things that appear to be ends in themselves. The model works for shipbuilding because a ship is not so much a good as rather itself an instrument; it is not so clear, however, that it works for medicine, generalship, and household management insofar as it seems possible to consider health, the city, and the family ends in themselves. Finally, to make the case for hierarchy, Aristotle must assume that each art exists as a part of a single hierarchical system of arts. But, while the subordination of bridle making to the art of horsemanship may be necessary, it is not so clear why horsemanship must lead to generalship rather than, say, to commerce or to arts dealing with leisure or exercise. The importance of this becomes clear when this string of arts subordinated to other arts ends with a sort of et cetera —saying that "others [*alla*] are under others [*hetera*]" (1094a14). Aristotle regularly takes advantage of the hint of difference between these two words for "other"—*allo* tending to mean other in an absolute sense and *heteron* one of a pair of two things defined in opposition to each other.[4] Their use here suggests that each art is linked to a specific other art (as *heteron*), only looking backward from the end and not forward. There is therefore no way to determine in advance—that is, from the vantage point of the lesser arts— the architectonic art that deals with the highest good and subordinates all other arts. The architectonic art thus exists solely as posited and not as experienced. The claim that the political art is architectonic is a hypothesis, not an observed phenomenon. This is why Aristotle briefly substitutes the word *dunamis*—"potentiality"—for *technē* at 1094a11. While the purpose of the art of shoemaking is clear, the end of the architectonic art exists as much by definition as by fact. Accordingly, it turns out that we pursue ends perceived as actually good—that is, perceived initially as *energeiai*—for the sake of an end perceived only in its potentiality. Thus, the good of the city, a hypothetical unity, is said to supersede the good of its parts. Aristotle justifies this claim by saying the good of the city is more *kalon* and more divine (1094b10–11), once again linking the beautiful with what is so general as never actually to be experienced.

The argument of the first chapter of book 1, powerful on its face, on second thought is not really successful. Its failure turns on Aristotle's illicit use of *technē*, with its separation of the product or outcome of the activity from the activity, as a paradigm for the structure of all human behavior. And yet, it is perhaps worth looking at the beautiful things even thrice, for a third look suggests that it is the error of the argument that is in fact paradigmatic of the activity of the human soul and so deeply revelatory of its nature. What remains is to see how it is a paradigm for rational activity not only as thinking but also as morality.

In the second chapter of book 1, Aristotle introduces politics as the architectonic art; it orders all the other goods using as a standard "the good and the best" (1094a23), which is what "we wish on account of itself" (1094a19–20). And yet, it is not at all clear that the goal of the art of politics is the same as the goal of the one practicing the art. Who is to be satisfied, the city or the statesman? Put differently, what effect will knowledge of the good as political have on me as individual? That political life comes in at all here suggests that for human beings singly, the comprehensive good is not available. But this means that the *polis*, the city, is simply another way of placing the good *outside* the activity of the individual. The political art is supposed to be of great benefit—it is supposed to be good—by provid-

4 · Compare, for example, 1166a30 with 1170b7, and see *On Poetics* 1450b20–1451a15.

ing comprehensive knowledge of what to aim at in life, yet knowledge of what the *polis* should aim at is not the same as knowledge of what I should aim at. From the city's point of view, I make shoes; from my point of view, I may make money. Aristotle is aware of this difference, as is clear when he remarks that to secure the good "for one alone is estimable [*agapēton*], but for a tribe or a city is more *kalon* and more divine" (1094b10–11). With this he introduces a doubleness to the human good; it involves both satisfaction and self-sacrifice, and it is not clear how the two will be related.

This doubleness is related to the distinction Aristotle proceeds now to introduce between the beautiful (*kalon*) and the just. The *kalon* is the good in its character as for its own sake—an activity that is whole and self-sufficient. We come to believe such an activity exists by observing the various activities of our everyday lives that we at first take to be simply for their own sakes—dance, for example. But even these activities are parts of our lives taken as wholes, and their goodness is measured in terms of this wholeness. All the goods of our experience are thus experienced as "good for"; they are only apparent wholes that always turn out to be parts point-ing to a larger and more complete whole of which we have no experience and which tends to undermine the experience of the *kalon* that we do have by being understood as yet more *kalon* and divine. Politics substitutes for this illusive final good the collective good—the just or fair distribution of goods, and in this way makes the various original instances of the *kalon* parts of an observable whole—the *polis*. But in so doing, it conceals an ambiguity, for the good of the whole involves different goods for different people within the whole for whom its wholeness is not an issue, and this is not identical to the good of the one who oversees the whole, who will be happy only because in securing the general good, he experiences the good as a whole—as *kalon*. Now, directly after Aristotle stipulates that politics is the most sovereign and architectonic art because concerned with that good which is best, he says that it has as its double end the *kalon* and the just (1094b15). Its unity is chronically threatened by the demand that it be simultaneously part and whole.

These two, the *kalon* and the just, are therefore not altogether persuasive in their claims to be good. They seem conventional and not natural—the *kalon* because it is only a false whole and so is deceptive; the just because it leads to a multiplicity of goods with no organizing principle and so is insufficiently one. Accordingly, there can be no precision in an account of the good, for such an account will err in taking goods either as wholes or as parts. The one is complete but imprecise, the other incomplete but precise. How, then, are we to judge what is good? Aristotle says that to be a good judge is to judge beautifully (*kalōs*, 1094b29–1095a1) and that this means to judge what one knows. But, as we have seen, the sign of the *kalon* is the artificial whole—the exaggerated generalization. To be a good judge simply, then, one would have to know the whole. Such knowledge would be unlike knowledge of anything in the whole—any part—for knowledge of a part presupposes knowing that whole of which it is a part. Knowing the button means knowing the shirt. The whole, of course, cannot be put into a context in light of which it is experienced; it *is* that whole. To attempt to give an account of it will then be a sort of bookish knowledge that allows one to name the good without really knowing what it is. It will be like the *kalon* with which the *Nicomachean Ethics* begins—the good at which all things aim. Now, Aristotle connects this idealizing with the idealism of youth, the tendency of one who is without experience (*apeiros*) to compensate for being without a limit (*apeiros*) by invoking a theory—a structure into which things fit. This can be corrected only by experience (*empeiria*)—that is, the acknowledged inability to deny the reality of certain goods. Aristotle then takes back his hasty generalization, saying that "it makes no difference whether they are young with respect to age or youthful with respect to character, for it is not a defect that goes with time" (1095a7–8). He characterizes the double perspective of the good by the split between the many and the few (those who are refined and wise). The two groups agree that the good is happiness but disagree on what one needs to pursue to get it. The many think it is something straightforward and apparent—something like everything else, a part of experience. The few stand in awe of it as something "grand and above them," and so something quite unlike everything else and apart from our experience. Among these are men who "have some *logos*" (1095a30).

Before turning to the most plausible versions of a good that stands apart from the goods of the world, Aristotle seems to digress at length, first on methodology and then on the character of his audience. He starts with Plato, who was perplexed or questioned in a good way (*eu ēporei*) because he was in the habit of asking whether an argument was moving to or from first principles. Now, in asking such a question, Plato was clearly himself not moving from fixed first principles, and so the goodness of his inquiry seems to consist in having moved to them. Aristotle appears to be referring to the end of *Republic*, book 6, where Socrates distinguishes between mathematics, which assumes first principles, argues from them, and never returns, and dialectic, which treats first principles as hypotheses in order to get at what they presuppose. Now, both movements are necessary. To begin at all means to begin from something—what Aristotle calls the "that"—but what is to be done with this that? Not having begun with what is known "simply" but only "to us," one will have to revise one's "knowledge" over the course of the argument. Still (and this is the second part of the "digression"), those who study morality must have been led *kalōs* by habits (notice, they are not responsible for their own conditions), for only they will have had sufficient experience of the "that." Contrary to our first impression, this does not mean that those who are raised *kalōs* will have a specific moral predisposition, although, of course, this is also true; it means rather that they will be in the habit of thinking their lives together in terms of a principle. They will, as a matter of course, seek to make wholes of their lives and will therefore have the incentive to try to find the right way of making wholes of their lives. As idealists, they will be idealizers.

Here Aristotle supports his description of the appropriate audience for the *Nicomachean Ethics* with an oddly revealing quotation from Hesiod's *Works and Days*:

> He is best who himself knows all things
> but good as well is that one who is persuaded by him who speaks well;
> but he who neither himself knows nor heeding another
> will take it to heart, this one is a useless man.
> (293, 295–97)

On its face, this is both a justification of habituation as a second-best option when one does not understand oneself and points to Aristotle's discussion of three candidates for the best life in the immediate sequel. The theoretical life would be akin to Hesiod's first man, the political life or life of honor to the second, and the life of pleasure to the useless third (incidentally, by having quoted Hesiod, Aristotle would seem to have placed himself in the second rank of men). However, Aristotle has dropped a line in Hesiod that follows the first of the lines he quotes: "pointing out the things both after and in the end—which will be better" (294). Only by suppressing this line that points to the necessary incompleteness of knowledge so long as we do not know the end can Aristotle make the first life of Hesiod the theoretical life. In this way, he gives the superficial impression that the "that" is a first principle to be applied "mathematically" and not a hypothesis to be examined dialectically. But by truncating the quotation, Aristotle also gives a striking example of how "knowledge" of any part is deceiving without knowledge of the whole of which it *is* a part—we call this quoting out of context. At the same time, Aristotle playfully leaves us with the mistaken impression that he subordinates himself to Hesiod. Now, this *mis*representation of how we ought to begin is meant to be a correct representation of how we always do begin. In the sequel, for example, various claimants for the title of best life (pleasure, honor, moneymaking) will be discarded not because they are not somehow good but rather because of their claims to be *the* good. Men were moved to make these claims not so much out of a longing for pleasure, honor, or money as from an impulse inherent in morality as such. This impulse has to do with a need to make a whole of one's life.

This need, in turn, is rooted in the very nature of the soul as that which goes out of itself in order to affirm itself.

The issue of morality is not so much goods as *the* good; it is not surprising, then, that Aristotle should turn to the *Republic* and *the* account of *the* good-itself in Plato.[5] He begins by defending his criticism of those men whom he loves and who introduced the ideas by saying that "it would be perhaps better and what one ought to do for the purpose of preserving the truth even to give up one's own, especially for those who love wisdom; for, while it belongs to both to be loved, it is holy to honor first the truth" (1096a14–18). But is not Aristotle's preference for the holy over one's own akin to his friends' placing the good-itself over the individual goods of experience? And so are we not invited to ask how all of the criticisms that follow of the good-itself affect Aristotle's own understanding of what is good in itself—namely, happiness? The general drift of these criticisms is that the good-itself is so good that it so dwarfs and ultimately cancels the goodness of the beings of which it was to explain the goodness that nothing is good but the good-itself. Looked at from the other side, this means that the good-itself is so far removed from the goodness of things in the world that it is of no use in determining what is good, and so, as this is the reason why it was introduced in the first place, the good-itself is of no earthly good. But could not similar things be said of happiness as it has emerged in book 1? Happiness is *the* good and the best; it is what makes all else "good for." Yet happiness cannot by itself be pursued; depending on our understanding of it, we will pursue food, drink, sexual relations, twelve-meter yachts, or perhaps virtue. These goods are *erga*, products apart from our activity; this makes them pursuable but incompletely satisfying. When we think of the good as complete, it must be an *energeia*; it must contain its *ergon* within itself, but then we have no idea what it is, for our every attempt

5 · The following is a literal rendering of how he begins: "But the universal better perhaps to inquire and question how it is said . . ." (1096a12–13). One's first tendency in reading the sentence is to take "the universal better" as its subject. In fact, *better* is the predicate adjective in a nominal sentence (one with the verb *to be* understood), which would begin "It is better to." The words *the universal* stand by themselves, and *good* is the implied noun that they modify, although it was last used nine lines earlier—a healthy gap in constructions of this kind in Greek. So one has to read, "But it is better perhaps to inquire and question how the universal [good] is said." That "good" left implied is interesting. It is a sign that it is entering the account indirectly, and in fact it comes in twice on the level of Aristotle's own action when he remarks on what it would be better for him to do. Thus, in this critique of Plato, the good first enters as relative and comparative. It comes in as the "good for" and the "better than." This is the heart of Aristotle's criticism of the apparent teaching of the *Republic*; it is a criticism not so much of what is said as of how it is said, for the teaching obscures the extent to which the primary experience of the good is as the "good for."

to understand the goodness of something takes the form of understanding what it is good for. Happiness, like the good-itself, looks to be riddled with a self-contradictory demand that it be both an object apart from us and something within us. But if happiness is as useless as the good-itself, what is the argument between Aristotle and those who introduced the ideas? The one obvious difference in how the good-itself and happiness "are said" is that the former, as a principle of the whole, leaves the impression that it is altogether independent of soul. Happiness, however problematic as a principle, makes manifest the relation between the good and the soul. There is no good without that for which it is good—something constituted by an "inside."[6] That Plato somehow knew this as well seems clear from the simple fact that he had Socrates name the principle of the whole "the good." Still, Aristotle's objection seems to be reasonable insofar as the "friends of the ideas" are too quick to mystify the good and so lose sight of the fact that it is in morality, the ordinary man's relation to things as good, that our rational natures become most powerfully manifest.

Happiness is like the good-itself insofar as it functions as a goal for inquiry, a regulative principle or hypothesis of unity that guides an investigation into what connects subordinate goods. On the other hand, Aristotle's project in the *Nicomachean Ethics* seems to differ from Plato's in the *Republic* in intending happiness also to function as *a* good that can be sought in action. This leads him to give happiness some content by characterizing it in terms of self-sufficiency. Aristotle seems intent here on saying that he does not mean anything mystical or invisible by happiness but only what is manifest to each of us in our ordinary lives. Yet, when the question of the good has moved in this way to the soul (or in this case the self), it becomes indeterminate in yet another way. The self of self-sufficiency cannot be characterized apart from the things that are for it. Lest the self become everything, Aristotle must place limits on how far it extends. The two he discusses are ancestors and descendants, on the one hand, and friends or kin (*philoi*) and fellow citizens, on the other. These are roughly our sequential or temporal relations to others in the world and our simultaneous or spatial relations. They are analogous to the double account of the good as good for in the first paragraph of the *Ethics*. If X is understood as a means to Y, it comes before Y and the relation is temporal or sequential; if the model is the hierarchy of the arts, the relation is logical, simultaneous, and so structural. The sequence is what it feels like when one intends something; it is internal. The structure is what it looks like from the outside. Sequence is thus connected to action—doing the good; structure is connected to in-

6 · Compare the discussion of the good in the account of the *Hipparchus* in part 4, chapter 10, below and *De Anima* 415b.

tellection—knowing the good. Now, when we ask ourselves whether we should do something, we need to envision some good not too far down the line that is for itself; the genesis of an action thus requires the *kalon* as an exaggerator or simplifier. However, in the process of realizing this good, we come to see that what we wanted is not really what we want—it is too simple. It is good only in a larger context, and yet the context deprives it of its goodness. That is to say, we jump outside of the sequence and consider the structure. This is presumably what would happen to Clytemnestra or Orestes were they to think through the implications of the *Oresteia* as a whole rather than remaining immersed in the flow of its action. Orestes would say to himself that he is not simply avenging Agamemnon and killing his mother but restoring right or justice. The individual action of the sequence would become a sign of a deeper willing of the structure. Paying taxes is not good in itself, but it contributes to a larger whole that is good. And because, in doing my part, I support the whole, my part becomes good in itself. I perform the means, but I will the end. The most common version of all of this arrangement is obviously the *polis*.

As virtue becomes progressively more reflective, it is inevitably exposed in its partiality. We are therefore moved to think the whole of which it is a part in order to restore its character as for itself and not instrumental. The consequence is that particular human actions become symbolic. Morality is necessarily tied up with this symbolic character of human action—this is what it means that we do the particular in time, in the sequence, as a sign of the whole, the structure. Morality is the constant attempt to restore the wholeness of particular actions by making them symbolic, an attempt that turns back on itself once these symbolic goals themselves willy-nilly become objects to be pursued in time.[7]

This difficulty emerges most clearly in Aristotle's attempt to disclose the *ergon*—the task, deed, or function—of human beings. Once again the account is progressively double. Aristotle first says that like any artisan, a human being will have "an *ergon* and action" (1097b29–30). However, he quickly leaves action behind and proceeds to give a double account of *ergon*—first based on the relation between an artisan and his product (his *ergon*) and then based on the relation of a single organ to the whole living body. In the one case, the *ergon* provides the limit or good in terms of which the art leading to it is measured, but a limit of which the artisan is not the cause. Given that there must be shoes, shoemakers have a task, but they do not give themselves this task. In the other case, one activity—for example, seeing—is a part of a larger activity that gives it meaning but itself remains

7 · Compare Aristotle *Politics* 7.1–3, along with the interpretation in my *Politics of Philosophy* (Lanham, MD: Rowman & Littlefield, 1996), 121–27.

undefined. Depending on which version we choose, the *ergon* as the defining feature of something is either clear but arbitrary or indistinct but necessary. Thus, either we move from parts and see natural *erga* that seem to presuppose an unstated *ergon* of the whole, or we posit an *ergon* of the whole, but it seems artificial.

Perhaps, then, Aristotle is not simply asking a rhetorical question when he asks if human beings are by nature without an *ergon* (*argon*), for we *are* in some way defined by our capacity for being idle (*argon*, 1097b31). We are always something in addition to being a carpenter, and so, like happiness, we are never altogether reckonable. Moreover, there are actually no carpenters in the world, but only human beings who are carpenters. In being defined by their function, carpenters are in no way detached from the world; they are simply of a piece with it. In not being altogether carpenters, and thus by being imperfect carpenters, we manifest our detachment from things in the world. While eyes do exist, and their activities are to be what they are, still, what they are is always defined in terms of some larger whole. The problem, then, is to give an account of human beings in terms of an *ergon* that is neither altogether apart from us nor so embeds us in a whole as to make us altogether parts. The two alternatives, equally unattractive, seem to reproduce the artificial wholeness of the *kalon* and the incompleteness of the just.

As is his wont, Aristotle finesses a direct acknowledgment of this problem when he says that if there is an *ergon* of human beings, it is an "*energeia* of soul according to *logos*, or not without *logos*" (1098a7–8). The claim is of course hypothetical; it is not clear that there is such an *ergon*. It is further diluted by the alternative "according to reason or not without reason," for the first makes the activity seem quite specific, while the double negation covers a much broader range of activities. We are not sure whether there is one activity that characterizes human beings so that its fulfillment would be something like Socrates' twenty-four-hour contemplative vigil on the snowy battlefield of Potidaea (*Symposium* 220c–d), or many. And if there are many rational activities, how will all of this help us to choose? How will we rank them? The double negation is thus Aristotle's way of introducing the problem of the multiplicity of the virtues versus the singleness of the human good. Finally, and for our purposes most important, is Aristotle's claim that the *ergon* of man is an *energeia*. If *ergon* is a way of characterizing what we aim for insofar as it is outside of and apart from us, and *energeia* is meant to point to another sort of goal that is internal, to say that the *ergon* of man is an *energeia* is to admit that there is no way of understanding the internal without externalizing it. On the one hand, this is what it means to be rational—to have *logos*. On the other hand, it is a feature of our natures as moral. The two are not really different. As ensouled beings, we are defined by our ability to go outside of ourselves in order to complete ourselves; we look for things to complete us—objects to consume. We then discover that it is not really the thing that we want but rather the activity in ourselves that results from appropriating the thing. Yet there is no end to this sort of appropriation of the external. Growth is, on the one hand, more than simply getting bigger (it must aim at an end or purpose). That we are capable of taking things *in* means that we must make a whole of the process. This wholeness, however, eludes us in the sequence of experience in time. Accordingly, we turn to ourselves in an attempt to take ourselves in as a whole; the particular deed is not so important as the state of character that underlies it, gives rise to it, and gives it meaning. Particular deeds are thus symbolic. Yet in our attempt to form character, we must make an object of it. To do so is to externalize it. Understanding happiness as an activity means understanding what we must pursue to become happy. This, in turn, means specifying the virtues and so making of them objects to be pursued. It is the nature of soul to go outside of itself in order to affirm itself; this nature necessarily shows up in a rational being as morality, the attempt to overcome time in time or seeking as an *ergon* an *energeia*. This is what it means that the good is the combination of the *kalon* and the just, where the structure of the just comes to be the object of internal longing.

That Aristotle has something like this in mind becomes clearer in one of the strangest features of book 1. In reflecting on what it means to be happy, Aristotle sees that happiness belongs to a whole life. Priam would look to be the happiest of human beings before the last ten years of his life, when the king of a great and prosperous city with many successful and talented children lived to see his city captured, burned, and pillaged; his sons killed; his wife and daughters carried off; and himself slain by the son of Achilles. Solon is apparently right; it is only from the perspective of the end, death, that one can be correctly judged happy. At this point, Aristotle asks whether even death is a sufficient vantage point; can't one be made unhappy by what one's descendants do after one dies? Aristotle devotes a full chapter to this question, and it is at first not at all clear why. Yet, if to be happy rational beings must know that they are happy, then either strictly speaking we can never be happy or there would have to be a place like Hades, a vantage point from which one could assess one's whole life which is at the same time immune from the incomplete and precarious nature of life. By raising what seems a rather bizarre question of whether the shameful deeds of our great-great-grandchildren can destroy the happiness of our lives, Aristotle is gently pointing to the problem of Hades (*Aidēs*)—the invisible (*aidēs*) place that is treated as though it were just like any other place. Hades looks to be absurd. Either you do not live on, in which case there seems to be no vantage point from which to sum up your life, or you do live on, in which case

your life has not really ended and you are still subject to its precariousness—
Hades is simply graduate school. In either case, you will not be able truly to
count yourself happy and so will not be able to be happy in any final sense.
You cannot say, "I am happy," because the "I" is in time and does not remain
constant. To overcome this problem, the poets invent Hades, but Hades is
simply the poetic version of morality, the attempt of the soul to do something in time that will allow it to stand apart from time.[8] The *Nicomachean
Ethics* means to display this tendency as the defining characteristic of the
animal that by virtue of being rational can be only imperfectly rational[9] and
thereby can be only imperfectly happy.[10]

II. "For the friend is another self"

The beginning of Aristotle's *Nicomachean Ethics*, on reflection, proves to be
remarkably self-reflexive. To grasp the good, we must turn it into an object,
but in so doing, we place it forever out of reach. In thus alienating us from
the good, our inquiry itself proves to reflect our necessary imperfection, revealing the structure of incompleteness characteristic of soul. This problem
is, in turn, the key to the progressively dyadic structure of the *Nicomachean
Ethics* as a whole. We have already set out the argument of book 1 leading to the split between moral virtue and intellectual virtue with which
book 2 begins. And we have seen its consequences for the account of choice
in book 3. The problem of the soul's unity emerges in a slightly different way
in Aristotle's treatment of friendship.

Aristotle begins his account friendship in books 8 and 9 of the *Ethics* in
the following way:

> After these things, it would follow to discuss friendship, for it is a vir-
> tue or with virtue. And further it is most necessary with respect to life
> [*bios*]. For without friends no one would choose to live [*zēn*], even hav-
> ing all the remaining goods. (1155a1–6)

This remark reminds us of another early in book 1.

> If indeed there is an end of actions which we want on account of itself,
> and the others [*t'alla*] on account of this, and we do not choose every-

---

8 · Compare the account of identity in Euripides' *Helen* in part 3, chapter 6.

9 · See Seth Benardete, "On Greek Tragedy," *The Argument of the Action* (Chicago and
London: University of Chicago Press, 2000), 140–41.

10 · The explicit argument of the *Nicomachean Ethics* does not make the impossibility of happiness clear until the end of book 7, where Aristotle indicates that our
natures are not simple but require change, and that only the simple nature is good
(1154b22–31).

thing on account of another [*heteron*] . . . , it is clear that this would be the good and the best. (1094a19–23)

Considered together, these two remarks come very close to suggesting that friendship, *philia*, is that for the sake of which we choose everything else. It is the "good and the best." Our age may consider it an appendix to the body of moral philosophy. Aristotle, who devoted a full fifth of the *Nicomachean Ethics* to its discussion, obviously thought otherwise.

At the very least, what this means is that, for Aristotle, happiness, in the name of which we choose everything, has to be understood relative not to ourselves alone but also to others. While this is consistent with his earlier claim that if there is a highest good, its science would be *politikē* (1094a29), and with the high status of justice as the sum of the virtues (1129b30), it seems not to consist so easily with the understanding of happiness as self-sufficiency that runs throughout the *Nicomachean Ethics*. The status accorded to *philia* is therefore initially puzzling.

Most of book 8 is concerned with what friendship is; only at the beginning does Aristotle say anything explicit about why it is so good. Here he emphasizes how much friends are in need of each other—whether rich or poor, old or young. His single example of those in their prime of life and of virtue is peculiar. Quoting from *Iliad*, book 10 (224–25), to the effect that when two go together, one will notice before the other how gain may be gotten, Aristotle calls attention to the nighttime reconnaissance of Diomedes and Odysseus. In the course of their spying, these two capture a Trojan, Dolon, sweet-talk him into telling them what they want to know by promising to let him go, kill him, and then raid the Thracian camp, killing the Thracians in their sleep and stealing their horses. None of this seems obviously helpful in explaining what it is that makes friendship good.

In book 9, Aristotle connects friendship as love of another to self-sufficiency, and so to happiness. "The friend is another self" (*esti gar ho philos allos autos*, 1166a30). One needs a friend as a mirror of oneself, for one cannot by oneself see oneself, and yet one cannot be happy without seeing oneself. If happiness requires complete virtue, this does not mean simply acting in a certain way. It means esteeming oneself worthy of great things while in fact being worthy of them (*dokei dē megalopsukhos einai ho megalōn hauton axiōn axios ōn*, 1123b3). It means not only being good but also knowing one is good. Self-knowledge is thus an ornament (*kosmos*, 1124a2) of the virtues. Yet it proves deeply problematic when first appearing in book 4 in the form of pride or greatness of soul.[11] To redeem the possibility of self-knowledge seems to be the task of *philia*. The friend, as an

11 · At the very least, one must wonder at the intellectual acumen of a man who because nothing is great to him is not even inclined to wonder (1125a3) when, for

externalized, objectified version of oneself, is the indispensable condition for the self-awareness without which we can never say of ourselves that we are good. And failing this awareness of our own goodness, "even having all of the remaining goods, no one would choose to live."

Yet this mirroring function of *philia* is double-edged, as Aristotle indicates by way of an apparently insignificant change in how he speaks of the friend. "For the friend," he says, "is another [*heteron*] self" (1170b7).[12] The small difference between *allos* and *heteros* is crucial. As indicated above (p. 63), the one (*allos*) suggests something like "simply other," whereas the other (*heteros*) regularly suggests a comparison. It is a correlative term—another that belongs with another—so that the introduction of one *heteros* leads us to expect that another will not be far off. That the friend moves from being an altogether other self (or same—once again, *autos* can mean either) to another self understood as one of a pair suggests that the self must be as much understood in terms of the friend as vice versa.[13] On the one hand, one understands the friend to be an externalized version of oneself—that's why we like friends. On the other hand, if to know oneself means to know another self, then to know oneself means to know oneself as other. The friend, who is the condition for the possibility of self-knowledge, is simultaneously the sign of self-ignorance. And, if loving a friend is like loving oneself, then to love oneself must mean to love oneself as other. Self-love is possible only when we are somehow split off from ourselves—alienated. And self-love of a certain kind is the defining feature of the being that always aims at the good understood finally as the good for itself—happiness. The account of moral virtue in the *Nicomachean Ethics* thus culminates in understanding the self in terms of the friend, the other, because it has from the outset been the nature of the only being open to morality to think of itself as other. Morality too seems to demand a soul that goes out of itself for the sake of itself.

Aristotle, it is owing to wonder that human beings first philosophize (*Metaphysics* 982a12).

12 · A similar change from *allos* to *heteros* occurs in Plato's discussion of friendship in the *Lysis* (see 211d and 212a).

13 · Accordingly, Aristotle says that friendship is possible toward oneself only insofar as the self is two or more (1166a33-b1).

PART TWO

HERODOTUS

The Rest and Motion of Soul

De Anima defined soul in its connection to various objects in the world. In the *Nicomachean Ethics*, Aristotle is primarily concerned with soul in its relation to other souls—to subjects in the world. Soul's relation to other souls involves a disposition of soul, character, which is on the one hand objective and on the other hand never simply determinative. Because the formation of character depends on habituation, it depends on external surroundings and so on society or politics. Accordingly, Aristotle begins the *Nicomachean Ethics* by announcing that *politikē* is the science that deals with morality and concludes by pointing to the completion of this science in the *Politics*. The *Nicomachean Ethics* therefore prepares us to see how Herodotus's *Historiē*, his history or inquiry, with its comparison of the laws and customs that distinguish various peoples from one another, may be understood as an account of the various forms that soul may take.

The *History* as a whole, and the first four books in particular, is designed to show us how the details of what we have come to call "culture" form "national character."[1] Egypt (to which we will turn in chapter 4) and the Scythians (to whom we will turn in chapter 5) mark the extreme possibilities of this character formation. The principle of the one is stability or rest and the iron rule of tradition; the principle of the other is change or motion and a freedom that is incompatible with fixity or tradition. Egypt proves hostile to poetry—stability means that a thing simply is what it is and doesn't

Part 2 owes a great deal to Seth Benardete's account of Egypt and of Scythia and Libya in Herodotean Inquiries *(The Hague: Martinus Nijhoff, 1969), 32–68, 99–132. While I will cite Benardete frequently, citation cannot really do justice to the extent of my debt to him.*

1 · For a thoughtful articulation of the problem with the word *culture*, see Leo Strauss, "What Is Liberal Education?" in *Liberalism Ancient and Modern* (New York and London: Basic Books, 1968), 3–9. I have nevertheless chosen to use *culture* in discussing Herodotus as it is the word we regularly use for the part of *nomos* that is not written but forms a people as a people.

point beyond itself. The Scythians seem to speak poetically (the snow of the north is "feathers"), but their sense of their own freedom prevents them from acknowledging the disjunction between what they say and what is—they speak metaphors without realizing that they are suppressed similes and so, because they do not know that they speak poetically, do not really speak poetically. In books 2 and 4, Herodotus shows us both how natural and inevitable these tendencies are and how, when pushed to their extremes, they strangely turn into each other. The slavish Egyptian adherence to stability leads to unrest; the Scythian wholesale rejection of institutions in the name of freedom leads to slavery. Herodotus thus reveals the intrinsic limits to how far character can be formed or manipulated. In articulating these limits, he articulates the boundaries of soul, thereby revealing the soul while scarcely mentioning it,[2] for soul is what guarantees the presence of the active even in what seems at first altogether passive and the presence of the passive even in what seems at first altogether active.

Herodotus displays the soul by letting what limits culture play itself out in his accounts of the extremes of culture—Egypt and the Scythians. At the end of book 4, he points to Greece as the culture that is most human because it is genuinely political and that can be genuinely political because of the presence of poetry. Its citizens, as self-governing, represent the togetherness of motion and rest. In making themselves objects for themselves, they are not simply what they are and so are alienated, but it is this alienation that humanizes them. The poetry of Greece—Hesiod's "lies like the truth"—amounts to an acknowledgment that the world is and is not what we say it is.

2 · See, however, Herodotus, book 2.123.

· CHAPTER 4 ·

Rest in Motion

Herodotus's Egypt

To try to understand anything at all means first to confront the fact that it seems strange—foreign—to us. We are always tempted to tame the foreign by reducing it to what is altogether familiar.[1] Thales, traditionally understood to be the first philosopher, is supposed to have said, "Everything is water." Had he said, "Everything is matter," it would have ill served him since, not knowing what this stuff matter was, it would have been equivalent to having said, "Everything is something, but I don't really know what that is." Yet, having made his initial claim, having reduced the unknown to something known, Thales faced another, perhaps irresolvable, difficulty: if everything is water, why isn't everything wet? Or, perhaps better stated, if *everything* is water, how can anything be wet? We cannot understand what is unknown in terms of what is known without making a mystery of how it was unknown to us in the first place, and yet without in some way relating it to what we already know, it is not clear how we could have begun to inquire at all. It is therefore a puzzle how we ever understand anything, or for that matter how we could even come to ask the question just asked.

One cannot be a stranger to Thales' problem if one has ever had to cope with being immersed in a foreign culture. This immersion poses a double danger. On the one hand, everything is new, and so we are full of wonder. We are rendered dumb in the face of difference.[2] On the other hand,

---

1 · See Aristotle, *On Poetics*, chapter 21.

2 · Many years ago as a graduate student in Germany, I passed each day by a wood of what seemed marvelously strange trees—they were sort of like spruce but with a texture and color somehow softer, and they were deciduous—they lost their needles in winter. How marvelous these German forests were, filled with these strange trees called Lärchen. Upon returning home to central Pennsylvania to the school where my wife taught and where we had lived before we went abroad, I discovered that on the path I had taken to school every day for two years before going abroad, there was a stand of larch trees. I simply hadn't noticed the wonderful German trees in my own backyard. Sometimes we stand so much in awe of the other that we too quickly

there is always the very real danger that we are too quick to judge what is other, to say that it is "just" or "merely" like what we have back home. There seem, then, to be two equally unattractive approaches to foreign cultures. We may either attempt to understand them by way of our own categories and principles, thereby closing off the possibility that they have anything to teach us about the most fundamental things. Or we may approach them by way of their own understanding of themselves, borrowing as best we can their categories and principles, thereby allowing ourselves to feel nonjudgmental, but, since in the end being nonjudgmental means not making any judgments—that is, being altogether passive and receptive—this path does not promise to be very interesting. What, then, are we to do?

Of course, this scheme of alternatives is itself much too pat. Culture does not simply perfectly impose its stamp on the souls of those who dwell within it. There are at least two obvious indications of this; culture shock and criminality each show that there are unsettling places either between cultures or within cultures from which one might begin to ask questions of them.[3] How, then, is it possible to harness the fact that our souls are never simply slavishly formed by culture in a way that will allow us to learn about culture? One finds one such attempt in the second book of the earliest account of comparative culture known to us from Greek antiquity—Herodotus's *History*.

The *History* begins with the following sentence:

> This is the showing-forth of the history of Herodotus of Halicarnassus, in order that neither the things issuing from human beings in time become eradicated, nor the great and wondrous deeds come to be without fame, whether exhibited by the Greeks or by the barbarians, both with respect to the cause on account of which they warred with one another and with respect to the rest.

Herodotus announces a double goal, the first part of which concerns things common to all human beings and the second, things peculiar to Greeks and Persians. Now, the *History* as a whole has the following structure.[4] In the first book, Herodotus turns to the mythic and historical origins of the conflict between Greece and Asia; this leads him to an account of Lydia and then of Persia's gobbling up of Lydia. The second book deals with Egypt, the third with Persia, and the fourth with the Scythians and Libya. In the fifth

---

grant it a free pass, giving up any attempt really to understand it on the grounds that it would be imperious (not to say imperialistic).

3 · I am grateful to Sarah Davis, who, both in writings and in conversation, has helped me to understand the nature of culture shock.

4 · For an alternative understanding of the structure of the book, see Seth Benardete, *Herodotean Inquiries* (The Hague: Martinus Nijhoff, 1969), 3–4.

book, Herodotus turns to a preliminary account of Athens in relation to Persia and in the sixth to an account of Sparta in relation to Persia. In books 7–9, Herodotus turns to the war between the Persians and Greeks. Roughly speaking, then, one can say that in dealing with the underlying principles of non-Greek peoples, books 1–4 provide something like an alphabet of culture. Books 5–6 deal with Greece, which is in a way more complex because it is compounded from principles clearer in the simpler peoples of books 1–4. Books 7–9 put this more complex people into time. In the first four books, then, Herodotus will deal with the things issuing from human beings—that is, with the permanent principles underlying the differences among all human beings generally. Books 5–6 deal with a special case, the Greeks, which, because less pure than any of the others, is finally more interesting. And in books 7–9, we see how these permanent principles show up in a real event—the Persian War. Herodotus's book, as a whole, then, seems to be an attempt to understand the permanent, fixed, and stable principles underlying the manifest variety, change, and motion of human history. One of the permanent principles that govern peoples proves to be the longing within the human soul for permanence. It is this to which Herodotus turns in book 2, on Egypt.

Herodotus's treatment of Egypt is distinctive in a number of ways. Book 2 is *the* religious book of the *History*. Herodotus tells us that "in reverence for the gods, the Egyptians are the most excessive of all human beings" (2.37) and traces the origins of most of the Greek gods to Egypt (2.50). Words having to do with piety, reverence, and holiness occur with far greater frequency here than in any other of the books of the *History*. The word *hosios*, "holy," for example, occurs sixteen times in all of Herodotus—eight of them in book 2. And this is the book as well in which Herodotus himself several times conspicuously, if not altogether convincingly, calls attention to his own religiosity.[5]

The structure of book 2 is also very different from the other books.[6] In book 1, we get accounts of a series of peoples. Each begins by tracing their history back five generations and then moves to a discussion of their laws or customs (*nomoi*). In book 2, we get a very long account first of Egyptian geography (first in terms of its land and then in terms of the Nile River), followed by an account of Egyptian *nomoi*. This is then followed by Egyptian history, but rather than simply going back five generations, we first get a long account of what one might call mythical history (at any rate, it is known or accepted only by the Egyptians) and only then do we move to the

---

5 · See, for example, 2.3, 61, 65, and 132.
6 · For a similar, but not identical, account of the structure of book 2, see Benardete, *Herodotean Inquiries*, 36.

history that has a parallel in the accounts of other peoples. There is a sense in which the first three-quarters of the book is a long digression; in any case, it is unique to the treatment of Egypt. What is especially peculiar about the structure of the book is the way in which it falls into a continuous proportion so that the account of land : the account of the Nile :: the geography as a whole : the account of the *nomoi* :: the geography plus the account of the *nomoi* : the mythic history :: geography plus the account of the *nomoi* plus mythic history : actual history. The principle at work in this proportion is the relation between what is fixed, stable, and at rest and what is changing or moving. In Egypt, Herodotus seeks to give an account of change in terms of what is fixed. This way of thinking will prove to be *the* characteristic of the Egyptians and has something to do with why religion is so prominent for them. The movement of Herodotus's own writing in book 2 is based on his acceptance of this Egyptian model for understanding. In book 2, Herodotus attempts to speak the language of the Egyptians. The results of this experiment will prove very interesting.

Close to the beginning of book 2, Herodotus tells a story about one of the Egyptian kings, Psammetichus.[7] The Egyptians had always believed themselves to be the oldest race, but Psammetichus set about to prove it. He took two newborn children and gave them to a shepherd to raise. The children were to be isolated from all human contact except periodic visits from a shepherd, who would bring his goats and give the children their fill of milk. He was prohibited from speaking to them. Psammetichus wanted to learn what word they would first utter, thinking that if it were Egyptian, he would have his proof. The word turned out to be *bekos*—after investigating, Psammetichus discovered that it was the Phrygian word for bread. He then concluded, sadly, that the Phrygians must be the first people to have existed, but that the Egyptians were second.

This is, of course, an utterly preposterous experiment and on multiple grounds.[8] Even were we to accept his method in principle, it is not clear how Psammetichus's conclusion would follow; that is, why should the Egyptians be the second oldest people? He seems also to conflate the view that language as such is natural to human beings with the view that there is a specific language natural to us, so that he assumes not only that the children will learn to speak without being taught but also that any child put in this situation would learn to speak the same language. It never occurs to him to

7 · See Benardete, *Herodotean Inquiries*, 32–35.

8 · For an attempt to understand it as a model of the scientific method, see Antoni Sulek's "The Experiment of Psammetichus: Fact, Fiction, and Model to Follow," *Journal of the History of Ideas* 50, no. 40 (Oct.–Dec. 1989): 645–51.

think that the children's first word might be their imitation of the sound of the goats. He doesn't see that being the animals with *logos* might have something to do with being the most imitative of animals. It never occurs to him that when, upon the arrival of the shepherd, the children clasp him by the knees and hold out their hands to him, they are already speaking in gestures. It does not occur to him to ask why, if all they are regularly given is milk, their first word should be "bread"; if they mean it to stand for food generally, why should their first word be synecdochal? It also never occurs to Psammetichus to ask why, if language is natural in this way, all human beings do not speak the same language. These mistakes prove to be grounded in what Herodotus takes to be the deepest feature of the Egyptians as a people—of the way in which the Egyptian soul is formed by the distinctively Egyptian misunderstanding of soul. The Egyptians so fully identify their own ways—their *nomoi*—with the nature of things that they mistakenly take the first things historically to be the first things understood as the ground or foundation for everything else.[9] Believing that the first things are not in principle qualitatively different from subsequent things allows them to think that the capacity for language is the same as a specific language. They do not understand the degree to which the first things are essentially hidden and not available to us in the way other things are available.

Stephen Hawking tells a story about a lecture, probably given by Bertrand Russell, on some topic in cosmology.[10] After Russell had finished, a woman raised her hand and asked him where exactly the cosmos was, what supported it—one might say, what it was grounded on. Russell turned the question back on her and asked her what she thought, to which the woman replied that the cosmos rested upon a giant turtle. Russell, amused, asked her what supported the turtle. She replied that it sat upon another turtle. To which he asked the obvious question of what supported this turtle. The woman responded that she was on to Russell, and he couldn't trap her in this way; it was turtles all the way down. The woman in this story is speaking Egyptian. Like the Egyptians, she does not see that the ground of everything else cannot be of the same order as what it grounds; being cannot be a being. The cosmos cannot be understood to be in a place or a time. Because the Egyptians understand the world in terms of what came first, they mistake history for philosophy.[11] They do not see that finally what is in time cannot be explained by way of a cause that is in time.

9 · Compare Plato *Minos* 318e–321b.
10 · Stephen Hawking, *A Brief History of Time* (New York: Bantam, 1988), 1.
11 · For Herodotus, *he historiē* does not yet mean "history" but rather something like "inquiry."

Herodotus moves from this story to his account of the geography of Egypt—starting with its land. But the land proves to be defined in terms of something less solid. The Egyptians have an oracle that tells them that Egypt is all the land that the Nile waters in its course (2.18). This proves to be not an altogether stable account since the yearly flooding of the Nile and silt it deposits lead to the constant formation of new land called "Lower Egypt." Also, the Egyptians never really settle on the precise limits of the Nile (2.19). They define themselves by its movement and yearly flooding, but for them it just is. It is the Greeks Herodotus cites as having various explanations for the "peculiar property the Nile possesses that is the opposite of every other river in the world" (2.19) of flooding in summer and receding in winter. On the boundaries of Egypt, Herodotus is content with a more conventional view: "Egypt is everywhere the Egyptians dwell" (2.17).

To define the solid land, the Egyptians point to the more fluid water, the Nile. Because they have no knowledge of why the Nile floods, they have no knowledge of who they are. Accordingly, the inquisitive Psammetichus launches another experiment, this time to discover the *archē*, the beginning, source, or principle of the Nile (2.28). He braids a rope thousands of fathoms long and lowers it into the spring that is *archē* of the northern and southern branches of the Nile. But the rope proves too short. The depths of the source of the Nile prove unplumbable, and so, contrary to the oracle of the god, Ammon, the river does not suffice to circumscribe the land and make clear what makes men Egyptians. Men cannot be characterized by the conditions that give rise to them, for these conditions cannot be perfectly determined and have an ever receding character; it's turtles all the way down.

Herodotus tells another story that points to this difficulty. Sailing south down the Nile, one eventually comes to the land of men called the Deserters, originally Egyptian soldiers who, having been on border duty for several years without relief, rebelled against Psammetichus and joined the Ethiopians. Psammetichus pursued them and, having caught them, upbraided them for having deserted their ancestral gods, their children, and their wives. In response, "one of them, it is said, showing his genitals, said, 'Wherever this is, there also will be for me both children and wives'" (2.30). There are always deserters possible—men who can begin afresh in a way that is not simply determined by their origins. Men *are* generated—they are effects, but they are also generators, and so causes. They are both in and out of the causal web of the world. The mistake of Psammetichus is once again typically Egyptian. The Egyptians affirm our status as effects while denying we are causes. Accordingly, in Egypt, nothing is understood to change. This is deeply problematic, for the gods of the fathers, or ancestor gods, or ancestors, can determine us only by being our generators. But, as we are of the same kind as they, we too will necessarily be potential generators. Accordingly, ancestor worship cannot stand against the claims of the Deserters.

Where have we come thus far? We want to know what characterizes the Egyptians' souls—what makes them what they are. We want a stable principle, an *archē*, a category under which to place them. Herodotus starts with the land. The land proves peculiarly unstable and determined by water—a moving principle. And the principle that governs the water is hidden and unclear. So book 2 proceeds by way of a loosening of the fixity of Egypt in the direction of motion or change. This is confirmed by the stories that bookend the account of Egypt. Psammetichus sought to show that Egyptian is the oldest, the first, language and seeks the fixed origin of the Nile. The account of Egypt ends just prior to the Persian invasion, with the reign of Amasis.[12] Amasis became king after the overthrow of Apries, the great-grandson of Psammetichus. When the army that Apries had sent on an expedition against Cyrene met with great disaster, the soldiers blamed Apries and revolted. Apries sent Amasis as his minister to negotiate with them, but the army proceeded to crown him king; Amasis then attacked, deposed, and replaced his former sovereign. Now, to depose the king, Amasis had to be not entirely the creature of conventions. So it is no accident that he was a commoner and in addition a lover of things Greek. However, these very things that facilitated his coup made it difficult for him to rule a xenophobic people in which stability is prized above all. To justify his rule, Amasis melted down a golden foot basin and had the gold recast into the statue of a god, which the Egyptians came to hold in great reverence. Then he assembled them and revealed that the statue had been made of a footbath in which they had previously vomited, pissed, and washed their feet. He proclaimed himself to be just like the footbath, previously a commoner but now their king, whom they should honor and respect. During the reign of Amasis, Herodotus tells us, Egypt prospered greatly "both with respect to what the river did for the land and what the land did for the people" (2.177). Amasis, this Hellenophile, teaches the Egyptians that things are not what they come from; the essence of a thing derives rather from its shape or form—Plato would have called it its *eidos*—than its origin. He also teaches them that the high and the low are necessarily linked. While recognized for his industry in attending to public affairs, he was also criticized for the low pleasures he pursued in private. Amasis replied, "Those who have bows string them when they need to use them and leave them loose when not in use. For if they were always strung, they would break and prove use-

---

12 · See Benardete, *Herodotean Inquiries*, 65–67.

less when needed. So too is the condition of human beings. Were he always in earnest and never to devote himself to play, he would unawares go mad or have a stroke" (2.173). Amasis thus makes a permanent principle out of the necessity for change or motion. In so doing, he points to the underlying puzzle of Egypt and of Herodotus's account of it in book 2: in its seeking for absolute stability, the soul must always engender motion or change. The attempt to get at what is first shows that what is first is permanently unavailable. We are *always* second, always already under way. This is what it means that our concern to define Egypt by way of its land leads us first to its water, then to its *nomoi*—its fixed laws or customs, and then to its history. But how exactly does this occur? Is it possible to give a stable account of it?

Herodotus gives an elaborate account of the *nomoi* of Egypt. A glance at some of its strange details is revealing. He begins with an explanation:

> About the Nile, let these sorts of things have been said, but I am going through the *logos*/account about Egypt at much greater length because it has more wonders than all the rest of the earth, and it produces more works greater than *logos*/account relative to all the earth. For these reasons, I will say more about it. (2.35)

In claiming to lengthen his *logos* out of a need to describe works greater than or beyond *logos*, Herodotus begins by acknowledging his task to be, strictly speaking, impossible. The particular problem and the idiosyncrasy of Egypt generally is that, just as its climate and its river operate in a way opposite to the rest of the world, so too are its habits and customs the opposite of what we find elsewhere. Herodotus provides the following list of examples of this reversal (2.36):

1. Women sell in the market; men weave at home.
2. Others push the woof up; Egyptians push it down.
3. Men carry burdens on their heads; women on their shoulders.
4. Women urinate standing; men sitting.
5. Egyptians defecate indoors; they eat outside.
6. Women are not priests; men are priests of both gods and goddesses.
7. Sons are not forced to care for parents; daughters are.
8. Other priests grow their hair; Egyptians shave their heads.
9. Others shave their heads to mourn; Egyptians grow their hair.
10. Others live apart from animals; Egyptians with them.
11. Others eat wheat and barley; Egyptians only spelt.
12. Egyptians knead dough with their feet; mud and dung with their hands.
13. Others leave genitals alone; Egyptians circumcise.
14. Men wear two garments; women only one.

15. Others fasten rings and ropes [*kala*] of sails on the outside; Egyptians on the inside.
16. Greeks calculate and write left to right; Egyptians right to left (but call it left to right).
17. Egyptians have two sorts of writing—sacred and demotic.[13]

This list involves a series of reversals of expectation having to do with relations of space (inside/outside, up/down, and left/right), of male and female (1, 3, 5, 6, 14), sacred and profane (6, 8, 9, 17), shameful or ugly and clean (5, 10, 12, 13), and visible and invisible (1, 5, 14, 15).

The key to understanding how to think them together is the excessive reverence Herodotus attributes to the Egyptians (2.37). Of the eleven customs he lists that have to do with this exaggerated religiosity, the first six have to do with cleanliness (2.37). For the Egyptians, the opposite of the word *aischron* (shameful or ugly) is not, as one would expect, *kalon* (beautiful or noble) but *katharon* (clean or pure).[14] They also connect the private, inside, hidden, or invisible with the unclean, shameful, and profane, for they say that "the necessary and shameful things ought to be done in secret, and the nonshameful things in the open" (2.35). There are some surprises in the list of clean things. Hair and genitals are unclean; shaving and circumcision are acts of cleansing. Dough is not clean, but mud and dung are clean. Rope (which, with a change of accent, would become *beautiful*) is unclean. Animals are clean. The customs concerning mourning are especially revealing. Other peoples cut their hair to indicate that at times of mourning, they have no concern with their appearance. The Egyptians let their hair grow and thus indicate that all by itself, in its natural condition, the body is shameful or ugly. This is why they find even food unclean. So, while it would seem that the clean deserves to be seen and the unclean in its shamefulness hidden, human life itself is unclean because body is somehow unclean. This, in turn, means that the only thing perceptible or available to the senses is unclean. And so, by an odd reversal, what is sensed, what is visible, what is seen—that is, body—gets understood as unclean. Accordingly, but nevertheless unexpectedly, the hidden and the clean get identified. This has dramatic consequences, but we first need some additional details.

In Egypt, we are told, all the gods take animal form when they show themselves, even though this is not their real form (2.42). And while the Egyptians have a Herakles in their pantheon, for them, he is solely a god.

---

13 · The list, and some conclusions with respect to it, are borrowed from Benardete's *Herodotean Inquiries*, 42–44.

14 · See Benardete, *Herodotean Inquiries*, 43–44.

Although the Greek Herakles clearly derives from the Egyptian, Herodotus can find no hint in Egypt of the Greek stories that speak of Herakles as having been first a man. Herodotus himself on occasion swears by gods and heroes (2.45), but the Egyptians do not seem to have anything like heroes. For them, gods and men do not mix. None of their gods take human form, for the human form is shameful. For this reason, although Herodotus is shocked by the public display of the mating of a he-goat and a woman, because both he-goat and Pan are called by the name Mendes in Egypt, this act is not so shocking to the Egyptians (2.46). Animals and gods seem to be clean, human beings not.

What, then, ties all of these customs together? Herodotus tells us that the Egyptians

> are the first to make it a matter of religion not to have intercourse with women in temples nor without washing to go from a woman into temples. But almost all the rest of human beings except the Egyptians and the Greeks have intercourse with women in temples and come from women into a temple without having washed, holding men to be beasts like the rest. (2.64)

The Egyptians are like the Greeks in distinguishing human beings from the other animals. But the Greeks make this distinction because they consider human beings the best of the animals—hence their anthropomorphic gods and their high regard for the beauty of the human form. Unlike the Greeks, the Egyptians consider human beings the worst of the animals. Human beings are shameful and unclean; other animals are held to be sacred (2.65).

If revulsion at the human is the key to understanding Egyptian *nomoi*, how does this show up in what actually happens in Egypt? The truth of Egyptian religion is born from an attempt to get at what is absolutely fixed and stable. The instability closest to us is our own mortality. An awareness of this instability leads to a contempt for the human and a corresponding elevation of what is *not* human. But just as there is a natural dyad stable-unstable, there is a natural tendency to distinguish human from animal. Once made exemplars of the "not-human," however, it is only a small step further to give animals the status of the visible manifestation of the invisible and pure source of things. Animals become stand-ins for gods. This leads to consequences that are at once intelligible after the fact and yet in no way predictable before the fact. Resentment against change or motion thus first leads to resentment against life—that is, one's own change or motion. This, in turn, leads to self-contempt, which leads to animal worship (despite the fact that animals too change—albeit they do not know that they change). In Egypt, this movement, ironically, culminates in worship of mortal gods.

So, for example, every so often a bull calf is born from a cow thereafter unable to conceive. When this calf is all black save for a white triangle on its forehead and the likeness of an eagle on its back and has double hairs on its tail and a knot under its tongue, it is believed to be an appearance of the god Apis. The Persian king Cambyses, otherwise rather mad, was perhaps not so crazy when, wondering how a mortal being could be a god, in a pique of anger he stabbed the calf in the thigh, giving it a mortal wound (3.27–29).

The curious character of Egyptian religion is manifest in other ways. The Egyptians understand human beings in a double way. The human soul is immortal. When the body perishes, this soul always moves into some other animal that is being born. After a cycle of three thousand years, the soul reenters a human body. The soul is thus stable and unchanging, the body subject to change (2.123). And yet, once a human being's soul separates from the body at death, it is the Egyptian practice to attempt to honor the soul by preventing the body from decay inasmuch as it is possible to do so. To honor it is to stabilize it—to put it at rest. Accordingly, the Egyptians practice various degrees of mummification (2.86–88). Corpses, once the sign of the transient, in this way come to be relatively permanent and, as such, become objects of worship. Egyptian religion thus has two parallel but not altogether compatible strands. On the one hand, there is a total renunciation of body in its transience—priests shave their bodies daily. On the other hand, Egypt is the land of the pyramids—monumental tombs that Herodotus calls "beyond *logos*," which are meant to stand as permanent reminders. This is in its way reminiscent of the manner in which Psammetichus assumed that the fact that all human beings are by nature speakers of language must mean that there is a particular language natural to all human beings.

The Egyptians' powerful sense of the fleeting character of human life gives rise to a monumental effort to stem the motion of life. This is perhaps most obvious in mummification, but it is true as well of the rigid adherence to ancestral custom apparent in Psammetichus's appeal to the Deserters as well as his repeated attempts to get at what is most fundamental through what is oldest and in the xenophobia characteristic of Egyptian customs generally. However, the result of this defense against the vagaries of change is a rigidifying or an embodying of the divine. This, in turn, has the peculiar consequence that they treat the body, now purged of all corrupting influences, as divine. Yet, as they must acknowledge the mortality of things bodily, they end up with a world view at odds with itself, and so, when confronted with the incarnation of Apis, Cambyses can address them (invoking what most individuates them),

O bad heads, are your gods of this sort, things of blood and flesh and susceptible to iron? This is a god worthy of the Egyptians. (3.29)

Egyptians seek to understand what is not known in terms of a purified or cleaned-up version of what is known—they are, in a way, conventional Platonists. In his attempt to understand them, Herodotus seeks to understand how they understand. For this reason, in book 2, he repeatedly sides with them over and against other possible ways of understanding. He is, for example, especially hard on the Greeks, and their poetry in particular. But what does it mean to look through Herodotus's eyes? How does he break free of speaking Egyptian in book 2? Amasis (of the golden footbath), who comes to power at the end of book 2, is perhaps the least Egyptian of the Egyptian kings. He is a usurper among the most traditional and ancestral people, an innovator, a lover of things Greek, and an apologist for the constant flux of human life. How did he come to power? His predecessor, Apries, who never seems even to acknowledge the possibility of being deposed, sees Amasis only as what he is and not as what he might be. As in the case of the Deserters, the reigning stability cannot understand the concealed dynamism of its own principle. Change in Egypt occurs not because the Egyptians fail to adhere to their laws and customs but rather because they so strictly adhere to their laws and customs. By earnestly following through these principles—that is, by speaking Egyptian strictly—Herodotus discloses the inner contradictions of the Egyptians. He comes to a vantage point from which it is possible for him to judge Egypt from within Egypt.

There is perhaps a simpler way to speak of Herodotus's way of inquiry and its meaning for us. Ours is a very self-conscious age. Our virtue is that we are reluctant to impose our world view on others. We wince at the possibility of being cultural imperialists. We tell ourselves that we must avoid criticizing the world views of others, for our own view is surely only ours and has no special value or status. In constructing our self-congratulatory modesty, we fail to see that we have embraced a rather too simple notion of what a world view is. To use Herodotus's language, borrowed from the Greek poet Pindar, we think that "*nomos* is king of all." For, as Herodotus says,

> if someone were to make a proposal to all human beings that they select from all laws the most beautiful, having examined them, each would choose its own. (3.38)

While this is no doubt in large measure true, it is also the case that the dicovery of this principle by a Persian is revealed by quoting a Greek poet. Moreover, perhaps the most sacred of Persian customs is telling the truth, and Darius becomes king by way of an extravagant lie. Herodotus shows us in this way that a Persian is no more always a Persian than an Egyptian is always an Egyptian. The way of a people is never so utterly consistent and seamless as fully to determine the souls of its members. It contains contradictions, and these contradictions are always the means by which it is possible for some to examine the principles of their own way from within. An intelligent Egyptian can no longer be simply an Egyptian. Herodotus gives us a guided tour through ancient Egypt in order to afford us the wherewithal to become intelligent Egyptians. "Speaking Egyptian" is a perfectly natural deformity of soul induced by the soul's longing for permanence. By displaying this deformity to us through its consequences, Herodotus begins to show us the soul.

CHAPTER 5

Motion at Rest

Herodotus's Scythians

On the one hand, book 4 of Herodotus's *History* rings familiar. In various ways, its account of the Scythians invites comparison with the account of Egypt. Book 2 and the first part of book 4 of the *History* share a similar structure. In both, a brief allusion to the invasion of the Persians (2.1 and 4.1) is followed by a striking but difficult-to-interpret story (2.2–3 and 4.1–4). These puzzling introductions are both followed by long sections devoted to fixed features of their respective peoples—on the one hand, the geography (2.5–34) and laws and customs (*nomoi*, 2.35–98) of Egypt and, on the other, the origin, tribes, and location of the Scythians (4.5–58) and Scythian *nomoi* (4.59–82). Then come a pair of historical accounts (2.99–182 and 4.83–144) of events leading up to Herodotus's own day. In addition, Egyptians and Scythians are alike in going out of their way to avoid foreign *nomoi*—especially Greek *nomoi* (2.91 and 4.76). And finally, the lives of both peoples depend to an unusual degree on their great rivers, which are several times directly compared (2.26 and 2.33–34). The Nile and the Ister (Danube) are both said to have five natural mouths (2.10, 2.17, and 4.47), and the number of tributaries of the Ister is said almost to equal the number of canals from the Nile (4.47). The Egyptians are thankful that the flooding of the Nile—on which their agriculture depends—releases them from the rest of the world's dependence upon Zeus for rain (2.13). Herodotus credits rivers as being the allies of the Scythians in sustaining the core of their way of life, their nomadism (4.46–47). The Scythians, a brand-new and fluid people (perhaps *the* fluid people), are an inversion of the Egyptians, who pride themselves on their antiquity and stability. If the Egyptians are slavish and effeminate, the Scythians are free and all male. By "speaking Egyptian" in book 2, Herodotus reveals to us the destabilizing effect of the longing for what is altogether stable. In book 4, he speaks the language of the Scythians and in so doing reveals to us the strange and despotic stability that results when a people takes as its defining principle to be always in motion.

At the same time, the obvious need to compare Egypt and the Scythians ought not blind us to the likelihood that Herodotus means the account of Libya and Cyrene at the end of book 4 to be taken together with the account of the Scythians at the beginning. Like Egyptians, Scythians and Libyans do not use pigs as sacrificial animals (4.63, 4.186, 2.47). Also, Herodotus uses language that invites comparisons between Libyans and Egyptians (see 2.50 and 4.187), and between books 2 and 4 as wholes (see 2.49 and 4.45, 4.81, and 4.180 as well as 4.114 and 4.75). Whether or not Herodotus is responsible for the division of the *History* into nine books, what we have as book 4 is meant to be taken as a whole. Still, even if we are meant to put the Scythians together with Libya (not to mention the settlement of Cyrene), the principle of this togetherness is initially illusive, perhaps because the principle that unites the Scythians is so milky.

And yet, while book 4 is familiar, it is also strange. At first glance, there seem to be three instances of the word *Scythia* (*Skythiē*) in book 4 (4.8, 4.17, and 4.99), but, since the text of each is disputed, it is altogether possible that Herodotus never calls Scythia Scythia but always speaks of either Scythians or Scythes. Scythia does not seem to be a fixed place in the way that Egypt is a place.[1] This is doubly puzzling given the high status for the Scythians of the goddess *Histiē*, whom "they especially propitiate" (4.59). She is the goddess of the hearth whose name derives from the verb *histēmi*—to make something stand or stay put—and actually means "hearth" (4.68). Why on earth do the Scythians, who are nomads and never stay put, and who live in a land aflow with many rivers, and who according to themselves are actually descended from a river (4.5), and who think of themselves as the youngest or newest people (4.5), nevertheless worship the goddess of rest? If home is where the hearth is, where can the Scythian home be said to be?

Herodotus describes for us a people who belong to no fixed place, who were born yesterday, who are nomadic (although there seem to be Scythians who farm, 4.17–18) and xenophobic and especially hostile to Greeks (although there are apparently Greek Scythians, 4.17), who seem to be of all things free (although kingly Scythes, who are "best and most numerous," consider the other Scythes their slaves, 4.20), and who sometimes have the same laws and customs but sometimes do not and sometimes speak the same language but sometimes do not. What, then, is it that makes this people one people?[2]

1 · See especially 2.18.

2 · The illusive principle of the unity of the Scythian people is mirrored by the illusive unity of book 4, which contains, even for Herodotus, an unusual number of obtrusive digressions. For example, what are we to make of the account of the fact that mules cannot breed in Elis, which Herodotus himself identifies as an addition or appendix (*prosthēkē*) of the sort his *logos* has sought out from the beginning (4.30; see as well Seth Benardete, *Herodotean Inquiries* [The Hague: Martinus Nijhoff, 1969], 195),

Book 4 is strange in yet another way. It begins with the return of the Scythians from Asia. We were given an account of their invasion of Media in the first book (1.103–6). The Scythians are in pursuit of the fleeing Cimmerians, but, taking a wrong turn (*ektrapomenoi*) and mistaking the way (4.12), they end up fighting the Medes, conquering them, and ruling for twenty-eight years.[3] We are also puzzled that they can rule Media for so long, "holding all of Asia" (1.104), and still retain their essential nature as nomads. Moreover, when they finally repatriate and "go down to their own," we discover that the women they left behind have taken up with their slaves and the Scythians have to face "no less a struggle" than they faced with the Medes. Upon reflection, it is hard to make sense of this. The Scythians have been away for over a generation, during which time one would assume many (perhaps most) of the elders among them—their leaders—have died. This would have been true of the original women left behind as well; the survivors would be at the very least beyond childbearing age. So, many of these "Scythes" must be descended in part from Medes, and they "return" to somewhere they have never been. "Their women," whom they seek to reclaim from their slaves, are most probably women they have never met and offspring of slaves and the original Scythe women. And, of course, many if not most of the "slaves" they confront, having never tasted slavery, know only freedom.

To make sense of Herodotus's account as presented, then, would require that we suspend the passage of time. Saying that the Scythians return from Asia to reclaim their women is like saying that the Chicago Cubs last won a World Series in 1908. What do the Cubs of today (Jason Kendall, Derrek Lee, Cliff Floyd, Kerry Wood) have to do with Tinker, Evers, Chance, Mordecai Brown, and Wildfire Schulte? Identity here is a poetic fiction—however regularly it is invoked. Herodotus thus begins book 4 with a strange story depicting the fiction of a people as standing altogether apart from the individuals who make it up and who must be regularly regenerated. We first accept this fiction without thinking, and then do a double take. The problematic unity of the Scythians looks to have something to do with the problematic unity of peoples generally.

---

or the long account of the Hyperboreans (4.32–35) or of the mapping of the world (4.36–45)? And, most striking, why are the Scythian nomads coupled with other nomads who live on the other side of the world in Libya?

3 · During this time, they threaten Egypt, whose king, Psammetichus, buys them off. On the Scythians' return to Media, some of them plunder the temple of Uranian Aphrodite in Syria, with the consequence that they contract a malady the Scythians call the "female sickness," a disease apparently still quite visible generations later after they have returned to their native land. So whatever the "female sickness" is—and we get no help here from Herodotus—it must be inheritable.

As book 2 begins with an extended and strangely digressive account of Psammetichus's attempt to prove experimentally that Egyptian is the oldest language, book 4 also begins with a seemingly gratuitous description of a Scythian practice. The Scythians milk their horses by inserting a pipe into the vaginas of their mares. Then some of them blow into these pipes with their mouths, causing the mares' udders to descend so that others are able to milk them. The milk is poured into hollow wooden containers, which are then shaken by slaves who stand around them. The milk separates, and the cream, which rises to the top and is thought to be the best, is skimmed off.

Several things are peculiar in Herodotus's description. The sexuality of the account of the milking process is obtrusive. A pipe made of bone is inserted into the female sexual organ of a horse. The udder descends when men blow through the pipe. "They blow" (*phusōsi*) is almost homonymous with *phusousi*, "they will engender / beget / cause to grow." Reading the pun, the sentence would say "They will beget with their mouths, while those milk who are other than the begetters." Scythians beget with their mouths by blowing through what looks suspiciously like a musical instrument. It is not altogether fanciful to say that it is their practice to beget poetically. This is confirmed by a subsequent account of their origins in which we see the difference collapse for them between making (*poiein*) and coming to be or being born (*gignesthai*) on one's own.[4] Herodotus's digression on milking is immediately preceded by the sentence "The women of the Scythians, because their men were away for a long time, were resorting to slaves." The verb "to resort"—*phoitaō*—may also bear the meaning "to go into" in the sense of initiating sexual intercourse.[5] Herodotus thus goes out of his way to begin book 4 by collapsing into each other the natural process of generation and the artificial process of making—*genesis* and *poiēsis* become one.

But strangest of all is that Herodotus begins his account of their practice of milking by saying the Scythians blind their slaves "for the sake of the milk they drink," and he ends it by saying, "For the sake of these things, the Scythians blind everyone they capture." Although he writes as though the account of the milking procedure is at the same time an account of why the Scythians blind their slaves, Herodotus never makes explicit what this sameness consists in. Seth Benardete provides a compelling hypothesis, which needs some preparation before we spell it out.

Herodotus's account of milking is followed by the fight between the re-

---

4 · See 4.5 and Benardete, *Herodotean Inquiries*, 103–4.

5 · The mares' vaginas are indicated by the word *arthra*—a generic term for joints. It is the word used by Sophocles for Oedipus's eye sockets when he blinds himself. The milking description is perhaps meant to remind of us of what it would take physically to blind men.

turning Scythians and their onetime slaves. The battle doesn't go well for the Scythians until one of them has an idea.

> Scythian men, what sort of thing we are doing! Fighting with our own slaves and being killed, we become fewer, and killing them, we will rule fewer in the future. Now it seems [right] to me to drop spears and bows and, each taking a horsewhip, to go at them with that. For while seeing us bearing arms, they hold themselves equal to us and born of those equal to us. But if they see us holding whips instead of arms, learning that they are our slaves and understanding this, they will not stand their ground. (4.3)

Armed men are of course more dangerous than men with whips. What, then, is the Scythian logic here? Only if "whip-bearing" is taken as "master" will the tactic work. That is, the whip cannot be taken simply as an image of enslavement; it must be understood as the reality of enslavement. This is true, of course, not only for the "slaves" but also for the Scythians.

This, in turn, is connected to another obtrusively odd Herodotean observation. In 4.7 he remarks that the Scythians say of the country to the far north that it is possible neither to see nor to go through it because of "being showered with feathers. For both earth and air are full of feathers, and these shut out sight." Later (4.31), Herodotus provides his own interpretation of this claim: the Scythians are using feathers as an image (*eikazountas*) for snow. It is characteristic of the Scythians to see the image as the thing. In Egypt (book 2), Psammetichus conflates the origin of a specific tongue with the origin of language—Egyptians identify *glōssa* with *logos*. For the Scythians of book 4, reality is identical to its representation in the poetic images presented in *logos*; in the far north, Scythians claim to be blinded not by something *like* feathers (Herodotus interprets them to mean snow) but by feathers.[6]

Both *logos* and *nomos* necessarily idealize the real and by so doing introduce a certain duplicity to the world. We see what is in terms of what ought to be or is meant to be. Yet this duplicity tends toward univocity insofar as its whole point is to bring order to what is experienced as disordered. Egyptian double vision leads to identifying the ought (what regulates) with what was (the first things temporally), thus finessing the difficult problem of the ontic status of what regulates by making it identical to the ontic status of what it regulates. It's the same, just older.[7]

---

6 · In Persia (book 3), *logos* as speech is identified with *logos* as reason—a true Persian does not lie.

7 · This Egyptian version of Platonism leads to problems, not the least of which is the bodily character of their gods in a world in which the body, as corruptible, is held in contempt. Egypt is a land of great physical (and so corruptible) monuments meant to

By reducing meanings to things, the Egyptians of book 2 verge on losing all meaning.[8] In so doing, they place the doubleness of experience at risk. What, then, are we to make of the Scythian way—seeing images of reality as reality, seeing only feathers? Herodotus brings this issue home to us in several ways. He tells us that the Scythians, with one exception (to which we will turn in a moment), make no images (*agalmata*) of gods or altars or temples to them, but only give them names (4.59). When their fathers die, the Issedones eat them in a celebratory feast. They save only the head, which, when emptied and with hair removed, is gilded and used as an image (*agalma*) to which yearly sacrifices are offered (4.26). For them, household gods are not images of their ancestors; they *are* their ancestors. Similarly, when a Scythian king dies, fifty of his servants and horses are killed, gutted, and stuffed. The servants are then put astride the horses and placed around the king's grave in a circle. The Egyptians attempt to preserve the dead body by mummification; for the Scythians, the real becomes a statue (4.72). The exception to all of this is the god Ares, whose *agalma* is an ancient iron sword (the word, *akinakēs*, is Persian in origin, 4.62). Only the god of violence and disorder is given a sign and placed at rest. Histiē and Ares seem curiously understood in the Scythian pantheon—she constantly in motion and he forever at rest.

All of this brings us to Seth Benardete's interpretation of Herodotus's twice-stated but never explained claim that it is for the sake of the milk they drink that the Scythians blind their slaves (4.2).[9] In Homer, we find the phrase *nuktos amolgōi* five times; it seems to mean "in the dark or the dead of night."[10] In the *Iliad*, the phrase always occurs in a simile; in its single occurrence in the *Odyssey*, it introduces a dream in which an image (*eidōlon*) of Penelope's sister comes to her. In antiquity, *amolgos* was understood to derive from *amelgein*—"to milk."[11] Presumably, because milking is done in

---

withstand the ravages of time so as to call into question the being of what unfolds in time. The Persians do not make this mistake. Their gods are cosmic. We learn nothing of their monuments. For them, the law and the *logos* are what regulate, each unerringly. The law describes what cannot be transgressed—incest is held not to exist. The *logos* rules so powerfully that we cannot lie—we cannot say the thing that is not. And yet Darius comes to the throne of Persia by a clever ruse. The illusion that the world is perfectly ordered shows up as a reconfiguration of reality to conform with *logos*. The Persian views that the law is infallible and that they cannot lie manifest themselves in the end as an inability to distinguish lie from truth. Perfect *logos* amounts to the triumph of the will, for where *logos* admits of no imperfection by pointing to no reality beyond itself, it ceases to be *logos*.

8 · The Persians of book 3, by reducing things to meanings, verge on losing things.

9 · Benardete, *Herodotean Inquiries*, 100–101.

10 · *Iliad* 11.173, 15.324, 22.28, 22.317; *Odyssey* 4.841.

11 · For the references, see Benardete, *Herodotean Inquiries*, 100n2.

the darkness of night, "in the milking time of night" comes to mean "in the dark of night"—what happens coming to stand for when it happens. Benardete suggests that Herodotus further extends this verbal slippage in which one thing (milking) comes to be an image for another (darkness) by allowing the verb "to milk" to stand first for the verb "to make dark" and then for the verb "to blind." It is Herodotus who makes the Scythians commit this slippage, for the connection he takes advantage of is a feature of the Greek language. Still, in his own voice, Herodotus "speaks Scythian," by using an accidental (if retrospectively intelligible) feature of Greek, to fashion a story that, while pretending to provide a cause for the Scythian custom of blinding slaves, in reality is tautological; for in the end, that the Scythians blind their slaves for the milk means nothing more than that they blind them for the sake of blinding them. In so doing, Herodotus highlights the danger of poetry to which the hyperbolic Scythians, as *the* poetic people, seem to succumb. A simile first drifts into a metaphor, which, in turn, gradually supplants the reality it is meant to gloss. Among the Scythians, the doubleness appropriate to all vision disappears when the image, the very being of which is to point beyond itself, becomes so powerful as to obscure its own incompleteness. In this altogether poetic world, blinded to the presence of poetry, men believe tautology to be causality. For example, should we once identify soul as the principle of motion, were we speaking Scythian, we might run the risk of further concluding that soul cannot in principle cease its motion and that, accordingly, it, and so we, must be immortal. Men in an altogether poetic world read images on the cave wall as real; the cave they inhabit is sealed so as to prevent the entry of any glimmer of light from the outside.[12] Accordingly, they reproach the Greeks for celebrating the mysteries of Dionysus, for "they deny it to be seemly to discover this god who leads human beings into madness" (4.79). The Scythians are especially suspicious of Dionysus, who, in his connection to drunkenness, madness, ecstasy, and theater, most of all represents the power of the image to represent (and so misrepresent) the real. Herodotus, then, begins his book on Scythia in a Scythian way with a story that, because it cannot be understood nonmetaphorically, finally cannot be understood metaphorically either. He has given us this illusion of understanding so that we may begin to grasp what it might mean that there is no place and there are no people to which these returning "Scythians" can return.

So that we will not mistake this mistake to be uniquely Scythian, book 4 provides several examples of how we might all be Scythians. After the milking story, Herodotus relates a series of accounts of the origin of the Scyth-

---

12 · This is the meaning of Scythian xenophobia; see especially Herodotus's account of Anacharsis (4.76–77) and Skyles (4.78–80).

ians as a people—their own version (4.5–7), that of the Greeks (4.8–10), and finally the one accepted by Herodotus himself (4.11–12)—that is, that they were expelled from their homes by the Massegetae and subsequently did the same to another people, the Cimmerians. Herodotus then presents a slightly modified version of his account put forth by the poet Aristeas, who says that the Scythians were expelled by the Issedones, who had been expelled by the Arimaspians (4.13). This is perhaps the first time in the *History* that Herodotus allows his demythologized version of what happened to stand in agreement with the version of a poet—although it must be said that he has indicated earlier (3.116) that these one-eyed creatures, the Arimaspians, cannot exist. Still, the agreement gives Herodotus an excuse to digress in order to tell a story (4.14–16) according to which Aristeas dies, reappears after 7 years and writes a poem about the Arimaspians, and then reappears in Italy 240 years later. The puzzle, how a poet is able to vanish and then uncannily reappear, may be resolved if we reflect on how we routinely say that we are reading Homer or Wallace Stevens. The resurrection of Aristeas makes sense when we realize how we identify the product of the man, his *poiēma*, with the man so that his name takes on a new meaning. It is a slide in the language not unlike the way in which the Scythians hear stories from the Issedones about one-eyed men and then make a race of them by calling them Arimaspians—from the words in their language for "one," *arima*, and "eye," *spou* (4.27). The Greeks, who borrow the name Arimaspian to designate the fictional one-eyed people, do not know that there is no people separate from the claim that they are one-eyed. The name is the claim; that they are one-eyed is a tautology. No being grounds the image; the image is the being.

Herodotus's accounts in books 1–4 are meant to be perfect images of the fundamental modes of understanding, and so being in the world, out of which every people is constituted. Perhaps the strangest feature of book 4 is Herodotus's second example of the universality of this Scythian tendency to poetize, his extended digression on the question of the map of the world (4.36–45). He begins by laughing at mapmakers, all of whom irrationally demand symmetry and balance in the world, as though Asia must be the size of Europe. They impose symmetry even when it requires that they falsify the real features of the world they profess to describe. In other words, they regularly ignore the fact that maps are images and can be what they are only when it is possible to test them against what they map. Mapmakers who make the Scythian mistake are seduced by the image as though it causes the world to be what it is. Now, while Herodotus accepts the conventional division of the world into Asia, Europe, and Libya, he also recognizes this division as conventional (4.45). This perhaps sheds some light on his own "mapping" of the world in which features no doubt actually present in Egypt, Persia, and among the Scythians are exaggerated so as to become ideal types.

Another of these poetic exaggerations is that the Scythians are a people so perfectly poetic as to cease to recognize poetic images as poetry. As a consequence of this exaggeration, Herodotus can say that "by the Scythian race the one greatest thing of all the human matters we know has most wisely been discovered, although I do not esteem the rest" (4.46). This greatest thing is freedom. The Scythians cannot be conquered because, as Darius discovers when he invades, there is no there there for the Scythians. Having no settled cities, forts, houses, or farms, they are the perfectly mobile people. Because they have nothing stable, nothing can be taken from them. But what has this to do with their nature as the poetic people?

Poetry, at its most powerful and extreme, would deny the difference between images and things. But when there ceases to be a difference between snow and what is used to express the nature of snow, the being of things in the world as always pointing beyond themselves is rendered invisible. We behave as though we are in the presence of reality. Accordingly, the Scythians think they are blinded by feathers. But anything we see may be used as an image of something else—snow, after all, also reminds us of feathers; to see means never simply to see what is, for everything that is always evokes something other than itself. To see things simply as what they are would mean to remove from them this evocative power. But this would mean not to see them as they really are at all. To be means to be ambiguous. Perfect vision, removing this duplicity, is blindness, for, because all things are always also images, vision cannot be other than imperfect vision. Herodotus makes Scythians, who, because they cannot see images, cannot see at all and who, because they are blind, are enslaved. We need to see more clearly, however, how slavery and blindness are connected.

The Scythians are so committed to the surface of things that they kill their king, Skyles, for secretly living a double life and adopting Greek ways (4.78–80). As they do not recognize the being of what is hidden, for them there is nothing beneath the surface to bind the various surfaces together into a single being. In their refusal of ambiguity, the Scythians have turned stupidity (Herodotus tells us that the Euxine Pontus where they live is the location of the stupidest tribes, 4.46) and superficiality into wisdom and depth by identifying freedom with total lack of constraint; they are nowhere limited. The Scythians are the most extreme case of what we mean when we speak of a simple people. Their freedom requires a complete simplicity that can show itself only as perfect indeterminacy.[13] Because there

---

13 · When Xerxes wishes to count the Persian army during his invasion of Greece (7.59–60), he packs together ten thousand men as tightly as possible and draws a

is nothing to them, nothing can be taken from them. These anachronistic acolytes of Janis Joplin, for whom "freedom's just another word for nothin' left to lose,"[14] are indomitable. Scythian freedom is thus rooted in the permanence of total impermanence. This is what it means that the people of rivers, of change, and of freedom worships Histië above all other gods. The Scythian king may do anything he wishes except cease to be a Scyth, but to be a Scyth means nothing else than not being anything else—not being the other. The free people are altogether unduplicitous; they are what they are and nothing else. Ironically, this means that they are not.

In book 2, Herodotus displays the transformation of Egyptian devotion to the fixed and stable into a celebration of the mutable. The Egyptians' last king, Amasis, is a usurper in the most traditional and ancestral of cultures, an innovator, a lover of things Greek, and an apologist for the constant flux of human life.[15] In book 4, we get the story of the Scythians, the fully poetic people who pride themselves on being beyond compulsion—altogether free—and as a direct consequence of this prove to be blind and enslaved. And yet book 4 does not end with the Scythians but continues with an account of Libya (4.145–205), an account in which the origins of the city of Cyrene (4.145–67) is another of Herodotus's obtrusive digressions. The account of Libya begins at 4.145 with the words "While he [Megabazus] did these things [among the people of the Hellespont], there came to be against Libya another great expedition of the army. . . ." Herodotus does not discuss this expedition, which connects this part of book 4 both to the rest of the book and to the end of book 2 until 4.200–205. This would be comparable to his previous accounts if he moved immediately in 4.168–99 to discuss the geography and *nomoi* of Libya. Instead, he inserts the long account of Cyrene and so forces us to wonder about its significance.

Cyrene is a city that combines elements of Greece, Egypt, the Scythians,

---

circle around them. Then he builds a wall following the circle and proceeds to pack the remaining part of his army into the enclosure in groups—each group presumably will number ten thousand. The Scythians seem about to do something like this at 4.81. Wanting to know the number of his subjects, their king, Ariantes, requires each Scythian to bring a bronze arrowhead to Exampaeus, but instead of counting them, he melts them down to make a gigantic bowl. The Scythians cannot know how many they are because in the end their total commitment to freedom leaves them with no defining features, not as individuals and not as a group, but counting requires differentiation.

14 · Janis Joplin on "Me and Bobby McGee," in *Pearl* (1971), words and music by Kris Kristofferson.

15 · In book 3, a similar transformation occurs in Persia, where perhaps the most sacred custom is telling the truth, and Darius becomes king by way of an extravagant lie.

and Libya. It is a Greek colony on the coast of Africa founded by settlers from Thera, who were expelled from Sparta and before that Lemnos, and who are descendants of the Argonauts, who stopped in Lemnos on the way to Colchis in Scythia. Colchis, the home of the Golden Fleece, and also of Medea, who was carried off by Jason, was, according to Herodotus (2.104), an Egyptian colony. As usual, the details of the founding differ depending on the source of the account, but all the accounts agree in making Cyrene a hodgepodge of peoples and customs. The backstories of Cyrene's settlers all emphasize in various ways the uncertainty of origins and of the strict divisions of peoples into races. That none of these peoples seems really to come from where it is thought to come forces us to wonder about the strict connection between a people and a place. Perhaps all peoples are nomads.

The unstable connection between people and place is further emphasized by place names—which seem to be either specifications of generic features (for example, Kalliste) or derived from the names of those who founded them (for example, Thera). The story of Cyrene is also filled with names of men borrowed from their peculiar features—*Battus* means "stutterer," and *Theras*, "hunter." That Herodotus has naming on his mind is clear from 4.149: "For the son [of Theras] refused to sail with him, and so [Theras] said he would leave him a sheep among wolves [*oïn en lukoisa*]; from this mot, the youth's name came to be Oiolukos, and somehow this name prevailed."

As being unable really to trace themselves to a place, the Cyrenians belong with the Scythians, who in the end are bound together by nothing but will. But the Cyrenians differ from the Scythians in that, while they are a people from no place, they do found a place. To do so, they must constitute it in a manner heretofore unprecedented in the *History*. The story takes a while to work itself out, but eventually, with the help of a man named Demonax ("lord of the people"), who is brought in to be a *katartistēr*—a restorer of order—they form a stable political regime. Because they cannot simply follow ancestral ways, they are the first people in Herodotus's book really to engage in politics—the first people for whom *nomos* means not primarily custom but law in our sense. And Herodotus uses the Cyrenians at the end of book 4 as a first pattern for what it means to be Greek.

After book 4, the *History* changes character; it reads less like anthropology and more like a history—an account of conscious political decisions. Cyrene marks this change. Prior to it, political life is truncated; the way of a people, their *nomos*, so dominates as to characterize them without their knowing it does so; they are a little like plants. True political life in some sense requires that men be "first" uprooted—nomads—in order for them to know what it means to plant roots. When Herodotus turns to Greece in books 5–9, he shifts his attention to this self-rooting, to self-conscious political life. But to see what it means for a people to form the ways that will, in turn, form them, he needed to look first at how a people would appear if they were altogether formed and then at how another would appear whose identity consisted solely in their act of forming—of making. The one, Egypt, would be all effect and no cause; the other, the Scythians, would be all cause and no effect. Both extremes, of course, are unstable. Egyptian stability leads to unrest, Scythian freedom to enslavement. It is their way to have no way; one might say that will concerned solely with the act of willing—that is, will absent a specific object—is empty. It too ends up being all effect and no cause. The Greeks, on the other hand, are genuinely poetic because, being imperfectly poetic (they see, not *despite* but *because* they see double), they combine these two features—freedom and rule. By acknowledging this duality—wedding the soul's indeterminacy to its identity—the Greeks come to light, in a way not intended to be altogether historical, as the first fully human people in Herodotus's *History*.

PART THREE

EURIPIDES

Soul as Same and Other

Euripides' *Helen* and *Iphigeneia among the Taurians* are obviously a pair. In the *Helen*, we are told that Helen did not really go to Troy. She was replaced at the last moment by an image fashioned of air. The real Helen was borne to Egypt, where she remained incognito for the duration of the war. In the *Iphigeneia among the Taurians*, we are told that Iphigeneia was not really sacrificed by her father at Aulis. She was replaced at the last minute by a deer. The real Iphigeneia was borne to the land of the Taurians, where she became a priestess in the temple of Artemis and supervised human sacrifices. The Greeks went to Troy thinking her sacrifice had been the price for their passage. The two plays are further paired in their relation to Herodotus's *History*. The *Helen* provides an interpretation of book 2, the *Iphigeneia* of book 4. Euripides means to show us the consequences for soul of the extremes represented by Egypt and the Scythians (the Taurians are Scythians who live on the Black Sea). The focus of the *Helen* is the illusiveness of personal identity—of the stability and self-sameness of soul. Euripides experiments with the possibility that this sameness has to do not so much with monument-like fixity (this is the error of the Egyptians and, in the *Iliad*, of Hector and finally Achilles) as with the continuity of the story in which one is embedded; it is thus dependent on the poetry that, as we have seen, Herodotus understood to be the signal feature of Greek culture. The focus of the *Iphigeneia* is on the centrality and instability of ritual as a sign of the double way in which human beings see first objects and then themselves in the world—as at once real and pointing beyond themselves, as other than themselves (it is thus a commentary on the Scythians' "snow is feathers"). This too depends on poetry, and specifically tragedy, as the necessary means for preventing the decay of this double sense of the world into a uniformity and flatness that is the limit case of which various barbarisms are approximations. The self-consciousness of this instability and the attempt to address it poetically are what separate Greek from barbarian.

Still, the *Helen* and the *Iphigeneia* remain tragedies. Accordingly, each in its way also reveals its own ultimate failure—the poetry of the Greeks is, after all, a version of seeking for stability. In the end, the decay of a poetic understanding by way of the hardening of its images into "reality" is a necessary consequence of the initial power of the images themselves. Euripides thus shows us the soul at work in its attempt to mitigate through tragedy the sedimentation that occurs in any attempt to show the soul at work. He endorses Herodotus's celebration of the exemplary humanity of the Greeks and sharpens its focus. What most distinguishes the Greeks is not simply poetry but tragedy. Tragedy displays our humanity but, in the very act of so doing, displays that, why, and how there is no simple resolution of the tensions that constitute our humanity. We are none of us simply "Greek."

· CHAPTER 6 ·

The Fake That Launched a Thousand Ships

The Duplicity of Identity in the Helen

For Aristotle, tragedy as a form of poetry is a paradigm for human nature, plot or story is "the first principle and like the soul of tragedy," and the best stories require what he calls recognition.[1] If he is correct, tragic recognition should provide a portal to self-understanding. Now, Euripides' *Helen* is a play so teeming with mistaken identities that lead to recognitions or false recognitions that it ought to be a virtual primer on human nature. Accordingly, it should teach us something about the human soul and so about ourselves. That a play by Euripides should be a tool for self-knowledge is no surprise, for the tradition tells us that his plays were "patched up by Socrates" (*Sōkratogomphoi*).[2] And Socrates, of course, is the philosopher especially fervent in the pursuit of self-knowledge.

In search of ourselves, then, we hurry expectantly to Euripides' *Helen*, but when we arrive, we are perplexed. What exactly is this play? It was first produced at a tragic festival in 412 BC, so mustn't it be a tragedy? Yet in modern times, when not harshly judged and dismissed out of hand, it has received mixed reviews.[3] The *Helen* has been called "an elegant romance," "a parody of tragedy," "frankly funny" and "nearer to comedy and operetta than high tragedy" "though filled with unpleasantness and meaningless cynicism," a farce, a tragicomedy, a tragedy manqué, "in no possible sense a tragedy," "a brilliant failure," *un tragédie romanesque*, a "drama of ideas," and like *The Magic Flute*, "a half-lyrical, half-philosophical romance."[4] The identity of the *Helen* is thus something of a question.

1 · See *On Poetics* 1450a29–39.

2 · The phrase belongs to Mnesimachus; it is quoted by Diogenes Laertius (II.18).

3 · For the harshness, see, for example, Ulrich von Wilamowitz-Moellendorff, *Analecta Euripidea* (Berlin: Borntraeger, 1875), 241, 244.

4 · See Richmond Lattimore, *Euripides II* (Chicago: University of Chicago Press, 1956), 263; A. W. Verrall, *Essays on Four Plays of Euripides* (Cambridge, U.K.: Cambridge University Press, 1905), 43–133; G.M.A. Grube, *The Drama of Euripides* (London: Methuen, 1941), 337, 352; Anne Pippin, "Euripides' *Helen*: A Comedy of Ideas,"

The conceit of Euripides' play, borrowed in part from the lyric poet Stesichorus and in part from Herodotus, is that Helen never really went to Troy. She was neither abducted by Paris nor did she run off with him willingly. True, she was promised to Paris as a bribe to name Aphrodite more beautiful than Hera and Athena in the famous "Judgment of Paris," but before Aphrodite can pay this debt, Hera substitutes for Helen a phantom, an *eidōlon*, a perfect copy fashioned out of air. The real Helen is then concealed in a cloud by Zeus, who tells Hermes to deposit her for safekeeping at the court of King Proteus of Egypt, where she remains for the ten-year duration of the war and for the seven-year period in which Menelaus attempts to return home from Troy. During this time, Proteus dies, and his son, Theoclumenos, is smitten with Helen and wants her for his wife. He begins killing any Greeks who come to Egypt—presumably in the hope of preserving the secret that Helen still lives (although, since the chorus is made up of captive Greek women, it is not so clear that he hasn't been raiding Greek cities—for what reason, we are left in doubt). When Menelaus, with the phantom Helen, and his crew shipwreck in Egypt, he comes to the house of Proteus begging and is told by a philhellene portress to leave before he gets killed. He runs into Helen, who has just heard from another Greek, Teucer, that Menelaus is presumed dead and then from Theoclumenos's sister, the seeress Theonoe, that he is not only alive but nearby. After considerable confusion, including a report that the phantom Helen has suddenly vanished into the air, they recognize each other and plan an escape. They convince Theonoe to conceal Menelaus's presence from her brother. Then Helen tells Theoclumenos that she has heard from one of Menelaus's companions (in fact, the real Menelaus) that her husband is dead. She agrees to marry Theoclumenos if only he will allow a symbolic burial, a cenotaph, of Menelaus at sea. Menelaus's companion will officiate, and she must be present. The cenotaph, Theoclumenos is told, must be lavish and will require that a ship carry a suit of empty armor out to sea with a sacrificial animal and produce of the earth—in other words, provisions for a journey. What happens is by now predictable. Helen and Menelaus collect his shipwrecked crew, take over the ship, and sail away. Theoclumenos is about to send men to chase them and kill his sister in anger when Helen's dead twin brothers, now gods in heaven, intervene (a typical Euripidean deus ex machina) to stop him and tell us that after they die, Helen will become a god and Menelaus will live among the gods.

Classical Philology 55, no. 3 (1960): 151; Cedric H. Whitman, *Euripides and the Full Circle of Myth* (Cambridge, MA: Harvard University Press, 1974), 35, 68; Gilbert Norwood, *Greek Tragedy* (New York: Hill & Wang, 1960), 260; M. Patin, *Euripide II* (Paris: Hatchette, 1883), 75.

Now, the play does seem to end happily—although this is not at all unusual for Euripides. Still more strikingly untragic are the characters themselves. When we first encounter Menelaus shipwrecked in Egypt, he seems rather too worried about the state of his clothing, lest "the sacker of Troy" be mistaken for a homeless man (415ff.). As part of Helen's escape plan involves faking the death of Menelaus, she tells us (1085) that she is going into the house to cut her hair, change into black, and rake her nails across her cheeks—all this to look the part of a grieving widow. A hundred lines later, she reenters having cut her hair and wearing black, but we hear nothing more of scratches. Apparently, Helen could not bring herself to mar her beautiful face—*the* beautiful face. Early in the play, she had contemplated suicide with these words:

> To die is best. How would I die not beautifully?
> It's unseemly to hang by the neck,
> and deemed inappropriate by the slaves.
> But they hold cutting the throat to be something noble and beautiful,
> and the moment for the flesh to be released from life is brief.[5]
>
> (298–302)

So "shockingly out of place" and inappropriate for us is Helen's curiously self-centered comparison of the relative beauty of ways to die that the authenticity of the passage has been regularly called into question.[6] Helen and Menelaus seem perfectly paired. He is *the* Sacker of Troy (although he seems to have forgotten how much help he needed—remember that Homer even calls him a "soft spearman" at *Iliad* 17.587), and she is the most beautiful woman in the world (although, in this play, she is the only one ever to comment explicitly on her beauty). At first glance, then, these unusually vain and superficial people seem rather the stuff of soap opera or light comedy than of tragedy.

But what we are to call the *Helen* is an identity crisis that pales to insignificance beside the question of what we are to call Helen herself. As Helen and Menelaus have a daughter, Hermione, they must have been married for at least a year before she was abducted, but it does not seem more than, say, three years, for if Helen were married at sixteen, this would make her thirty-seven when the play opens, and, since everyone seems to think she looks the same as she did seventeen years ago, it would be hard for her to be much older than this. So we have a woman who was married to a man for perhaps three years seventeen years ago. Meanwhile, the phantom Helen slept with

---

5 · Throughout I have quoted Gilbert Murray's text as reproduced in A. M. Dale's *Euripides: Helen* (Oxford, U.K.: Clarendon Press, 1967). The translations are my own.
6 · See Dale, *Euripides: Helen*, 86.

Paris for ten years, then, when rescued, slept with Menelaus for seven more, and at no time did either of them doubt her identity. So why is the real Helen the real Helen? Because the phantom was made of air? But how was Helen "made"? One version has it that Zeus took the form of a swan fleeing from an eagle, swooped down on Helen's mother, Leda, and impregnated her. Helen was born from an egg, a story so implausible that even Helen can bring herself to believe it only about half the time (20–21, 257–529). Would such a fabulous story, in any event, make her reality more believable than the phantom's? This is an issue of considerable importance, for everything in the play depends on what it means for Helen to be real, and so on which Helen is real—the one hibernating in Egypt or the one who actually did what Helen is so famous for having done and thereby made possible the war that established what it means to be Greek over and against barbarian. One is reminded of the old joke that Shakespeare's plays (or in an alternative version, Homer's poems) were written not by Shakespeare but by another man of the same name. Our puzzle might be put in the following way. In the prologue of the *Helen*, a character steps on stage and says, "This is Egypt," and, "I am Helen." Of course, it is not Egypt but the *skēnē* of the theater of Dionysus on the slope of the Acropolis in Athens, and "she" is really a male actor wearing a large mask. Why do we accept her claim? We suspend disbelief for the sake of the story—the *muthos*. This, of course, makes Helen not so very different from her phantom; both are who they are by virtue of being embedded in a story.

Helen's is not the only identity question in play. The second half of the prologue is her meeting with Teucer, the half brother of Ajax exiled by his father from their home in Salamis for having failed to prevent his brother's suicide at Troy. Teucer comes to Egypt to ask the seeress Theonoe for directions to Cyprus, where Apollo's oracle has told him he is destined to found a new Salamis. In a strange inversion of the main story, Teucer takes the real Helen to be a look-alike, an image. At first, he is overcome with anger and hates her for the destruction she has caused. He relents only when he considers that she is not real (it is not altogether clear why he is so sure she cannot be the real Helen, since he admittedly doesn't know precisely where she is other than with Menelaus, who is himself just about to make an appearance in Egypt). Only the bracketing of Helen's reality, seeing her as an image or phantom, allows him to see her as she really is. She, in turn, does not recognize him, although the tradition regularly places him among her original suitors. When she asks who he is, he first responds with a generic description—"one of the wretched Achaeans" (84). Then he says, "Our name is Teucer, the father giving me life is Telemon, Salamis is the fatherland which nurtured me" (87–88). The expression "our name" (although it is certainly not uncommon in Greek to use a first person plural pronoun as a singular) hints that many are called "Teucer" (it is, for example, the name of a legendary king of Troy). Teucer himself is the son of one of Priam's daughters. We know as well that Telemon sired another son and that Teucer is about to found a city bearing the same name as his fatherland. Teucer thus fails to describe himself in an altogether distinctive way, for every common noun by virtue of being common applies in principle to many individuals. We are moved to name things to overcome this generic character of language, but while we may name babies to honor their uniqueness, we also have books in which prospective parents shop for the perfect name. Telemon exiles his son for failing to protect Ajax, who committed suicide because he was not awarded the armor of the dead Achilles as a sign that he was now the best of the Greek warriors.[7] Apparently, for Ajax to be recognized as unique among the Greeks means for him to wear the armor of Achilles. To look like Achilles is the measure of uniqueness.[8] Accordingly, a name, like armor, is of necessity inadequate to its task, for it is an exterior mark of identity designed to render what is interior—a shell of armor posing as the inimitable core of a man. A name does not confer identity.

Several things emerge in the subsequent conversation between Helen and Teucer. Troy was sacked and set afire "so that not even a trace of its walls is manifest" (108). There is thus no external sign remaining of the war, which therefore might as well have been an illusion or phantom—something in a poem. Teucer says that he saw Menelaus carry off Helen "with my own eyes, just as I see you—no less" (118), and then, when questioned about whether "this seeming seems steadfast" (121), he replies, "I myself saw with my eyes; and mind sees too" (122). He confidently takes sight to be the gold standard for identification at the very moment that he misidentifies what is before his eyes. At the same time, even after pressing Teucer to distinguish between what he saw and what he heard (117), after asking about the fate of her family, Helen too quickly jumps from a report of Menelaus's death to the fact. Later she will announce to the chorus that Teucer "said clearly that her husband was destroyed" (308). Even had Teucer said this, why would she believe him? Helen is surely not shy about declaring how wrong others can be in the face of apparently decisive evidence. Teucer reports only reports of Menelaus's death; are there not also many reports that Helen ran off with Paris to Troy? The explanation of the chorus, that fear leads us to assume the worst (312), is just a sign of how much mind determines what we think we see. Sight reveals identity no more than a name.

Finally, Teucer becomes impatient with stories (*muthoi*, 143) and presses on to his own business in Egypt; he has come to find the way to Cyprus.

---

7 · Compare 40–41.

8 · Consider in this regard the fate of Patroklos in *Iliad* 16.

Apollo had prophesied that he would found a new Salamis there, but Teucer doesn't know where to start. He has been told his story, but it has no contact point with reality. Helen tells him that "the journey itself will signify" (151). The story must suffice, for there is no way to anchor it to reality. Teucer replies that she has spoken beautifully (*kalōs*, 158); beauty apparently need not be connected to the real. Identity, what something really is, is neither a question of body nor a matter of name. It might be thought to be established by context—the story in which something is embedded. But with no connection to reality, a story may well be mere poetic fancy. The report of Menelaus's death is as false here as it will be at the end of the play when Helen uses it as a ruse to effect her escape.

No one can claim an unproblematic identity in the *Helen*. Menelaus is shocked that the old woman who is the gatekeeper at the house of King Proteus does not recognize "the sacker of Troy," even though he has just finished lamenting how perfectly awful he looks. Still, he thinks himself "not unknown in any land" (504). Helen, who announces to the chorus that she has just been told by the seeress Theonoe that her husband is not dead and in fact is in Egypt (528–40), immediately turns her head and discovers a man she does not recognize to be Menelaus.

Then there are the Egyptians. Proteus shares a name with a sea god described in *Odyssey*, book 4. There Menelaus is describing how his ship was becalmed at an island off the shore of Egypt. In order to learn how to get away, he must lay hold of Proteus, who has the power to change into anything, and hold on until Proteus becomes himself. The identity of the god whose name means "first" is to be somehow all things. His namesake is a king of Egypt who is said to "dwell in this house" (460) but turns out to have died sometime before the play opens. His tomb sits conspicuously before the house, and his son, Theoclumenos, now king, regularly greets him when entering and leaving (1165–68). Hermes left Helen in the safekeeping of Proteus, and now, in order to avoid the advances of Theoclumenos, she takes refuge at the tomb as though in a temple. Since Proteus still protects Helen, it is not altogether clear what the distinction between living and dead means in Egypt. His body is, after all, still there—entombed at the entrance of his house.

The Menelaus of the *Odyssey* learns how to seize the sea god Proteus from his daughter, Eidotheia, whose name means something like "look [or "shape"] of a god." The Proteus of the *Helen* also has a daughter. At first, her name was Eido—"form" understood either as "shape" or as "principle of knowledge"—but upon reaching puberty (apparently, you must be named what you are in Egypt), she acquired the power to understand "all the divine things that are and will be" (13–14) and thereafter was named Theonoe—

"god-knowing." Euripides thus splits Homer's Eidotheia into the problematic identity of the preadolescent Eido and the grown-up but still virginal seeress Theonoe. Theoclumenos, whose name means "listening to god" or "obeying god," also has a namesake—a fugitive and a prophet who becomes a friend and an ally to Odysseus's son Telemachus (*Odyssey*, book 15).

To summarize, there are two Proteuses—two "firsts." The one not in our play is a god whose identity it is not to have a fixed identity. The identity of the one in our play is thoroughly ambiguous. He is dead and yet not. He sires two children; the name of one means "to know the gods," of the other "to obey the gods" (Euripides thereby invents the tension between Athens and Jerusalem). Theonoe, the knower, divides into what she was in her youth (something to be known) and what she is now (someone who knows). The action of this play ends when her brother conforms to his name and obeys the gods; his namesake, of course, like his sister, was a seer.

That the identities of everyone and of many things in the *Helen* are doubled is paradigmatically manifest in Helen's twin brothers—Castor and Pollux. They are called the Dioscuri—the sons of Zeus. As with Helen, however, it is not clear what this means, for we are repeatedly told that Tyndareus may also be their father (137). When Helen asks about them, Teucer says, "They are dead, and they are not dead; there is a pair of stories [*logō*]" (138). Either they killed themselves out of shame over Helen, or they have become "most like stars and are a pair of gods" (140). These twins alternate appearances in the night sky, since Zeus granted each immortality only every other day.[9] It is, of course, hard to know what this means. What would it mean for two identical beings to alternate existence in the very same place? Why wouldn't the two simply be one? At the end of the play when the Dioscuri address Theoclumenos to forbid him to kill his sister, they say, "*We* the twin Dioscuri call you" (1643–44). Then they turn to address Helen and say, "*I* speak to my sibling" (1662) (emphasis mine). The *Helen* is a play in which no one seems to recognize anyone else—apparently, for good reason. That immortal twins should appear on alternate days in the heavens as gods signals how problematic Euripides has made the question of identity in this play. The ambiguity of twins who are both two and one, alive and dead, god and mortal, bodily and not, is somehow paradigmatic for the ambiguity at the core of our being.

Let us see if we can unravel some of these difficulties. Like many Greek tragedies, the *Helen* has a conspicuous "recognition scene." Since recognition must turn on the question of identity, perhaps we can gain some clarity by looking closely at the scene in which Helen recognizes Menelaus. Helen

9 · See *Cypria* I.

has just returned from following the advice of the chorus and asking Theonoe about the fate of her husband. She has learned that he is alive and even "somewhere near this land" (538). Addressing him in his absence, Helen says, "When will you come? How far would you come?" (540). Then she turns her head, sees Menelaus, and utters her next line: "Oh, who is this?" (541). Although the groundwork for the recognition has been rather well prepared, Helen does not take the bait. He, on the other hand, recognizes her body but knows that she cannot be Helen—"Never have I seen a body more similar" (559). The moment of recognition itself is rather strange and surprisingly difficult to pin down. It begins with a sentence that no one translates literally because it is just too odd. Helen looks at Menelaus and says, "O gods—for even [or "also"] to recognize friends [or "those dear"] is a god!" (560). We are first puzzled and then inclined to think that the sentence must mean something like "What a divine thing to recognize a friend!" But the immediate sequel makes this difficult.

Menelaus: Are you a Greek or a woman of the country?
Helen: Greek, but I would learn yours too.
Menelaus: Woman, I see that you are especially like to Helen.
Helen: And you indeed to Menelaus; I do not even grasp what I'm saying.
Menelaus: You have rightly recognized a most unhappy man.
Helen: O, after a long time, you have come into your wife's arms.

(561–66)

Now, when Helen says that even to recognize friends is a god, this cannot be an exclamation of joy over having recognized Menelaus, for then her next line would be altogether unintelligible. Are we to believe that she recognizes the husband she hasn't seen for seventeen years in one line and in the next asks him what country he is from? Accordingly, the recognition must occur later, when she makes it explicit at line 566. Menelaus, on the other hand, does not accept her as Helen until after the messenger arrives to tell him that the phantom Helen disappeared into the air (605–21). So, despite never having seen "a body more similar," Menelaus doesn't trust his eyes. The general point might be put this way: Helen "recognizes" Menelaus at 566 because she expects him; not until he expects her to be Helen does he recognize her. The problem is once again the relation between the eyes and the mind; expectation, whether dread or longing, shapes our thoughts and determines what we "see."[10] Menelaus gives expression to this connec-

10 · This problem is the theme of Helen's *kommos* with the chorus at 330–85. Anticipation leads us to poeticize our world and endow its particulars and our own with more significance than they deserve. We suppress chance at the cost of reality.

tion when he responds to Helen's claim to be his wife by saying, "Am I to suppose I do not think well? Are my eyes diseased?" (575). Helen responds, "Who else will teach you but your eyes?" (580). Were this correct, of course, the phantom Helen would be the real Helen.

Let us begin again. Why doesn't Helen recognize Menelaus immediately? It has been seventeen years. She may have agelessly retained her beauty, but Menelaus has changed. Helen knows who he is *supposed* to be but cannot quite believe her eyes. Menelaus's name has remained constant, but he changes. The odd sentence at 560, then, does not mean it is divine to recognize a friend. Rather, Helen is disappointed. You may always believe that you will know the one who is dear—*philos*—but even with those closest to you, it is as impossible to grasp their unchanging core as it is to recognize a god. To recognize friends *is* a god, for only a being with the power to see within others could genuinely know them.

Were Helen and Menelaus *philtatoi*—most dear to each other—they would see into each other so as to know each other perfectly. Yet the relation between them is thoroughly cynical; they use each other. Menelaus does not recognize Helen in a moment of divine insight but acknowledges that she is Helen only when he learns that the phantom Helen has vanished. Now, there is no reason in principle why he should accept the existence of a phantom at all. The two Helens are never seen together; as soon as one disappears, the other appears. There is no temporal difficulty, for Helen could have made her way to the house of Proteus while Menelaus was making his way. The slave who arrives to announce that "your wife has gone soaring up invisible to the air" (605) eleven lines later says, "Greetings, daughter of Leda, were you here then?" (616). Menelaus now accepts her as his wife because he needs *some* Helen lest he have to return home embarrassingly empty-handed after ten years of war and seven years of wandering; he needs her to justify the plot line of his life. At first, Menelaus refused to acknowledge her because he needed to justify another plot line—"the greatness of toils there [Troy] persuades me, not you" (593). He cannot afford to have the great deed of his life reinterpreted as the pursuit of a phantom.[11] At the same time, neither does Helen exactly recognize Menelaus. She needs him, for without him, "never again will I come to Greece, my fatherland"

11 · Even after he acknowledges who Helen is, Menelaus expresses doubts about her fidelity (794). That is, even when he identifies her, he admits that he cannot know her. This occurs directly after Helen has called into question Menelaus's claim that when he came to the door of the house of Proteus begging, he did it in deed but not in name. She does not automatically accept his understanding of his inner nobility, the nobility that allows him to denounce crying to Theonoe at 948 after having "eyes wet with tears" at 456.

(595–96).[12] And she tells him what she knows in stages, revealing only as much as she thinks she needs to persuade him of her identity—for example, feigning complete ignorance of the phantom (572, 574) and springing it on him only when it is clear that she has no other choice (582). Trying one tack and then another, Helen behaves exactly as she would if she were an imposter. When the two finally agree to acknowledge each other, then, it is not because they trust each other but because they need each other. They see what their minds tell them they must see.

If really to recognize friends is a god, what sort of being is a god, and how can it be a verb? When Menelaus first hears from the gatekeeper that Helen, the daughter of Zeus or perhaps of Tyndareus, she who once lived in Sparta, is now living in the house of Proteus (470–72), he is perplexed: "What am I to say? What am I to think?" (483). That the two are not simply the same for him suggests a distinction between internal cause and external manifestation. That there could be living on the Nile another woman named Helen born of a man named Zeus (a man because it is clear that in heaven there is only one Zeus), that there could be another Tyndareus and another Sparta, these all seem unlikely to Menelaus. Still, "it is likely that in so much space many have the same names, both city with city and woman with woman; this is nothing to wonder at" (497–99). What is obviously left out here—so obviously that one intelligent translator, Richmond Lattimore, simply supplies it anyway—is the claim that the world also contains many *men* with the same name. But Menelaus balks at this conclusion, for he cannot quite admit that there could be another Menelaus somewhere. His whole reflection on the possibility of doubled names has as its purpose to find a way to explain his own singularity and uniqueness as "the sacker of Troy." This sheds some light on why Menelaus has been so careful to indicate that while there might be another *man* named Zeus, there was only one Zeus in heaven. There cannot be two Zeuses, one in Egypt and one in Greece, because to be a god means to be a universal particular. Ares may be a god of war whose name sometimes simply means "war," but he is also unique—a person who gets caught sleeping with Aphrodite. Gods are combinations of significance (they mean something) and individuality (they are something).[13] Menelaus longs for this status and believes it belongs to

---

12 · Helen knows how deeply those who are held captive long for home; later, to ensure their cooperation, she will make a promise to rescue the Greek slave women at the court of Theoclumenos with absolutely no explanation of how or whether she plans to keep it (1385–89).

13 · In this way, the question *quid sit deus* ("What is god?") is the same as the question *ti to on* ("What is being?"). In the latter case, the question of being constantly moves between two poles. On the one hand, the being of a thing is its permanent and unchanging form—its *eidos*; on the other hand, the being of a thing is whatever

him as "the sacker of Troy," as it belongs to Helen as "the face that launched a thousand ships." Apparently, not only is the recognizing of friends possible only *for* a god; what it means to *be* a god is to be the sort of being that cannot itself be recognized—a being that consists of the impossible combination of perfect intelligibility and intelligence. Gods are simply perfect representations of what we mean by souls.

We long to be gods but do so at our own peril, for, if Ares stands for war, then he is a kind, and as a kind, he is something that has instances—he can be duplicated. If Menelaus is not careful, then, he will turn into an *onoma*, a name or a noun—something fashioned out of air that, because it stands for one thing, can also stand for something else and so is necessarily detachable from the thing it identifies. In principle, no name is unique even though it is meant to be our personal ID tag, for a sign of uniqueness cannot itself be unique. This problem is present from the very first line of Helen's opening speech. *Neilou men haide kalliparthenoi hroai* may refer either to the Nile's beautiful virginal streams, presumably virginal because receiving water only from melting snow and not from tributaries, or to the beautiful virgins, nymphs—personifications of the streams of the Nile. The streams of the Nile are either gods to be named or things to be described by godlike adjectives; the language does not permit us to settle the issue. Helen goes on to speak of Proteus, his wife Psamathe (sand), Theoclumenos, Eido, and Theonoe, all of whom share this doubleness; they are both names and nouns.

The crucial action of the *Helen* occurs before it begins, when Paris judges Aphrodite to be the most beautiful of the goddesses. Suppose Hera had won. Would she not then have been the most beautiful of the goddesses, and so the goddess of beauty, and so Aphrodite? Remember the joke about Shakespeare. The Judgment of Paris makes sense only when we put together universal quality with particular identity. *Ouranos* means "sky," and *gaia* means "earth." At the same time, they are the names of specific gods. When the two couple, they produce a generation of gods—among them a son, Kronos, whose name is very close to *khronos*—time. Kronos castrates Ouranos, and a new generation of gods takes over. At the same time, time deprives space of its unrivaled dominion. The coupling of *ouranos* and *gaia*, on the one hand sexual, on the other describes the fact that the two cannot exist without being together. There can be no earth without something enveloping it, and there can be no envelope without something inside. To recognize friends, kin, those most dear and most loved, is a god. To recognize what we most love involves the togetherness of universal and particular,

---

makes it particular—its *tode ti*. The latter clearly has something to do with body but oddly cannot simply be identified with body. The locus classicus for this problem is Aristotle's *Metaphysics Z*.

even though we regularly identify what we most love as unique—my one and only. Aphrodite is the combination of universal significance in a particular individual. In the *Helen*, Euripides has experimented with the separation of these two elements. The phantom Helen is a symbol for everything that led the Greeks to Troy. The particular individual Helen is hidden in Egypt. Euripides has in this respect simply taken a hint from Homer. In the *Iliad*, the Trojan elders admire the sight of Helen at the city wall, saying that "there is no cause for indignation for Trojans and well-greaved Achaeans to suffer for so long a time for a woman like her; in her face, she resembles in an uncanny way the deathless goddesses" (3.156–58). Later Helen tells Hektor that the whole war has occurred for her sake and for that of Paris "so that we may be made subjects of song by men of times to come" (6.356–57). Homer's Helen is likened to a god and understands herself as a figure of solely poetic significance. She thus testifies to her own unreality.

What, then, would it mean that the Greeks unwittingly went to Troy and fought for ten years for the sake of a breathing phantom made of the sky (34), a cloud (706), what was only a name or word (43)? That the Trojan War was undertaken in the name of something unreal would seem to compromise not only the name of Helen as the face that launched a thousand ships and that of Menelaus as the sacker of Troy but also to call into question the significance of the single most important event in the history of the Greeks—their greatest deed; indeed, what gives them their identities as Greek as opposed to barbarian.[14] On the one hand, it seems preposterous to have gone to war with Troy for a phantom. On the other hand, were Helen only a particular being, it would have been equally preposterous; it is not as though Helen herself would have been restored to each member of the army. As accounts of human behavior, both idealism and realism fail; they make our lives tragically ridiculous.

Before this play begins, we believe there is only one Helen. The recognition comedy calls this into question and forces us to ask whether we can ever be sure of another's identity, or for that matter, our own identity. This applies most obviously to those we most think we know—those we love, our friends, and those we hate, our enemies. Helen may say, "O gods, for even to recognize friends is a god," but, upon first seeing and "recognizing" her as the Helen he hates, Teucer says, "O gods, what sight have I seen? Do I see the most hateful deadly likeness of a woman who destroyed me and all the Achaeans?" (72–74). We invoke the gods not only to say "thank god"

---

14 · The importance of the Trojan War is acknowledged in an interestingly backhanded way by Thucydides, who wants to make the case that the Peloponnesian War, between Athens and Sparta, is the "greatest motion that has come to be among the Greeks and some part of the barbarians, and in a word, among most human beings" (1.1.2) but cannot do so until he dispenses with the prior claim of the Trojan War.

but also when we say "goddamn." The most common Greek definition of justice is helping friends and harming enemies. Our inability to recognize friends would therefore call into question our ability to be just.[15] This, in turn, calls into question the justice of the Trojan War, a war that begins with a violation of the laws of *xenia*—guest-friendship.

The question might be put somewhat differently: short of recognizing friends, how is it possible to share with them, since friends are supposed to hold all things in common? It is not uninteresting that when Menelaus's slave arrives to inform him of the disappearance of the phantom Helen and is then convinced of the identity of the real Helen, he asks to share Menelaus's pleasure (700).[16] Menelaus replies with, "Indeed, old one, share in speeches [*logoi*]" (701). Speech serves as the limit of sharing. In mediating between us, it is simultaneously the sign that there is no perfect "us." The slave then begins a long reflection on causality (711–33). The god is the cause of everything, but nevertheless everything has the appearance of chance. There is thus a split between what happens and its significance. The slave first had respect for the events of Helen's wedding, but after her disgrace, he lamented them; now, when her reputation is cleared, he has renewed respect. But, of course, the events of the wedding did not change—only their significance. Life unfolds in time as if it were a tragedy—the significance of its events intelligible only in light of the end of the story. The slave uses himself as an example. A good slave, he says, shares the goods and ills of his master and so is like his master. He may be named a slave, but he is noble by nature—his spirit is free. In other words, this slave dares to claim that he shares in Helen's plight. As it has her, chance (*tuchē*) has plagued him with a bad appearance that conceals a good inside. What she thinks of as her extraordinary fate or destiny (*tuchē*) is really the ordinary and necessary discrepancy in all human beings between what they seem to be and what they really are. Real friendship means sharing pleasures (700), faring well (736), and luck (738—*tuchē*). It means "joining in one fortune [*tuchē*]" (742). If the necessary condition for a common life together is sharing pleasure and toil, then political life requires something that is, strictly speaking, impossible. Our souls are not available to others—even to our soul mates. The existence of the phantom Helen brings to the surface the inner distrust that plagues Helen and Menelaus, but in revealing the hollowness of the Trojan War, it also brings to light the deeply problematic status of political life.

The story of the Trojan War, whether in the traditional version or in

15 · See, for example, Plato's *Republic* 332a–c.
16 · The slave addresses Menelaus in either the dual or the plural; in either case, it is peculiar unless it is meant to go back to 646, where the chorus use the dual to call Helen and Menelaus a pair.

Euripides' revisionist account of Helen, begins with the Judgment of Paris, a judgment about which of the gods is most beautiful. Our experience of something beautiful is complicated, for on the one hand, we experience it as in a class by itself, as unique, and at the same time as in some way paradigmatic of the class that, in its beauty, it is threatening to surpass. This is even more telling in Greek, where *to kalon* means not only "the beautiful" in the sense in which it attaches to Helen but also "the noble" in the sense in which it attaches to Achilles (and in which Menelaus wishes that it attached to him). The *Iliad* is therefore a poem about the beautiful across its whole range. Now, if experience of the beautiful combines in itself an experience of what is particular with an experience of something universal, then it might seem to be a model for what it means to combine the two when we identify something. This experience, while showing up most powerfully in beautiful things, would really point to our underlying ability to see anything at all as apart from other things—as one. However, *the* premise of the *Helen*—the phantom—means to show that this powerful urge is a mistake. Accordingly, every recognition in the *Helen* is in some way defective. *To kalon* is a general name for what shows up in each of the gods—the illusion of the unity of universal principle with particular being.

In its concern for identifying the beautiful, the Judgment of Paris lays the groundwork for all trials. Any judgment has two parts—a universal principle of right and the particulars of the case. What is the crime, and did he do it? Accordingly, perfect justice would require that the one judged both be an individual, and therefore be deserving of praise or blame, and fit perfectly under a universal rule, and so be a type. The shifting meaning of the Greek *tuchē* in the *Helen* points perfectly to this doubleness, for it may mean either chance or destiny. From the perspective of the one, I am free and hence responsible; from the perspective of the other, my fate is sealed.[17] This is the meaning of Paris's choice of Aphrodite; all gods somehow embody this tension, but Aphrodite as *the* beautiful is the exemplar of it.

There are two trials in the *Helen*. They occur simultaneously and deal with the same issue—whether Helen and Menelaus will be allowed to leave Egypt. Zeus is the judge in one case, Theonoe in the other. Here is Theonoe's description:

> On this day, in an assembly before the seat of Zeus, there will be strife among the gods concerning you. On the one hand, Hera, who was ill disposed toward you before, is now well disposed and wants you to be safe in your fatherland with this one here [Helen], in order that Greece

17 · This is just the double perspective of all tragedy, which Aristotle refers to as the likely and the necessary. See *On Poetics*, chapters 7–8, with my *Poetry of Philosophy* (South Bend, IN: St. Augustine's Press, 1999), 52–54.

may learn that Cypris's [Aphrodite's] gift of a bride to Alexander [Paris] was false. Cypris, on the other hand, wants your homecoming to be wrecked, so that it will be neither argued nor manifest how she bought beauty on account of Helen for a vain marriage. The end is with us, either what Cypris wishes, I will destroy you by telling my brother that you are here, or again siding with Hera, I will save your life, concealing you from my sibling, who ordered me to say when you should chance to come to this land on your journey home. (878–91)

So Zeus will hear this case and decide between Hera's wish to reveal that Aphrodite cheated and Aphrodite's wish to cover it all up. And yet Theonoe goes on to say that she will decide the case of Helen and Menelaus and proceeds to listen to their arguments on their own behalf. How can both of these be true? While we do know that Zeus will decide, we do not know what he decides. Much in the same way, we can preserve our freedom of action in particular while believing in general in destiny. This tension is preserved within the human side of the case in the quite different arguments given by Helen and by Menelaus. Helen urges Theonoe to lie to her brother and say that Menelaus is not in Egypt. Her reasons are curious. She turns herself into a piece of property belonging originally to Menelaus and about to be stolen without right by Theoclumenos (this is, of course, meant to remind us of the abduction of Helen by Paris). So important is this right of ownership that even "a rich man [*ploutos*] who is unjust must be let be" (905). Helen never asks how the rich man first got his property. Her example is of interest since *Ploutos* has been once used in this play as a name for Hades (69)—the god of that place, or the place itself, where the issue of first ownership cannot come up because there is no time.[18] Helen can have such a clear-cut notion of justice only because she stops the clock at a certain time; this is appropriate enough for the gods perhaps and for Hades, and it may well be appropriate for the Egypt where Helen has remained frozen in time for seventeen years, but it cannot really hold for a human being. Helen's argument posits absolutely fixed and unchanging ownership— a first owner. Not only does she forfeit any freedom for herself, but her insistence on fixity describes a world governed from a first beginning by a necessary order. Menelaus, on the other hand, argues that Proteus made an agreement to keep Helen safe until the war was over and she could be taken home. An agreement is an agreement; when a man indicates his will, that is all there is to it. In Menelaus's world, nothing counts but freedom. Soul can exist only in the uneasy combination of these two. Perfect soul—a god— would be the impossible total reconciliation of the two.

18 · That we are meant to think of Hades is also clear from the reference to Persephone at 913.

The story of the *Helen* is about an escape from Egypt. Why Egypt? The king's name is Proteus—first. Despite his death, he is still called king. His tomb is outside his house, and his son regularly talks to him. His daughter "recognizes gods" and wants to remain a virgin—that is, not participate in generation. The main feature of the country itself is the Nile—the very first word of the play. Its streams are virginal; they come from a first source and are not part of a larger motion. When Menelaus first sees the house of Proteus, he calls it one of the "houses of the rich [*plousiōn*]" (432). The word is very close to *Ploutōn*—an alternate name for Hades, the god of the dead. Egypt is where things stay put; they are what they are, and so the names of people are the nouns that describe them. There is no difference between the universal and the particular. Egypt is Hades, in which Helen has "lived" for seventeen years without changing, which is to say, she has not lived at all. We have seen Herodotus point out that the Egyptians have such contempt for the impermanence of the human body, its susceptibility to change and decay, that they worship what is other than it. This leads to some strange practices, for in their rejection of the human, they turn to animal worship (despite the fact that animals too change and die), and in their attempt to stabilize the body, they mummify corpses, leading them to the odd and contradictory practice of having contempt for living body on the one hand and worshipping dead body on the other. But the principle underlying these practices is always traceable back to an attempt to find something within the bodily realm that has permanence—to find a first thing. Egypt is thus a place where a particular individual gets transformed into a universal principle. Menelaus and Helen, who have each in their way achieved a certain permanence as phantoms, want to go home. But to go home means they must escape Egypt, which is simply another version of the longing for permanence.

Their escape proves to require three things. First, Theonoe must lie. Teucer had come to Egypt to consult her even though he already had an oracle from Apollo (144–50). Theonoe is apparently a better seer. She is less ambiguous. She tells it straight. However, once she lies for the sake of justice, she will no longer be simply believable. Egypt will cease to be the Egypt where things simply are what they are. Put differently, really to tell the future would mean that there is no future. For human beings, having a future means not knowing, not being a finished product, not having an already settled identity, being a verb rather than a noun. Second, Menelaus must "die." He must put the Sacker of Troy behind him. Third, Helen must cut her hair, wear black, and scar her face; she must put behind her the Face That Launched a Thousand Ships. Of course, it turns out that Menelaus does not really die; he simply reasserts himself as the hero of a new story. And Helen cannot bear to scratch her face. So, in order to escape being characters in a poem, phantoms, nouns rather than real human beings, Menelaus and Helen have to launch a plan that turns them into characters in a new poem, the *Helen*. It is therefore no surprise that at the end, the twin brothers, who, when they become gods become indistinguishable from each other, tell us exactly what is in store for Helen and Menelaus. Helen will become a god, and Menelaus will live among the gods on the isle of the blessed. It is appropriate that on the basis of a very fanciful and forced etymology, they rename the island that guards the place where she was stolen away by Hermes *Helenē*, saying that it derives from *klepsas*—taking by stealth. Euripides thus makes Helen meaningful and a goddess.

One of the peculiarities of the *Helen* is its use of choral odes—*stasima*. Ordinarily in Greek tragedy (although the practice is by no means strictly adhered to), after a prologue, the chorus enter singing an ode, the *parodos*. An episode follows made up of dialogue among the characters; this, in turn, is followed by a *stasimon*. Episodes and *stasima* alternate until the end of the play, which ends in an exit song, an *exodos*. In the *Helen*, a *kommos*, a sung interchange between the chorus and a character, occurs where one would "ordinarily" find the first *stasimon*. The next ode, the first "*stasimon*," is so abbreviated as scarcely to be a *stasimon* at all; it is only thirteen lines long (515–27). The first real *stasimon* in the play therefore does not occur until line 1107—two-thirds of the way through the *Helen*, and further into the play by some three hundred lines than any other first *stasimon* in Euripides. The upshot of all this is that the appearance of the more "poetic" part of tragedy is delayed for quite a long time. When the *stasima* do find their way into the play, they turn out to seem formulaic—as though Euripides pulled stock songs out of his repertoire and inserted them with only the slimmest connection to the plot of the *Helen*. The choral *exodos*, their exit song, turns out to be something Euripides uses word for word as the *exodos* for three other tragedies (the *Alcestis*, *Andromache*, and *Bacchantes*) and with only a slight variation for the *Medea*. Now, as it turns out, this is only deceivingly haphazard, for Euripides has a thematic purpose in mind. The second *stasimon* is perhaps most striking in this regard. For apparently no reason, Euripides introduces the story of Demeter, Persephone, and Hades—Persephone, the daughter of the goddess Demeter, is taken away to Hades for half the year each year. Her mother mourns her loss and the earth goes infertile. This is the mythic account of the change of seasons. But in the version in this *stasimon*, no proper names are used; we are left to infer the identities of the characters in this plot from its action. And it is a story about the tension between permanence and generation, at the end of which we are puzzled to find Helen compared not to the mourning Demeter (Helen, after all, has several times mentioned the fate of her daughter, Hermione) but to the permanent virgin, Persephone. We are given a generic account of the loss of the daughter by the mother, and Helen is somehow blamed in terms of this relation. She sinned against the mother by being so preoccupied with her own beauty—the sign of her permanence. Despite affirming her own reality over and against that of the phantom, Helen wants her name back. In the *Helen*, the poetic, the symbolic, is the realm of the phantom. It comes back late in the play as the real Helen, despite her own self-understanding, is about to once again become a poetic fiction. Euripides knows that poetry necessarily detaches its characters from the real; it beautifies them and turns them into proper names—*eidōla*. It is thus not accidental that the *stasimon* that attacks this process should have within it no proper names. The phantom Helen, who did go to Troy, was an image in a Greek poem. Greek poetry embodies the ideal. At first, it seems that the *Helen* means to solve this problem—to be a poem about the real in its opposition to the ideal. It turns out, however, that Egypt, which may first seem to be a sign of this resurrection of the real, in fact idealizes the body. The *Helen* is the story of a woman who, to avoid becoming a phantom image, becomes a mummy.

Euripides writes a play concerned with the problem of identity—of things, of other human beings, and finally of ourselves. He shows that recognition or identifying requires fixing something or stabilizing it and so necessarily lifting it out of time. He shows as well that while we do long for such fixity, at the same time we want to be alive and so changing. This perfectly expresses the impulse to deify. The double character of our longing is described by alternate translations of a biblical sentence: "I am what I am," and "I will be what I will be."[19] Menelaus and Helen, each in a way having gotten only half of what they long for, want out. So they devise a way to escape. But the escape proves to be a reenactment of what they are escaping from, for to do anything, human beings must set before themselves models—ideals. As ideal, these objects of longing are of necessity not real; they are shadows—beautiful *eidōla*. The *Helen* is in the end a tragedy because Helen and Menelaus do not realize that their attempt to penetrate the *kalon* (the beautiful or noble) for what is real and good (the dear, or *philon*) necessarily involves them in a projection that idealizes and is itself an illusion. Or, when Helen utters her now famous sentence "O gods, for even to recognize friends is a god," she may be expressing her doubt in the reality of the gods, but in order to do so, she has had to begin by making an appeal to them. Invoking a phantom in order to show that it is a phantom, Helen displays for us the elusive and peculiar character of the identity of her own soul.

19 · See Exodus 3.13.

CHAPTER 7

Euripides among the Athenians

The Double Vision of Soul in
Iphigeneia among the Taurians

According to Aristotle, Euripides is the most tragic of the poets.[1] Since "plot is the first principle and like the soul of tragedy," and the most beautiful plots involve reversal and recognition, and, of these, in the best, recognition comes to be "from the events themselves," it is not surprising that Aristotle should cite the plot of Euripides' *Iphigeneia among the Taurians* as exemplary.[2] The "most tragic of the poets" perhaps ought to have written the best of the tragedies, and the *Iphigeneia* appears to be Aristotle's candidate. Yet Aristotle also says that in the most beautiful tragic plot, a better-than-average man moves from good to ill fortune.[3] In the *Iphigeneia*, Athena arranges things so that all ends happily for Orestes, Iphigeneia, and even for the captive Greek women who make up the chorus. Is this a movement from good to ill fortune? How can this play be the best of tragedies? How can it be a tragedy at all? Of course, not having read Aristotle, Euripides may have been ignorant of what he was supposed to do. But didn't Aristotle read Aristotle? How could the celebrated celebrator of plot have been so filled with praise for a tragedy with the story of a fairy tale? That "*Iphigeneia among the Taurians* is usually regarded as an exceptionally well-made play, more transparently coherent and unproblematic than, say, the kindred *Helen* or *Ion*," only deepens this puzzle.[4] An unproblematic and coherent tragedy is only problematically tragic.

The *Iphigeneia among the Taurians* opens with a speech in which Iphigeneia reveals that she, who is presumed to have been sacrificed by Agamemnon at Aulis so that the Greeks could sail to Troy, was in reality whisked away by Artemis at the last minute and replaced by a deer. Iphigeneia was brought to Artemis's temple in Scythia among the Taurians, where either

---

1 · *On Poetics* 1453a29.

2 · See *On Poetics* 1450a38–39, 1452b30–31, and 1455a16–18.

3 · *On Poetics* 1453a7–12.

4 · See Christian Wolff, "Euripides' *Iphigeneia among the Taurians*: Aetiology, Ritual, and Myth," *Classical Antiquity* 11, no. 2 (1992): 307.

the goddess or Thoas (34), the local king, made her priestess and responsible for preparing human victims for sacrifice. Iphigeneia has just had a powerful dream, which she interprets to signify the death of her brother, Orestes. In the meantime, Orestes and his cousin and brother-in-law, Pylades, arrive on the Taurian shore, sent by Apollo to steal the statue of Artemis from the temple and take it to Athens. Success will release Orestes from his labors, presumably meaning that he will no longer be pursued by the Furies for the killing of his mother. After conducting a ritual funeral for the "dead" Orestes, Iphigeneia is brought a report that two Greeks have been captured. She is to prepare them for sacrifice. A long scene follows in which Iphigeneia discovers the prisoners to be Argives, questions Orestes about affairs at Argos, and offers to free him if he will carry a letter to someone there. He agrees on the condition that not he but his friend, Pylades, be the one to go. When Iphigeneia makes Pylades swear an oath that he will deliver the letter, he asks what he is to do if it is lost at sea. Iphigeneia makes him commit the letter to memory, and in the process, its addressee (Orestes) and its content (that she was not really sacrificed) are revealed. Pylades immediately meets the conditions of his oath by handing the letter to Orestes, who reveals who he is and offers some proofs. How all three will escape is now the problem. Iphigeneia determines to tell Thoas that Orestes and Pylades are matricides who, before being sacrificed, must be purified in seawater, as must the statue of Artemis tainted by their touch. After using her authority to ensure that everyone else will remain inside, Iphigeneia takes Orestes, Pylades, and the statue down to the sea. They are about to escape in Orestes' ship, but the wind turns against them. Thoas is in the act of sending men for their recapture when Athena intervenes. She instructs Orestes to set up a new temple of Artemis at Halae, where each year a ritual human sacrifice will be performed. Iphigeneia is to become the priestess at Artemis's temple at Brauron; when she dies, she will be buried there and offerings will be made to her of the fine clothing of women who have died in childbirth. The Greek slave women who have made up the chorus will also return home. Thoas agrees because to disobey a god is crazy, and so, with the possible exception of Thoas, all live happily ever after. Or do they?

At some level, the *Iphigeneia among the Taurians* is clearly about two things—the difference between Greek and barbarian and the significance of human sacrifice. The first word of the play is *Pelōps*, the name of an ancestor to whom Iphigeneia traces the origin of her Greekness. Tantalus, king of Lydia and Pelops's father, was said to have murdered his son and served him to the gods as dinner in order to test their divinity by seeing if they could discern that they were eating human flesh. All the gods but Demeter knew immediately; she, apparently brooding over the loss of Persephone, was inattentive and took a bite of shoulder. Tantalus was punished severely.

The gods reassembled the pieces of Pelops (with an ivory shoulder) and brought him back to life, after which he went to Greece, married Hippodamia of Pisa, founded the Peloponnesus, and fathered Atreus, father of Agamemnon. Iphigeneia thus begins the play by reminding us that Greeks were originally Asians, albeit Asians reassembled as a result of a divine rejection of human sacrifice.[5] Iphigeneia repeatedly understands the distinction between Greek and barbarian in terms of human sacrifice, even though the originator of her line served his son to the gods for dinner (386–91), her grandfather similarly served his brother's children to him out of revenge (179–90, 811–17), and her own father meant to sacrifice her to Artemis as the price for setting sail for Troy (6–27, 203–28).[6] According to an ancient law in the city where "barbarian Thoas is lord among the barbarians," Iphigeneia now prepares for sacrifice any Greek man who comes to the Taurian land. She calls it a festival "only the name of which is noble [*kalon*]." Out of fear, she remains silent as to the rest—the unspeakable things done within the temple (28–41). Later Iphigeneia doubts that the gods could demand such sacrifices and even doubts the stories about her ancestor Tantalus. It must be "those killers of men here" who attribute their own baseness to the goddess (385–91). Just before putting her escape plan into action, Iphigeneia prays to Artemis.

> Mistress [*potnia*], who saved me in the glens of Aulis from the terror of a hand of a murderous father, save me also now as well as these men; or because of you the mouth of Loxias is no longer true for mortals. But kindly [*eumenēs*] go from a barbarian land to Athens. For it is not fit for you to dwell here when there is a happy city at hand for you.[7]
> (1082–88)

5 · The *Iphigeneia* also begins by reminding us that beneath the problem of human sacrifice lies the still darker problem of cannibalism. Sacrifices to an Olympian god involve offering the fat and bones of the sacrificed animal to the god but eating the meat. See Hesiod *Theogeny* 507–60; and Jean-Pierre Vernant, "Greek Religion," in *Religions of Antiquity*, edited by Robert M. Collier (New York: Macmillan, 1989), 176–81.

6 · The chorus too emphasize their exile from Europe (135) to barbaric Asia (180). Thoas, on the other hand, asserts that no barbarian would dare matricide (1174).

7 · In the plural, *potnia* (*potniai*) is used to refer to the Furies (Sophocles' *Oedipus at Colonus* 84, Herodotus's *History* 9.97), who, of course, are given the name Eumenides, or Kindly Ones, in Aeschylus's play of that name when they acquiesce in the acquittal of Orestes and take up residence at Athens. Here Iphigeneia urges her *potnia* Artemis to be *eumenēs* and take up a new home in Athens. The plot of the *Iphigeneia* makes clear that Orestes has not yet been cleansed. Euripides means to revise Aeschylus's version of the story. Orestes has not yet come to terms with what it means to have killed his mother for killing his father for killing his sister. Iphigeneia remains as un-

Were Artemis, who once saved Iphigeneia from being sacrificed, to be perfectly consistent, she ought to save her now as well. It is because they practice human sacrifice that the Taurians are not fit to keep Artemis's temple. Iphigeneia effectively identifies the barbarity of the barbarians with the fact that they practice human sacrifice. On the other hand, presumably because she is a Greek, she finds the suggestion terrible (*deinos*) that they, as visitors, kill a host/stranger (*xenophonein*), even to effect their escape (1021).[8] Iphigeneia seems to think it less barbarous to kill your own than to kill strangers.

Given the importance of human sacrifice in the play, the ambiguity surrounding its practice by Iphigeneia is doubly puzzling. Beginning with her interpretation of her dream, she regularly collapses the distinction between anointing those who are about to be sacrificed and actually killing them. She says her art is to slay strangers (53), even though others in fact cut the throat of the sacrifices. But is even this true? The queerest of the puzzles of the play emerges in Iphigeneia's conversation with the herdsman from whom she hears of the capture of Orestes and Pylades and to whom she says that "never yet was the altar of the goddess made red with streams of Greek blood" (258–59). In her dream, Iphigeneia makes much of the auburn (*xanthas*) hair that grows out of the cornice of the one pillar that remains standing after the fall of her ancestral home (52). In the immediate sequel, Pylades remarks that the cornice of the altar is auburn from blood (73). This would seem to settle the matter, and yet directly after Iphigeneia makes her puzzling remarks about never having spilled Greek blood, the herdsman introduces into his story the fact that capture occurred near a shelter for those fishing for *porphura*, the fish from which purple dye is made (263), and then goes on to tell of how they sounded an alarm by blowing on *kochloi*, shellfish from which purple dye is also made (303). All of this might be thought to be included only for adding color to the description were it not for the fact that in the *Iliad* (17.361) and in Aeschylus's *Persians* (317), *porphureos* refers to the color of bloodstains. We thus have a bloodstained altar (73), a claim that no blood has been spilled (258–59; this seems to follow from the fact that the ancient law specifies the sacrifice of Greek men), and finally the gratuitous introduction of material for making dye the color of blood (263, 303). We seem to be meant to wonder whether the human sacrifice practiced by the Taurians might be an elaborate hoax.

That said, we must immediately answer that it cannot be. Iphigeneia has

---

finished business since Orestes seems to have taken her death rather lightly. Another Fury has to be made kindly. Aeschylus and Euripides seem to agree, however, that this is what distinguishes Greeks from barbarians.

8 · This is, of course, a version of the issue of the status of strangers at stake in the Trojan War.

a letter written for her to Orestes by a captive who pitied her and held that the law, not her hand, was responsible for his death. This can only be the law that prescribes the death of Greek men. So one Greek at least has died. Euripides seems to have made it impossible for us to solve this difficulty on the level of the plot. On the one hand, and contrary to our initial impressions, no sacrifice has been performed; on the other hand, at least one sacrifice has been performed. But perhaps the contradiction is the point. By being made to wonder whether a human being has been sacrificed, we are made to wonder what it would mean for a human being to be sacrificed. When Agamemnon sacrifices Iphigeneia, he is fulfilling an oath to sacrifice "the most beautiful thing a year would bear" (23), much as Abraham is told to sacrifice his "only son Isaac, whom [he loves]."[9] Human sacrifice has meaning insofar as we are offering up our ownmost—what is of the greatest importance to us. Piety demands that the gods be given what we value most. A lamb may be dear, but a human being is more dear. Understood in this way, killing one's child is a sign of great piety. At the same time, the very moment a human being is placed on the sacrificial altar, his humanity is diminished.[10] On the one hand, the greatest piety requires human sacrifice; on the other hand, to sacrifice a human being is to render it less than it was—no longer the greatest sacrifice but just another animal to be burned and eaten. The gods place an impossible demand on us. No sacrifice is sufficient unless it is a sign that we give what is most our own, and yet in the act of sacrificing it, our own ceases to be our own. The *Iphigeneia among the Taurians* is ambiguous with regard to the question of human sacrifice because human sacrifice is by its very nature ambiguous. To perform it is not to perform it; human sacrifice is impossible.

The *Iphigeneia* begins by acknowledging that what was thought to be a human sacrifice was not; at the last minute, a human being turned into an animal. The Greeks, altogether unaware of the change (perhaps human flesh tastes like venison), have to be taught its significance. This play, the instrument for their education, will make them fully Greek. Iphigeneia herself still confuses the intent, acknowledgment, or meaning of sacrifice with the act itself. She does not carefully distinguish her office from that of those who cut animals' throats, and she assumes that because her dream showed her performing the rites of her office over what she took to be Orestes, this is tantamount to the death of Orestes. Not sufficiently understanding the

---

9 · Genesis 22.2.

10 · It is for this reason that Euripides has Iphigeneia go voluntarily to the altar at Aulis (*Iphigeneia at Aulis* 1368–1401) and in this play has her stipulate that Orestes and Pylades must be untied before they can be fit sacrifices (468–71). An unwilling human sacrifice strips a human being of humanity, but even a willing sacrifice involves a devaluing of the worth of a human being.

distinction between the significance of a deed (one might say the poetic representation of the deed) and its reality, Iphigeneia makes a typically barbarian mistake—a Scythian mistake; it is as though everyone were like Thoas, whose name describes his most significant feature—as though the swift of foot were all named Swift, and all Carpenters were workers in wood (2, 31–33), and as though those bearing whips were of necessity masters. But by distinguishing the meaning of a deed from its reality, might it not be possible to preserve the lofty piety of human sacrifice without indulging in the low savagery of the deed? "For the sake of the holy"—*hosias hekati* (1461)—would then take on its idiomatic meaning, "for form's sake." The *Iphigeneia*—which is, after all, about thwarted human sacrifices—would in reality be about the superiority of ritual, fake sacrifices.

That Euripides has the duality of reality and significance in mind is also clear from our first glimpse of Orestes and Pylades. As the two enter cautiously, Pylades twice speaks of looking around in a double way.

> I am looking [*horō*], turning my eyes in every direction, I am inspecting [*skopoumai*]. (68)

> But looking round with my eye [*egkuklounta ophthalmon*], I must inspect [*skopein*] well. (76)

Pylades tacitly distinguishes between seeing what is present and a metaphorical seeing that involves understanding the meaning of what one sees. Similarly, when the herdsmen first encounter Orestes and Pylades, while there is no argument with respect to what they see, there is an important disagreement about what it means. To some, the strangers are gods (*daimones*, 267) or images (*agalmata*, 273) of a god; to others, they are simply wayward sailors (276). This duality gets resolved only in madness or in dreams. For Orestes, who mistakes the dogs and cattle of the Taurians for the Furies (whose sounds are said to be *mimēmata* of the sounds of cattle and dogs, 293–94), and Iphigeneia, for whom anointing her brother is killing him, vision is not double. There is no difference between feathers and snow.

Had Orestes made the distinction between ritual and reality, he might have understood Apollo's instructions quite differently. We do not know the precise words of the oracle, only Orestes' versions of them:

> You said for me to come to the boundaries of the Taurian land where your sister Artemis has altars, and to take the image [*agalma*] of the goddess, which they say fell into this temple from heaven. (85–88)

> There, sounding a voice from his golden tripod, Phoebus sent me here to seize the image [*agalma*] fallen from Zeus and set it in the land of the Athenians. (976–78)

It is possible, of course, that Apollo told Orestes to go to the land of the Scythians to fetch his sister, which in Greek might be indistinguishable from "the sister."[11] Both the *agalma* of Artemis and the person Iphigeneia fell from the sky (29). This ambiguity is perfectly expressed at the end of the play when, to effect their escape, Orestes lifts Iphigeneia into his ship while she is holding the *agalma* of Artemis (1381–85)—the act of rescuing Apollo's sister being the same as the act of rescuing his own sister. *Agalma* has a variety of meanings in Greek ("delight," "honor," "glory," "gift," "image," "statue," and so forth), as Euripides reminds us when he has one of the herdsmen, upon first seeing Orestes and Pylades, suggest that they are *agalmata* of Nereus (273). They are surely not thought to be statues but rather something like favorites. If the word were used in this way, Iphigeneia could easily be understood as an *agalma* of Artemis. Of course, were she simply an *agalma* of Artemis, she would be little more than a statue. As priestess, she performs the duties of her office, but she asserts her humanity by doubting her patroness, blaming Artemis's "sophisms" in accepting human sacrifices while she keeps from her altars any who are stained by murder or by touching a woman in childbirth or a dead body (380–83). A human being can no more be an *agalma* than a sacrifice. Iphigeneia is and is not an *agalma* of Artemis. None of this ambiguity ever gets through to Orestes, however. He thinks only that he has been sent to fetch a statue; finding Iphigeneia is a stroke of luck, but it never occurs to him to see one event as an image of the other. Neither he nor his sister sees double.

Yet there is reason to believe that for Euripides, as for Herodotus, seeing double is the defining feature of the human soul. Iphigeneia begins the play by lamenting the death of her kin (*philos*, 59), Orestes, although she can scarcely have known him. She places all her hopes in him even though, when she last saw him, Orestes was an infant. He is her friend in name only; before she learns his name, she is content to see him die. On the other hand, Orestes and Pylades are *philoi* in a deeper sense. The herdsman reports that while the Taurians attacked the mad Orestes, Pylades protected the dear man (*philon andron*) at the risk of his own life (310–14). This account leads Iphigeneia to assume that the two are "a pair of brothers [born] of one mother" (497). Orestes responds that they are brothers in love (*philotēti*) but not in blood (498). The friendship of the two men is confirmed when, having been offered a chance to save himself by taking Iphigeneia's letter to Argos, Orestes wants Pylades to go in his stead because he is his *philos* (597–608). Pylades, lamenting this as misfortune ("unenviable is the death of friends to friends," 650), wishes to die with Orestes, for he is his friend.

11 · See Moses Hadas, *Introduction to Classical Drama* (New York: Bantam Books, 1966), 108.

It would be shameful for him to do otherwise (674–86). Orestes replies that this would pain him even more; he asks Pylades to suffer the shame of abandoning him so that he, Orestes, will not have to suffer it and calls Pylades the dearest of his friends (*philtaton . . . philōn*, 708). Friends seem to be those who identify their friend's good with their own; they are as one.

Why has the *Iphigeneia* suddenly become preoccupied with the issue of *philia*—kinship or friendship? For Orestes to love Pylades as a brother is possible only because Pylades is not his brother. *Philia* in the highest sense can become manifest only when two human beings bound together by mutual consent behave as though they had been bound together by something, like birth, altogether beyond their consent. And yet to be bound together by necessity is precisely not to be friends. At its most powerful, will appears to be necessity, but at precisely that point, it ceases to be will.[12] Just as perfect meaning or single vision is no longer meaning, perfectly free willing is no longer willing. Orestes says he and Pylades are brothers in love but cannot mean what he says, for, were they brothers, there would be nothing special in behaving like brothers. But *philia* is special. Its metaphorical meaning, which can be understood only as imperfect or incomplete, is thus the measure of its "real" and so "perfect" meaning. Metaphorical brotherhood, a simulacrum of brotherhood, is ironically real *philia*. It requires that we understand ourselves as being something we are not in order to understand what we are; we must see double. Significance must be at odds with reality to be the measure of reality. At first, it seems as though the metaphorical level of our lives is interpreted in terms of a more fundamental reality, but the metaphor turns out to be the reality of our lives. Ritual is not a reminder of a deeper reality; it constitutes a "deeper" reality, which it then interprets. The plot of the *Iphigeneia* serves as an example. Iphigeneia overinterprets her dream to mean that Orestes is dead—she cannot know that he is the last male of her family since she knows neither that her father is dead (543–45) nor that Orestes was the last of her mother's children (compare 917–19). She then stages a funeral, during which she sprinkles libations, cries, and would put her auburn hair on his tomb if she could (158–78). Her misinterpretation of the dream thus leads to a ritual that could itself be the meaning of the dream. A dream is interpreted as a ritual that is then interpreted back into what it is a ritual of. Iphigenia says that a dream about sprinkling libations over a pillar with a red top is an image of her doing her priestly function, and so represents death. This then causes her to perform a ritual

---

12 · Accordingly, in the *Iphigeneia*, the word *daimōn* and words compounded from it are used to mean sometimes fate or destiny (157, 202–4) and sometimes god (267, 391, 570). At 1486, Athena tells Thoas that "necessity is stronger than both you and the gods."

burial that can, in turn, be understood as the true meaning of the dream she first interpreted—she saw herself sprinkling libations over Orestes, who is really alive.

Fraternity among real brothers could show itself only after the rejection of the blood bond that ties them together; fratricide points to the rejection of the merely animal connection. To be willing to kill your brother seems to be the prerequisite for loving him simply as a human being, for only in this way can you be sure that you love him for himself and not because he is your brother. The plot of the *Iphigeneia* reflects this difficulty. Not only does Iphigeneia literally come to know her brother as her own by planning to kill him, but she also demands that Orestes separate himself from one who is *philtaton philōn* for the sake of his own escape (595). To know what you love, you must forsake it, and yet to forsake it is to deny your love. Friendship no less than piety makes impossible demands on us and for the same reason. The significance of both depends on a reality that undermines their significance.

Iphigeneia among the Taurians is a story about what happens when the reality of things is replaced by their significance. The fundamental "fact" of the play is that although Iphigeneia did not die at Aulis, the Greeks were allowed to sail to Troy. The Trojan War required not her death but its significance—something like acknowledging the harsh cost of war before going to war. Ironically, a real sacrifice would not serve this purpose so well. Ritual forces us to acknowledge that we are really concerned with the meaning of the action we are imitating, not its reality. By separating the significant from the real, it forces us to acknowledge the presence of the significant within the real. It is like dreaming, which seems almost a natural ritual—an experience of the separation of experience from reality that induces us to look for a meaning within reality.[13] The Taurians seem to have sacrificed strangers before Iphigeneia dropped into their midst (39), and it is not clear that they sacrifice only Greek men since Iphigeneia is told to prepare for the sacrifice of Orestes and Pylades before she asks what land they have the look of (241–46). What is clear is that the Taurians have come to interpret their practice as just reprisal for Agamemnon's "sacrifice" of Iphigeneia at Aulis (336–39). But once a practice is acknowledged to exist for the purpose of expressing something else—not simply the hatred of strangers but the symbolic avenging of Iphigeneia—then it no longer really has to be done. The symbolism is important, not the deed.

Greeks differ from barbarians in that they are aware of this primacy of significance. In the *Iphigeneia*, Euripides experiments with the complete rationalizing or Hellenizing of the Greeks—in a way, with giving them single

13 · See 1234–82.

vision; the play is a declaration of their utter independence from Asia. For there to be no stain of savagery on the Greek war against Troy (the deed that more than any other constitutes them as a people), the sacrifice of Iphigeneia has to be denied.[14] If Iphigeneia was not killed, then the murder of Agamemnon was not justified, and if Clytemnestra was altogether in the wrong, Orestes was altogether right. The Tantalids begin to look squeaky-clean. Still, there are problems. The play begins with a reference to the origin of the Greeks in Asia; these Greeks—Iphigeneia, Orestes, and Pylades—institute a plan designed to free them, like Pelops, from Asia. The scheme involves the sort of untrustworthiness that Iphigeneia attributes to Greeks (1204) and the messenger to women who happen to be Greek (1298). This is no idle charge. Iphigeneia's escape plan involves taking advantage of the Taurians' naive piety.[15] But to use the purification of the statue of Artemis as a ruse to reach Orestes' ship means that they do not treat it as a sacred object. What they do reminds us of what Artemis did at Aulis; both involve manipulating the holy for ulterior motives. There are several other events of this sort in the play. When Iphigeneia realizes that she lacks a way of being certain that Pylades will take her letter to Argos, Orestes asks her what she is perplexed about (*amēchanein*, 734). She asks that Pylades swear an oath. Pylades does (749) but then says that they have forgotten something (753), to which Iphigeneia replies that it doesn't matter because they can just swear a new oath (754). Oaths are apparently subject to ongoing revision at the convenience of the oath taker. Here the gods are no more than devices—*mēchanai*. But when god becomes a deus ex machina used to extricate characters from difficult situations, it is not really any longer a god to be worshipped. Does the substitution of a deer for Iphigeneia at Aulis demonstrate the power of Artemis or her irrelevance? To understand Artemis as an *agalma*, one must understand the power she has. For that, she must be taken deadly seriously; she must be thought real. But then she will no longer be understood as an image—as what she stands for. The significance of Artemis is at odds with her reality or power; she both does and does not want to be called by the name Artemis. Perhaps the tragedy of the *Iphigeneia among the Taurians* is that its "happy ending" points to the vanishing of the sacred. The triumph of guile or significance (Greekness) means that all constraints are negotiable. Ritual seems at first to establish the primacy of significance over reality, but it is a curiously insignificant significance.

Ritual preserves the significance of something done without preserving

---

14 · For the same reason, Iphigeneia is moved to deny the story of Tantalus and Pelops (386–90).

15 · See also Euripides' *Helen* 1049–66.

the doing itself.[16] The blood on the knife of the rite performed at Halae each year stands for human sacrifice without being human sacrifice. Ritual is pure significance, but once the actual doing is taken away, it risks losing its significance. It is initially done *hosias hekati*, for the sake of the holy, but it ends by being done *hosias hekati*, for form's sake. It is done because it is done. The very end of the *Iphigeneia* points to this problem. The escape of Iphigeneia, Orestes, and Pylades is about to fail when Athena saves them. But if now, why not at the beginning? All the action of the play is rendered meaningless in light of the end; it is simply for form's sake. Athena's intervention deprives it of reality; had they known she would save them, their efforts would have been like the ceremony at Halae, a ritual, but that is to say they would have been tongue-in-cheek—for form's sake. The cleverness of the Greeks thus threatens to undermine the very meaning that distinguishes them from barbarians. The *Iphigeneia*, as the story of the complete triumph of ritual and Greekness, is thereby also an account of the death of Greekness. Here, as in book 4 of Herodotus, the Greeks are the paradigm for the human. But as it is characteristic of the human soul "to see with parted eye," to unify soul is to render it blind.

The dependence of the Greek on the barbarian comes out in a curious way after Iphigeneia discovers that Orestes is her brother (869–99). She first tacitly compares her boldness in almost sacrificing Orestes to the boldness of her father (862, 869) and then laments Orestes' present plight.

> By what way [*poron*] discovered for you out again from the city will I send you away from murder to the Argive fatherland before sword comes near to your blood? This, this, unhappy soul, you must discover. Will you go overland, not by ship but by swiftness of foot? Then you will draw near to death, marching through barbarian tribes and ways that are not ways [*hodous anodous*]. Going through the narrows [*stenoporou*] of the dark rocks is a great journey for escapes by ship. Wretched me, wretched me. With respect to these things, who, whether god or mortal or something of the unforeseen, by finding a way out of trouble [*poron aporon*] will bring to light a release of evils for the only two offspring of Atreus? (876–99)

The issue is how to leave Asia and the barbarians behind. Orestes cannot go by foot, for that would take him through barbarian lands where there are ways that are not ways—*hodous anodous*. Now, *anodos* is not only a privative *an-hodos*. It is also a compound of *ana* ("up") and *hodos*. It means not only

16 · It is as though *phantasia* could be utterly wrested free of sensation so as to eliminate the otherness of what is sensed. See chapter 2, III.A, above.

"no way" but also a "way up." So the barbarian way is both a dead end and an ascent. Similarly, when Iphigeneia asks what god, mortal, or whatever of the immanifest things will find a way out of the problem, "way" is *poros* and "problem" is *aporon*—lack of a way. Without realizing it, Iphigeneia thus calls for a wayless way.[17] She asks for a solution to their problem that in not being a solution will provide a solution. She likens this to making a way up, an ascent, out of the nonway of the barbarians. But this is just a description of a peculiar kind of ritual—tragedy. The *aporos* of the barbarian, when displayed and made self-conscious, becomes the *poros* of the Greek. What seems no way is really a way up. The experience of the savagery of human sacrifice by way of ritual is like the experience of tragedy. Tragedy civilizes, for to be civilized is to be a ritualized barbarian.

Tragedy sketches a problem, an *aporia*, in all its intractability. Then it represents it in such a way as to make the experience of the problem a solution. Yet the success of this procedure is incomplete. Insofar as tragedy, as play, undermines the seriousness and reality of what it is about, it tends to commit suicide and thus paves the way for forgetting the problem that it describes. It is like ritual cut free from the reality of which it was an image, Greekness so complete as to be utterly nonbarbaric. But a problem that has come to be a solution soon ceases to be understood as a problem and therewith ceases to be a solution. When we become convinced that the irrational attachment to family is a necessary feature of human nature (we all have mothers), it becomes something everyone has to "cope with." Yet it no longer has a powerful hold on us that makes it possible to understand a tragedy based on it and revealing it. When Oedipus and Electra simply need therapy to take care of the complexes bearing their names, tragedy is no longer possible. But when tragedy is no longer possible, these complexes are no longer intelligible. Perfect Hellenization is thus impossible; to be Greek (that is, to be fully human) means to retain the memory of what it is to be a barbarian—to see double. The *Iphigeneia* begins with a reference to Pelops and constantly reminds us of the Greek origins in Asia. It is the being of us all to be lapsed barbarians; to be Greek means somehow to acknowledge this fact.

The plot of the *Iphigeneia among the Taurians* presents the replacement of actual human sacrifice by ritual sacrifice. This involves the movement from the land of the Scythians to Athens, from Asia to Greece. The action of the play is made possible by Iphigeneia's clever use of the *agalma* of Artemis to effect their escape. The significance of the change involved in this

17 · This seems to be a reflection by Euripides on Sophocles' *Antigone* 360ff. See also Seth Benardete, *Sacred Transgressions* (South Bend, IN: St. Augustine's Press, 1999), 40–50.

ruse is made manifest in the expression *hosias hekati*; what was for the sake of the holy gradually becomes for form's sake. On one level, the *Iphigeneia* is a story about the superior humanity of Greeks over and against barbarians. Euripides celebrates the fact that, unlike barbarians, Greeks in recognizing common humanity display their humanity. They do not sacrifice human beings; instead, they ritualize such behavior, distilling its significance—the sacrifice of what is most dear—into nonbarbaric action. On a deeper level, however, the *Iphigeneia* points to the fragility of all ritual. Its success is its failure, for insofar as it suppresses its barbaric origin, it becomes unintelligible. Accordingly, the *Iphigeneia* provides accounts of the forgotten "realities" at the source of at least three Athenian rituals.[18] Orestes tells Iphigeneia that when he stopped over in Athens, he was not denied hospitality, but, because the Athenians did not wish to drink from the same cup as a matricide, each man drank from an individual small cup. He says that this has since become a rite at Athens—the *Choes*, or pitcher feast (947–60). At the end of the play, when Athena instructs Orestes and Iphigeneia on what they are to do, she is in fact offering accounts of already existing rituals at Athens. She speaks directly to Orestes (1446), telling him to hear her *epistolē*—her message. The word can also mean "letter" and was used by Iphigeneia to describe the message written for her by the Greek whom she sacrificed (589). What might the two "letters" have to do with each other? Iphigeneia's *epistolē* says that she did not die; her sacrifice was only an illusion—a symbol. Athena's *epistolē* directs Orestes to establish a symbolic Taurian land in Athens. He is to set up a temple at Halae for the statue of Artemis, who will henceforth be called *tauropolon*. This was an epithet of Artemis at Athens prior to the *Iphigeneia among the Taurians*; it could mean either "worshipped by the Taurians" or "hunting bulls." Starting with an already existing temple, Euripides has settled the ambiguities surrounding it and provided a story to give it significance. Similarly, although with a significance less obvious, Athena instructs Iphigeneia to become a priestess at Artemis's temple at Brauron. When she dies, Iphigenia will be honored with *agalmata*—the finery of women who have died in childbirth. This too seems to be an existing ritual for which Euripides is creating a "reality."

Euripides has thus written a tragedy that restores an awareness of the original reality to rituals that have become so much for form's sake that it is no longer clear why they are practiced. But if the reality underlying ritual is its barbaric origin, it would be fair to say that Euripides' tragedy rebarbarizes rituals that have become so civilized as to cease to be significant. In fact, this is what the whole of the *Iphigeneia* is meant to do. Tragedy is a

18 · See the whole of Wolff's "Euripides' *Iphigeneia among the Taurians*" for a discussion of these three.

ritual restoration of the reality that underlies ritual. When the vehicle for ambiguity becomes so perfect as to make double vision impossible, it must be artfully made less artful. This process is the truly distinguishing characteristic of the Greeks. They do not simply shake hands; they provide stories adequate to restore our awareness that shaking hands was originally a sign that men would refrain from drawing their swords. If this is not to be simply a bit of quaint antiquarian knowledge, these stories must reproduce the fear that swords might indeed be drawn. They must rebarbarize us. Similarly, the ritual of human sacrifice at Halae is unintelligible apart from the terror of human sacrifice that a tragedy like the *Iphigeneia* is meant to inspire.

Isn't this still a happy ending? Tragedy goes one step beyond ritual. In this play, Euripides provides an imaginary context for an existing ritual so as to rebarbarize us in thought, and thus in reality civilize us. He provides a model for bringing together reality and significance by providing us with a poetic (that is to say false) reality to bolster the significance of the rituals of our day-to-day life. Tragedy reveals to us the *phusis* underlying our *nomos* and, by doing so, causes us to wonder again at what we have come to take for granted. For, as Aristotle says, "The lover of myth is somehow a philosopher."[19] As a result, we get knowledge without suffering—a perfect coincidence of significance and reality.

In the end, however, even this solution is incomplete. On the obvious level, Athena's intervention is not simply a happy ending because Iphigeneia is not allowed to go home. She and Orestes must remain separated. Orestes was sent to the land of the Taurians to accomplish two things that looked like one thing. He was to rescue his sister and steal the statue of Artemis. Reality and significance were adroitly confused. In the end, the statue of Artemis is to be housed in a temple at Halae where a ritual is conducted each year. A man will be brought to the temple as if to be sacrificed, and when the knife is brought near his throat, a drop of blood will be drawn *hosias hekati*. This ritual, a fake sacrifice, is meant to remind us of the significance of human sacrifice. Iphigeneia, on the other hand, will be housed at Brauron, where, after her death, ritual offerings will be made to her to acknowledge the real sacrifice that mothers make so that their children can be born. In the first ritual, the death is intended but unreal; in the second, it is unintended but real. The first ritual is used to make the significant real; the second is used to make the real significant. Each of these is, in its way, an attempt fully to close the gap between the soul and the world so that the objects of the soul (images and thoughts) are identical to objects in the world, making the soul not "somehow all beings" but simply all beings. As we have

19 · *Metaphysics* 982b18–19.

seen, this would mark the disappearance both of the world as "outside" and of the soul as "inside."

While significance and reality are of necessity "somehow" related, their separation at the end of the play suggests that Euripides knew that their complete togetherness is never simply possible. In the end, tragedy too is a ritual, the significance of which must be lost in time. *Iphigeneia among the Taurians* is Euripides' self-consciously imperfect attempt to provide a ritual for its renewal—perhaps this is why Aristotle called him the most tragic of the poets. The nature of this self-conscious imperfection is the issue that underlies all Platonic dialogues; in its nontragic form, it is called philosophy. It is to Plato, therefore, that we must now turn.

PART FOUR

PLATO

If Euripides challenges us with the potentially tragic character of the human soul, Plato may be said to accept this challenge, for at the center of Platonic philosophy, perhaps more than for any other thinker, is the awareness of the necessary imperfection of soul that always threatens to end in tragedy. In a way, the question for Plato is simple: If philosophy is the best of lives, and yet is incomplete and incompletable, why isn't human life tragic? Why is philosophy not simply a more complicated version of the irresistible and yet unfulfillable human longing for perfection already exemplified by Achilles? Like Euripides, Plato reflects on an issue he finds in Herodotus (we turn to this in chapter 8). In *Republic*, book 2, Plato reworks the Gyges story from the first book of the *History*. What ties the two stories together is their recognition that tyranny and the longing for justice have a common root in the soul's *erōs* to be whole and its subsequent misunderstanding of itself so as to be able to imagine this wholeness to be possible. This self-misunderstanding is embodied in the law, which, because it must assume the pure agency of soul in order to justify punishment of those who defy the law, also must assume the potential self-sufficiency of soul that is at the heart both of Glaucon's tyrannical longing and of his demand that Socrates show the just man to be perfectly happy by virtue of his justice alone. The longing for justice is a longing for things, and oneself, to be perfectly in their place—at rest. When allowed full rein, it leads to tyranny.

The *Cleitophon* (chapter 9) examines this movement from justice to tyranny, showing us how a world in which it was possible to give an objective account of justice (this is what Cleitophon demands of Socrates) is a world where there would be no subjects to be just—an utterly passive world in which soul could not exist. In willing a perfectly ordered world, Cleitophon would unwittingly exclude the possibility of the will to be just, without which justice does not really exist.

The *Hipparchus* (chapter 10) looks at this problem from the other direction. When Socrates introduces the partial truth that the measure of goodness is ultimately the soul, he means also to point to the danger of this truth—the tyrant's misunderstanding of his soul as the object of all longing. Here, in taking itself deadly seriously, the soul objectifies itself and disappears.

The *Phaedrus* (chapter 11) reveals *erōs* as the soul of these errors, for as going out of itself for the sake of itself, the soul inevitably mistakes itself in the process. When soul attempts to understand itself, it objectifies itself. Even when seeking to understand itself as pure agent, as something altogether active, it renders itself passive. It is in *erōs* that the tension that constitutes soul between nature and structure, between agent and patient, becomes most manifest. And yet, as the soul is one—we do have identities—must there not be something between the active and the passive, grounding the dilemma they generate and more fundamental than either of its horns?

Plato's *Euthyphro* (chapter 12) is an extended reflection on this curious in-betweenness of soul by way of a reflection on the middle voice of Greek grammar and on Socrates as a subject of imitation for those whom he "corrupts." The *Euthyphro*, conspicuous for not even mentioning the word *soul*, means to show us that, while soul tends to disappear as soon as it is mentioned, it can nevertheless be displayed in this act of disappearing. The *Euthyphro* makes clear why Platonic philosophy must be dialogic—presenting us with the philosophical life by, on the one hand, teaching us through speeches and, on the other, seducing us with the person of Socrates.

CHAPTER 8

The Soul of the Law

Gyges in Herodotus and in Plato

The second book of Plato's *Republic* begins with a spirited outburst. Glaucon, not satisfied with Socrates' arguments proving the goodness of justice in book 1, demands a new proof. At once deeply tempted and deeply repelled by the life of injustice, he wishes to be purged of his longing for tyranny and, accordingly, wants Socrates to show that justice itself, by itself, is good (despite the fact that they have just agreed that it is one of those things good both for its own sake and for the sake of its consequences)—that is, that justice is not simply a necessary evil, something good by law or *nomos* but not by nature (359b). To explain what he means, Glaucon tells a story. It is worth quoting in full.

> That even those practicing [justice] practice it involuntarily by virtue of an inability to do injustice we would especially perceive if we should make [*poiēsaimen*] something in thought of the following sort: once we give the possibility to each (both to the just man and to the unjust) to do [*poiein*] whatever he wants, let us follow, seeing where desire will lead each. We would catch the just man in the act, going toward the same thing as the unjust on account of a longing for more, which [thing] every nature pursues by nature as good, while only by law is it led astray by force to the honor of the equal. The authority which I mean would be especially like this if the sort of power should ever be theirs that they say belonged to the ancestor of Gyges, the Lydian. [They say] he was a shepherd in the service of the one then ruling Lydia when there was a great thunderstorm and earthquake, breaking open the earth so that there was a chasm in the place where he pastured. Looking and wondering, he went down and saw, in addition to other wonders about which [men] mythologize, also a bronze horse, hollow and having little doors, through which he peeped in and saw a corpse buried within that appeared larger than human, and this wearing nothing else than around its hand a gold ring; after stripping it off, he went

out. During the usual meeting of the shepherds in order that they might bring a monthly report to the king about the herds, he came bearing the ring. While sitting with the others, he chanced to turn the collet of the ring around toward himself, to the inside of his hand. When this happened, he became invisible to those with whom he was sitting, and they conversed as though about someone absent. He wondered at this, and, again feeling for the ring, he twisted the collet outward, and, in twisting it, he became apparent. Thinking about this, he tested whether the ring held this power, and it happened thus: by turning the ring inward, he became immanifest, and outward, [he became] manifest. Perceiving this, he immediately brought it about that he was among the messengers to the king, and after arriving, committed adultery with his wife, and, with her, setting upon the king, he killed [him] and so gained the rule. (359c–360b)[1]

Glaucon goes on to draw conclusions about what all would do should they possess this power of becoming invisible so as to be able to avoid the consequences of their actions. The final nine books of the *Republic* are Socrates' extended reflection on this poem invented by Glaucon to make visible the power and naturalness of injustice in the soul and the weakness and conventionality of justice.

Now, whether wittingly or no, Glaucon's poem about the visible and the invisible, the usurpation of a throne, and Eros for a woman has an ancestor. Toward the beginning of the *History* (1.8–12), Herodotus gives an account of the ascent of Gyges to the throne of Lydia. It is the first extended story in the book and contains the first of many quotations of which Herodotus cannot possibly have had direct knowledge, the event having occurred some seven generations before his own day.[2] As the quotation must be an invention, this story too is a poem. Herodotus tells us that the king of Lydia, Candaules, so loves his wife that he finds her the most beautiful of women. He praises her frequently to his trusted bodyguard, Gyges, but, troubled lest this claim not be believed because her beauty is never publicly visible, Candaules urges Gyges to hide unseen in the queen's bedroom so that he might see her naked form (*eidos*). Gyges demurs but, when Candaules insists, obeys his king. On the fateful evening, Gyges conceals himself and secretly observes the queen, but as he leaves, she sees him. The queen does not at once indicate her discovery but the following day assembles her most faithful servants and sends for Gyges to give him an ultimatum: he must

---

1 · Translations from the *Republic* are my own and follow the Greek text of John Burnet (Oxford: Clarendon Press, 1978).

2 · Herodotus implies that his version owes a debt to the poet Archilochus of Paros (1.12).

choose either to die at once or to kill Candaules, marry her, and become king of Lydia. Thus compelled to consider his own good, Gyges naturally chooses the latter alternative and founds a dynasty that endures for five generations until the fall of Croesus. Now, the deepest of Herodotus's themes in the *History* is embedded in this story—the power of *nomos* or law in its relation to nature. Like Glaucon's story about the ring, it provides a structure for the nine books of the *History* that follow. And like Glaucon's story, it is concerned with the relation between nature and *nomos*. While Glaucon may not know the origin of his tale, Plato surely knows, thereby suggesting to us that something might be learned by comparing the structure of the *Republic* to the structure of the *History*. This would, of course, be a very long task, but perhaps what we are to learn is writ small in the two stories themselves.

Let us begin at the beginning of the *History*:

> This is the showing forth of the inquiry [*historiē*] of Herodotus of Halicarnassus, in order that neither the things having come to be from human beings in time come to be eradicated, nor the great and wondrous deeds, on the one hand shown forth by the Greeks and on the other hand by the barbarians both with respect to other things and with respect to the cause on account of which they warred with one another, come to be without fame.[3]

Herodotus has a double intention. He writes in order to prevent what comes to be *in time* from being eradicated *by time*.[4] This is a universal principle and seems to apply indifferently to everything that time produces and consumes; Herodotus means somehow to overcome human temporality. On the other hand, he intends to reward with fame the great and wondrous deeds that attach to a specific event, the Persian War. That Herodotus's *History* will be simultaneously so all-embracing and so very particular is a version of the problem of history simply: to give an account of change in terms of fixed principles.[5] Perhaps this particular war with these particular antagonists interests Herodotus so because he perceives its cause to be especially revelatory of our common nature as temporal beings.

We are at first a little taken aback to discover that, for Herodotus, this cause has so much to do with rape. To be fair, the Greek word he uses here, *harpagē*, and its cognate verb, *harpazō*, like the Latin *rapio* and the less customary, but older, meaning of our word *rape*, all have the more general sense

---

3 · Translations of Herodotus are my own and follow the Greek text of Carl Hude (Oxford: Clarendon Press, 1988).

4 · The construction of *tōi khronōi* permits one to read it both ways.

5 · If history, properly understood, amounts to an account of the togetherness of motion and rest, it would be an account of being. See Plato *Sophist* 250a–d.

of seizing or carrying off. Still, of the fifteen occurrences of *harpagē* in the *History* (the verb occurs much more frequently), nine have to do with the carrying off, and presumably the rape, of women; eight occur in the first six chapters of the book (which is less than 0.5 percent of the whole); and, of these, seven have to do with rape in the more common sense.[6] In addition, the verb *harpazō* occurs eight times in these same chapters. Rape is clearly the theme of the beginning. The Persians say that Io of Argos was carried off to Egypt by Phoenician traders and that the Greeks (different Greeks—these are Cretans) retaliated by carrying off Europa from the Phoenician city of Tyre. The Argonauts then doubled the Greek retaliation by carrying off Medea from her home in Colchis on the Black Sea.[7] The Persians say that when it became clear that the Greeks would pay no penalty (literally, "would not give justice") for the rape of Europa, Alexander of Troy decided that he would steal a Greek wife, who turned out to be Helen. The Greeks took this rather more seriously than he had anticipated, and the ultimate result was the destruction of Troy.

Now, Herodotus is aware that the Greeks tell a different story (1.2). They say, for example, that Hera became angry with Io for having had intercourse with Zeus. For protection, Zeus disguised Io, transforming her into a cow, but Hera nevertheless relentlessly pursued her all the way to Egypt, where Zeus restored her and she gave birth to the god, also a cow, that the Egyptians worship as Apis.[8] About Europa, the Greeks say that Zeus disguised himself as a bull and carried her away to Crete, where she gave birth to his sons Minos, Sarpedon, and Rhadymantus and then married the Cretan king.[9] Similarly mythic accounts are given of the abductions of Medea and Helen.[10] What Greeks feel the need to mythologize and seek divine causes for, however, Persians demythologize and make light of. Herodotus quotes the Persian learned men (*logioi*):

> Now, on the one hand, to rape men's women we hold [*nomizein*] to be a deed of unjust men, while to take in earnest the avenging of those having been raped [is a deed] of fools; but to have no care for those hav-

6 · See 1.2 (twice), 1.3 (thrice), 1.4, 1.5, 2.118, and 5.94; for those instances having to do with theft or plunder, see 1.6, 1.97, 3.47, 3.48, 3.104, and 9.42.

7 · Colchis, we later learn, is an Egyptian colony in Scythian territory—one might wonder with the Persians what this has to do with them (apparently, the Greeks easily identify one barbarian with another even though their cities are probably a thousand miles apart). See 2.104.

8 · See Aeschylus *Prometheus Bound* 823–76 and Herodotus 2.38. Io is frequently identified by the Greeks with Isis. See W. W. How and J. Wells, *A Commentary on Herodotus* (Oxford: Oxford University Press, 1928), 1:54–55.

9 · See *Iliad* 14.321–22.

10 · See *Theogony* 992–1002 and *Cypria* 1.

ing been raped [is a deed of] sensible men. For it is clear that if they themselves had not wished it, they would not have been raped. (I.4)

In what is probably the first recorded instance of this lamentable defense of rape—"She was asking for it"—Herodotus reveals something interesting about the Persians. They are the people about whom he will later say that "whatever is not allowed for them to do, these things are not even allowed for them to say" (1.138). Accordingly, one of the Persian laws or customs (*nomoi*) is that no one has ever committed matricide or parricide, so that wherever this seems to have happened, there must have been some sort of Gilbert and Sullivan mix-up at birth.[11]

The Persians trace their enmity toward Greece to the Trojan War, when Europeans invaded Asia "for the sake of a Lacadaemonian woman" (1.4). Herodotus seems to agree with their view of the relative insignificance of rape when he says first that he will tell us who was the first Asian to do unjust deeds against the Greeks (1.5) and then tells us that it cannot have been the invasion of Ionia by the Cimmerians, for that was simply a matter of *harpagē*—here apparently to be understood as plunder (1.6). But his agreement is only partial. Herodotus stands somewhere between the Greeks, who consider *harpagē* unjust and take it seriously, and the Persians, who consider it unjust and make light of it.[12] Insofar as the Medes are of all Asians closest to the Persians (1.134, 3.89)—Cyrus was half Mede—one can go even further. The Mede who is instrumental in bringing Cyrus to the throne and later in the defeat of the Lydians by the Persians seems to be an invention of Herodotus; his name is Harpagus—the masculine version of *harpagē*. "Rapist" seems a strange name to give to one's child.[13] It should tell us something about the Persian view of rape. The cause of the war between Greece and Persia that in its specificity will reveal a universal feature of human nature as temporal has to do with their different estimations of the importance of rape, and so of women in relation to sexuality.

It should come as no surprise that all these issues are present in the Gyges story.

---

11 · See Seth Benardete, *Herodotean Inquiries* (The Hague: Martinus Nijhoff, 1969), 71.

12 · While Herodotus seems to make light of *harpagē*, he does so by refusing to acknowledge that it is a case of injustice and, of course, also uses it in the sense of plunder. He thereby calls attention to what is most distinctive in the Persian view. They consider *harpagē* unjust *and* irrelevant. That the question of justice is not the most important question for them is connected to their failure to understand the seriousness of rape and so of women.

13 · While Harpagus is a central character in Herodotus's account, he is mentioned by no other historian of the period. This is especially important given that Xenophon's *Cyropaedia* is a history of the coming to power of Cyrus.

Now, this Candaules was in love [*ērasthē*] with his own wife, and because loving [her] held [*enomize*] his wife to be much the most beautiful of all women. So that holding [*nomizōn*] these views, since there was among his bodyguards Gyges, son of Daskylus, who especially pleased him (to which Gyges Candaules used to communicate the most serious of his concerns), he also used to go so far as to praise the beauty of form [*eidos*] of his wife. Not much time thereafter—for it was fated that Candaules should end badly—he said the following to Gyges: "Gyges, I don't think you are persuaded by what I say concerning the beauty of form of my wife—for the ears are indeed for men less to be trusted than the eyes. Contrive [*poiei*] a way to see her naked." Crying out greatly, Gyges said, "Master, what an unhealthy speech you speak, bidding me to see my mistress naked; for in laying aside her robes at the same time she lays aside the shame [*aidōs*] appropriate to woman. Long ago the beautiful things were discovered by human beings, and one must learn from them. Among them is this one: look [*skopein*] at what is your own. I am persuaded that she is the most beautiful of all women, and I beg you not to require unlawful things." (1.8)

Eros occurs three times as a noun in the *History*; the cognate verb *eraō* occurs eight times.[14] Of these eleven instances, two refer to Candaules' love for his unnamed wife. Of the rest, seven refer to a variety of illicit loves—Mycerinus's possible love and subsequent rape of his daughter (2.131), Cambyses' love of his sister (3.31), Ariston's love of the wife of his best friend, and Xerxes' love of his brother's wife and then of his niece (9.108). The remaining two refer to an *erōs* for tyranny.[15] Most of the women involved remain nameless (the one exception is Xerxes' niece, Artaynte). All of them are antinomian objects of longing—this seems to be the link to tyranny.[16] The whole *History* more or less concludes with an account of the illicit love of Xerxes, who elsewhere announces quite openly that his goal is universal empire so that his realm will be coextensive with that of Zeus, who is the sky (7.8). Is there a clue to this relation between eros and tyranny in the Gyges story?[17]

Candaules loves his wife and *therefore* believes her beautiful. He loves

14 · As a noun: 5.32, 6.62, and 9.113; as a verb: 1.8 (twice), 1.96, 2.131, 3.31 (twice), and 9.108 (twice). See Benardete, *Herodotean Inquiries*, 137–38.

15 · Deioces at 1.96 and Pausanias at 5.32.

16 · The *erōs* for tyranny of Deioces is especially interesting since its fulfillment proves to require that he become invisible. See Benardete, *Herodotean Inquiries*, 24–26 and 137.

17 · For the relation between the Gyges story and the story of Xerxes' seduction of his niece, see Benardete, *Herodotean Inquiries*, 212.

what is his own, what is private to him, but wants public confirmation of its attractiveness to him *as his own*. He cannot bear that the beauty of what he holds good should remain invisible; somehow, he wants it both to be his and to be universal.[18] Now, to contrive that the essentially private (the inner) should be seen publicly (outside) in its character as essentially private is to abolish shame (*aidōs* is used only here in the *History*).[19] Candaules wants the world to acknowledge his own experience that what is his is incomparable and the best. His desire for Gyges to confirm his judgment of his wife's beauty is tantamount to a desire that there be no distinction between his experience of the world and the world. This is, unwittingly but essentially, a tyrannical desire for truly universal empire—a desire to remake the world in his own image.

Candaules wants Gyges too to accept what he holds or believes (*nomizō*). He does not think this possible through speech, "for the ears are indeed for men less to be trusted than the eyes." Speech removes us one step from the reality that verifies it. To get at the truth, there must be no intermediaries between us and the evidence; we must be fully in the presence of being, doing away with what is between. But Candaules ignores the fact that his certainty about the beauty of his wife is a product of his *erōs*. To be fully in the presence of the evidence, Gyges would not only have to experience what is inside the king's private quarters; he would also have to experience what is inside the king. Gyges is to contrive, or *make*, a way to see the queen naked; the verb *poiein* also means to make poetry. It is not hard to see how the ambiguity is important here, for to do what Candaules wishes him to do, Gyges would have to put himself in the king's place in more than a spatial sense. Thinking himself into the king's position would be an act of poetic imagination. In requiring interpretation, it would be more akin to the speech that comes through the ears than the visions that come through the eyes. Candaules is peculiarly like the Persians in his trust in the self-evident significance of things as they appear.[20] His belief that the *eidos* of his wife

18 · It is probably not accidental that the word Herodotus uses here to refer to the beauty of Candaules' wife is *eidos*—a word deriving from the verb "to see" and meaning something like "looks" or "visible form"; it begins a long and distinguished career in Plato as "idea" or "form."

19 · See Benardete, *Herodotean Inquiries*, 12.

20 · Consider, for example, Xerxes at the beginning of book 7. He has heard arguments for whether the Persians should invade Greece, first decides that they should, and then thinks better of it. Then a dream comes to him in the night and tells him to go ahead with the invasion. Out of fear, he does so. But this is an appearance just like the appearances of the everyday world. Doesn't it have to be interpreted just as they require interpretation? Had Cambyses understood that meaning is never simply self-evident but is always the product of putting things together, he would not have

is something unproblematically visible is tantamount to a belief that there is no qualitative difference between inside and outside. Candaules thinks that you get a look at the inside of an orange by slicing it open; he does not realize that all you get is a new outside. He is like Cyrus's son Cambyses, who, when accused of madness, thinks to prove his sanity by demonstrating that he has a hand steady enough to shoot an arrow straight into the heart of Prexaspes' son (3.35). Afterward, he challenges Prexaspes to verify the success of his prediction by opening up the chest of his son. Cambyses treats the inside and the outside as though they are of the same order. This enormous exaggeration of the power of the visible is what will lead Xerxes to think that one becomes whole by conquering the world. Persians think spatially.

Candaules' trust in the visible is connected to the question of law. Twice Herodotus says that Candaules held his wife most beautiful—both times using the verb *nomizō*. Gyges begs not to be forced to do what is unlawful, clearly believing it unlawful to look at the naked queen, for it is one of the beautiful or noble things (*ta kala*) discovered of old that one ought to look only at one's own. This principle is expanded later in the *History* in a passage that follows directly after the account of Cambyses' madness.

> For if someone were to address all human beings bidding [them] to select the most beautiful *nomoi* from all *nomoi*, having considered, each would choose their own; thus each holds [*nomizousi*] its own *nomoi* to be by far the most beautiful . . . and it seems to me that Pindar was right to make a poem [*poiēsai*], saying *nomos* to be the king of all. (3.38)

Nomos operates in a double way; accordingly, we translate it sometimes as "law," sometimes as "custom." When the rules of our conduct are explicit, we must also be aware that there are alternatives to them; when they are only tacit, custom is so powerful that it seems to us simply to be the way things are. While Herodotus tells us that Candaules thinks his wife most beautiful *because* he loves her as his own, we do not know this to be Candaules' self-understanding. Making no distinction between what is his own and what is, Candaules could simply think his unnamed wife is beautiful. On the other hand, that he wants Gyges to confirm his judgment must mean that he is not altogether at ease with it. The beautiful things are the hidden measures of all our judgments that we wish somehow to bring into the light and make manifest. Gyges tells the king that one of the many beautiful

---

assumed that a dream that told him that Smerdis was on the throne was altogether straightforward and unambiguous in its meaning (3.30). Benardete has noted that in Herodotus's account of the Persians, there are a number of significant dreams but no oracles (*Herodotean Inquiries*, 24).

things discovered (or invented) of old is that one should look only at one's own. To disobey would be unlawful. This is the *nomos* that makes everyone likely to prefer his own *nomoi* above those of others. "Look to your own" means "Accept what is customary," but it is an injunction that cannot help calling attention to one's own as one's own. In doing so, it calls forth the lawful longing to vindicate one's own over against what is other. To say that *nomos* is king of all means that all hold (*nomizousi*) their *nomoi* to be most beautiful. Yet this lawful defense of one's own—let us call it patriotism—leads willy-nilly to the lawless violation of one's own. Candaules' behavior is thus not aberrant; it is the necessary consequence of the double structure of law, which, in telling us that our way is the only way, necessarily also tells us that there are other ways. In forcing us to reveal what it enjoins us to keep hidden, the law assures our shame (*aidōs*).

The story reveals this doubleness to us in a double manner, for what is true of Candaules is also true of Gyges. Gyges reveres the law; this seems to be why Candaules trusts him so. He therefore recoils from the command to look at the secret beautiful things—*ta kala*. But as his lawful king commands him, he must obey. The law forces Gyges to transgress the law. Given this tragic conclusion, it is perhaps no accident that Herodotus should make the story of Cyrus, in which Harpagus figures so prominently, a version of the story of Oedipus (1.108–29).

Now, what does all this have to do with women? Why should Candaules' unnamed wife stand for the law? The Gyges story calls our attention to the relation between clothing and *nomos*. When a woman removes her clothing, she removes her shame, for, as Herodotus tells us, "among the Lydians, and also, I dare say, among the rest of the barbarians, even for a man to be seen naked carries a great shame [*aiskhunēn*]" (1.10). The remark is clearly meant to call our attention to the fact that, for a Greek, this shame must seem a little provincial.[21] Exercising naked—*gumnazomai*—is a sign of what it means to be Greek. And yet, since the Greeks wear this practice as a badge of distinction, isn't it too a species of clothing? That is, ignoring for the moment that even for a Greek it is not so clear that female nakedness is of the same status as male nakedness, if the particular *nomos* to which one is so devoted is most obviously revealed in the character of the clothing one dons to cover one's shame, isn't pride in nakedness as what distinguishes Greek from barbarian simply a more complicated parochialism—a particular sign of a particular *nomos* and not the shedding of *nomoi* in favor of nature that it represents itself as?[22] The Greeks are a people who represent themselves to themselves as a people unlike any other people, as in some sense a universal

21 · See Benardete, *Herodotean Inquiries*, 12.

22 · In this regard, naked exercise is like tragedy—a ritual restoration of barbarism.

people—a chosen people.²³ Still, however special they may be, they do not simply escape the tragedy of political life.

As Darius, Xerxes' father, prepares for the invasion of Greece, he finds it necessary to name a successor in case anything should happen to him (7.2–3). Before becoming king, Darius had three sons, the eldest of whom was Artobazanes. After he became king, he had four more sons, now by a new wife, Atossa, daughter of Cyrus. Xerxes was the eldest of these. In pressing his claim, Artobazanes maintains that all men hold (*nomizō*) that the eldest should inherit the rule. Xerxes at first claims to deserve the rule by virtue of his relation to his mother, whose father, Cyrus, was the founder of the empire, but then, urged by the Spartan exile Demaratus, he cites a supposed Spartan *nomos* (it is not clear that there actually was such a law)²⁴ according to which sons born to a king after he became king have precedence over those born to him previous to his kingship. Darius accepts this claim, the implication of which is that it is not a man but a king who has offspring, as though one's being were totally exhausted by one's office and no distinction were possible between *nomos* and nature. That this is somehow the Persian view is confirmed in the immediate sequel. Having become king, Xerxes announces that he too plans to invade Greece, for imperial expansion is the essence of the Persian *nomos*.²⁵ The ultimate goal of the invasion is to "show forth a Persian earth coextensive with the sky of Zeus" (7.8). Needless to say, in such a world, there would be no difference between the natural laws of earth and sky and Persian *nomoi*. Comparative politics of the Herodotean variety would no longer be an option.

When Xerxes asks his advisers for their opinions of his plan, they are divided. Xerxes is at first especially angry with Artabanus's opposition but later reconsiders and decides to call the expedition off. That night, however, a dream comes to him in which a man who is great and cuts a fine

23 · Compare to 7.61–83, where Xerxes' army is enumerated on the basis of a division by tribes distinguished almost solely in terms of what they wear. There is an interesting related passage in the *Mishnah*. Proklos, the son of Philosophos, asks the following of Rabbi Gamaliel in Acre while he is bathing in the Bath of Aphrodite: "It is written in your Law, 'And there shall cleave naught of the devoted thing to thine hand.' Why then doth thou bathe in the Bath of Aphrodite?" to which he replies, "One may not answer in the bath." The editor glosses the story (note 11): "It is forbidden to speak words of the Law while naked"; *The Mishnah: Translated from the Hebrew, with Introduction and Brief Explanatory Notes*, by Herbert Danby (Oxford: Clarendon Press, 1933), 440.
24 · See How and Wells, *Commentary on Herodotus*, 2:125.
25 · "Men of Persia, I myself am not initiating this new law by laying it down, but I use it as something I have received. For, as I learn from the elders, never have we kept still since we took over this rule from the Medes" (7.8).

figure (*eidos*) warns him not to change his mind. Xerxes nevertheless goes ahead and announces his decision to cancel the invasion, but the next night the same dream figure returns warning him more sternly. Terrified, Xerxes summons Artabanus, to whom he announces a curious plan. To determine whether it is a god who speaks to him, Xerxes decides that Artabanus should dress up in the king's clothes, sit on the king's throne (this, by the way, was a crime), and sleep in the king's bed. Then, if the dream should come to Artabanus as well, it will be a divine sign. This is rather bizarre behavior, especially since it turns out that the dream figure is not fooled for a moment and addresses Artabanus as himself. In any event, Xerxes' ploy would make sense only if one assumes that there is no distinction between being the king and wearing the clothing of and behaving like the king. If it looks like a king and walks like a king, then it must be a king?[26] Xerxes' plan involves collapsing the realms of inside and outside, of being and seeming. It is typically Persian because it is understanding internal phenomena in an altogether external way.

The connection between this story and the succession crisis is that the Persians hold that what you are by *nomos*—what you wear—is what you are. This is why they cannot acknowledge the possibility of matricide or parricide. If your being is exhausted in your role as child, then you cannot behave as other than child.[27] There is no inner substance that eludes one's conventional role; one has a role but no soul. Now, at the conclusion of his account of the ascension of Xerxes to the throne, after having introduced the complicated Spartan *nomos* Darius was supposed to have used as the basis of his decision, Herodotus adds in his own voice that "even without this advice [of Demaratus], Xerxes would have become king; for Atossa had all the power" (7.3). Herodotus acknowledges what the Persians cannot—the power of women, a power that apparently grounds the *nomos* but resists being taken up into the *nomos*. It is what is hidden and needs to be hidden but cannot be dispensed with for political life to be possible. And it is what distinguishes the Persian attempt to bring everything into the light from the Greek acknowledgment of the importance of women. To return to where we began, unlike the Persians, the Greeks do not think that rape is trivial.

Insofar as it is idiosyncratic, the power of women is generation; this is

26 · This should be considered in connection with the story of Cyrus playing king with his young comrades (1.114–16).

27 · This is the true significance of the "one man, one art" principle in the *Republic*. You can do your particular job perfectly only if it is your only job, but this makes you a shoemaker or a guardian and nothing else. Your being is identical to your function, with nothing left as a remainder. For a similar problem, see Sophocles' *Antigone* (1) and Seth Benardete, *Sacred Transgressions* (South Bend, IN: St. Augustine's Press, 1999), 1–2.

the connection between women and temporality. Just before marching on Greece, Xerxes reviews his troops (we will later learn that they number 1,700,000—7.60). After looking at the whole of his fleet and army, he first declares himself blessed and then, reflecting on the fact that none of these men will be alive in a hundred years, weeps over the brevity of human life (7.45–46). Xerxes collects a vast host for the purpose of mastering the whole world. By obliterating the distinction between being a man and being a Persian, he will make his reach extend as far as that of Zeus. Still, one thing thwarts Xerxes' wish to be a god. While universal spatial dominion is thinkable, even Xerxes must relent in the face of the rule of time. He too will be dead in one hundred years.

Perfect political life would require that there be a *nomos* worthy of being king of all; it would justify a nonparochial patriotism. To be complete and perfect, such a *nomos* could leave nothing to chance. But if everything is subject to the law, then we are simply whatever we are by law. Everything is manifest; nothing is hidden. Herodotus begins the *History* with the Gyges story because it points to the impossibility of this Persian project for universal dominion. For there remains something that cannot be made public itself but without which the public cannot be. Women bear children and so put human beings in time—make them particular. No political order can exist without citizens, but citizens are first human beings who must be brought into being nonpolitically, to the embarrassment of the *polis*. Atossa has all the power because without her there would be no succession. It is a necessity of political life to be able to say, "The king is dead; long live the king!"; this is the illusion of the *polis* of its own atemporality. Men die; the king never dies. But this is quite absurd unless there is a stratum of life beneath, and not simply exhausted by, political life. Women, in their distinctive roles as generators, thus point to the fact that the political sphere is necessarily incomplete and cannot be other than incomplete. Yet, upon sensing this incompleteness, political life in its will to order has a natural tendency to seek to complete itself. It can do so only by way of an attack on the very private sphere that makes it possible. Xerxes' attempt to make his realm coextensive with that of Zeus, a universal homogeneous state, thus requires him to undermine the natural. That the Persians do not take rape seriously is the sign for Herodotus that they do not understand this fundamental fact of political life. Accordingly, by being too political, they are not really political at all. What distinguishes Herodotus's Greeks is an awareness of the necessary incompleteness of *nomos* in its dependence on the natural; this makes them the paradigmatic political people in the *History*, which proves to mean paradigmatic for the human simply. Whether by virtue of the unwittingly salutary disorder of the double kingship of Sparta (6.52), which conspired to make them the only Greek people never subject to tyranny, or by virtue of the quite conscious attempts of a man like Themistocles to attend to his private good at the same time as he was doing his public duty, Herodotus's Greeks are aware of the limits of the political. Still, as this is distinctive of them *politically*, they do not altogether escape the ultimately contradictory character of the political attempt to stabilize what comes to be in time. Perhaps only Herodotus's *History* may be said to succeed in this regard, and only insofar as it is knowledge of the political.

Close to the end of the *History*, after the Persians have suffered terrible defeats at Salamis, Plataea, and Mycalae, Herodotus shifts the scene briefly from political events to tell us of Xerxes' erotic longing for his brother's wife. Xerxes pursues her, but she will not give in, so in an apparent attempt to bring her closer to him, he arranges for her daughter to marry his son, Darius. It is hard to know exactly what all of this means, but it is clearly a little perverse, even though Herodotus tells us that Xerxes arranged for this betrothal by "doing *ta nomizomena* [the customary or lawful things]" (9.108). Xerxes then proceeds to develop an erotic passion for the same brother's daughter—his niece Artaynte. Not so virtuous as her mother, Artaynte gives in. In the meantime, Xerxes' wife makes him a gift of a beautiful robe in which he delights as he delights in his niece (Herodotus uses the same word for both attachments). Overcome by *erōs*, he offers his Artaynte anything; when she says, "Are you sure?" he says that he is, and she asks for the robe. So, Xerxes has received something from his wife that is meant only for him. To prove his love to the girl, he claims that he will give her anything. This is, of course, possible only if he is absolutely free to do so, but who is free if not the Great King? Xerxes must give Artaynte the robe to prove that his wife has no claims on him. For the Great King, there is no private sphere to limit the public sphere; the public sphere is the private sphere. Yet Xerxes behaves as he does only because his niece does have such a claim on him. Xerxes seems to be shamed into behaving as if shame has no hold over him.

As with Gyges, the story contains two versions of the problem at its core. When Xerxes' wife, Amestris, learns that he has given the robe to his niece, she believes it is for the sake of her sister-in-law. Accordingly, at the yearly feast for the king's birthday, when the king distributes gifts, Amestris asks Xerxes for her sister-in-law. This would appear to be the day on which even the Great King acknowledges his own *genesis*: he is a creature in time and so not a god. Xerxes thus cannot refuse his wife without violating the *nomos* that by forbidding him not to satisfy a request made during this feast, humbles him. There is thus a Persian *law* that by recognizing obligations to family, recognizes the limitations of law. Knowing that his wife is up to no good, Xerxes seeks to assuage his brother in advance by urging that he forsake his own wife and take Xerxes' daughter in her stead. The brother refuses and goes home to find his wife mutilated. This leads him to rebel, and, in putting down the rebellion, Xerxes has him killed. Once again, the whole course of events is set in motion by Xerxes' unwillingness to acknowledge that there are certain things he cannot do. Xerxes experiences *aidōs* in the face of the possibility that he might experience *aidōs*. Ironically, here he might have put an end to the whole matter by simply denying his wife's request. The *nomos* in question is clearly more of a custom than a law; its violation was hardly likely to foment a revolution. Xerxes need only have said to Amestris, "I cannot allow you to harm my brother's wife." But he is ashamed to admit that there is something he cannot do. Accordingly, to demonstrate that he is absolutely free and not at all governed by *nomos*, against his will, Xerxes must obey the letter of a trivial *nomos* about the limitation of *nomos* and so allow the mutilation of his innocent sister-in-law (with whom he was once infatuated) and the death of his brother. His law-abiding assertion of independence from the law leads to complete enslavement to the law. The placement of this story and the similarity of its terms to those of the Gyges story suggest that it is meant to mark the movement of the *History* as a whole.[28] This history of the Persian War is at the same time a history of the consequences of playing out within the political sphere the erotic longing for completeness.

By this time, the outlines of the connection to the *Republic* should be apparent. Glaucon's initial ambivalence about justice and injustice is no more an accident than Candaules' longing to have his internal vision of his wife externally confirmed. In fact, the *Republic* is remarkably similar in structure to the *History*. Coincidences of language seem to connect certain peaks of the argument of the *Republic*. The first word of the dialogue is *katebēn*—"I went down"; the verb appears in the accounts of the descent of Gyges' ancestor into the chasm, of the philosophers' descent into the cave, and of Er's descent into Hades.[29] When we are told that the collet of the ring is "turned around" (359e), we are reminded of the famous *peri agōgē* of the released prisoners in the cave (515c, 518d), and the chasm of the Gyges story reminds us both of the cave and of the chasms in the myth of Er (614c, 614d). These are not arguments, of course; they merely focus

28 · See Benardete's account of the relation between these two stories (*Herodotean Inquiries*, 212–13).

29 · The verb occurs infrequently in the *Republic*: twice in the introductory section (327a, 328c), referring to Socrates' going down to the Piraeus; once in book 6 (511b), referring to the downward movement on the divided line that characterizes dialectic; twice in book 7 (516e, 520c), in connection with philosophers returning to the cave; once in book 10 in the myth of Er, referring to souls coming down from heaven; and once, of course, in book 2, describing the movement of the ancestor of Gyges into the chasm that opens up before him.

our attention. Then we see that the passages serving as glosses on the Gyges story in Herodotus have their analogues in precisely these passages in the *Republic*. The power of *nomos* as potentially king of all (3.38), so that there is no distinction between being and seeming, is what is at stake in the cave. And the necessary failure of Xerxes' project to make himself like Zeus is the subject first of the critique of tyranny in *Republic* 8–9 and, perhaps less obviously but more tragically, of the failure of the men raised in the best city to choose their next lives wisely in the myth of Er.[30] Herodotus links the fairly innocent, if misguided, *erōs* of Candaules to the longing for tyranny and, in so doing, means to show that this is no aberration; it is the very nature of politics. Is this also what is underlying the argument of the *Republic*?

If the text is to be trusted, Gyges' ancestor discovers a ring on a corpse of more than human stature.[31] Now, if the ring is so powerful, why isn't it handed down from generation to generation? That is, why isn't Herodotus's Gyges already king of Lydia? Or, to put the same point differently, if the ring is so powerful, why is it found on a corpse? The problem for Glaucon, as it was for Xerxes, is death (his brother Adeimantus seems to understand this better than he). He means to make up a story demonstrating the utter superiority of the life of the perfectly unjust man, but the details of his own story make clear that the ring leaves the greatest human problem unresolved. It is useless for avoiding the ravages of time. One wonders, given the difficulty of this detail, why Glaucon chooses to make a story at all. Why does he need more than an extended example like Socrates' example in his conversation with Cephalus in book 1 of the man who deposits arms with a friend and then goes mad? Why be so elaborate? Why is Gyges' ancestor a shepherd? Is it simply to contrast his low birth with his ascent to the throne, or perhaps to allow Plato to use the verb "to pasture"—*nemein*—and so hint at its connection to *nomos*? And why the bronze horse or the little doors? Glaucon uses none of this detail but cannot seem to resist introducing it. By excessively adorning his story, Glaucon calls our attention to the fact that he is making visible something of which he has just finished denying the visibility.

When the ancestor first discovers the power of the ring, he is said to turn the collet around "toward himself, to the inside of his hand" (359e). Glaucon's choice of words is revealing. What does it mean to turn the collet of a ring toward oneself? Isn't Glaucon using a spatial category for something that is not really spatial—himself or, let us say, the soul? And doesn't his

30 · See Seth Benardete, *Socrates' Second Sailing: On Plato's* Republic (Chicago: University of Chicago Press, 1989), 225–29.

31 · There is considerable debate about whether it is Gyges himself who finds the ring, especially given *Republic* 612b, where Socrates (linking the ring with Hades' cap) refers to it as Gyges' ring.

entire argument depend on this understanding of soul as something that has permanence and does not unfold in time?

At the beginning of book 2, Glaucon demands that Socrates show him what justice is like in the soul—that is, stripped of all external consequences, of all seeming. Despite Socrates' claim that justice is the sort of good that is good both for itself and for the sake of its consequences, Glaucon demands that it be defended solely in terms of itself. His assumption that its two sorts of goodness are separable from each other is a little like assuming that it is possible to give an account of a form or idea—an *eidos*—independent of what it is an *eidos* of, as though one could give an account of the idea of the beautiful without recourse to the things it makes beautiful. Glaucon's demand would ultimately require that justice as an internal disposition be identical to happiness. In making this demand, he is consciously articulating his antinomian desires. *Nomos* has justice as its goal, but it is a compromise fashioned by the weak because they cannot do what everyone by nature really wants to do. Were they to become strong, to possess the ring of Gyges, those previously weak would sleep with the queen, kill the king, and so fulfill their deepest longing—to have the fulfillment of no desire denied them.

The greatest difficulty with Glaucon's game plan emerges in the poem he fashions to give voice to this antinomian desire. As in the story in Herodotus, the problem is visibility.[32] Candaules guarantees that he will find a way to allow Gyges to see without being seen, as though one could see body without being a body and so have nonperspectival vision. Gyges, of course, gets caught; human beings are not invisible. Glaucon, however, alters the story so that his hero *is* invisible, but this does not really solve the problem. He does not see that the real desires we have require visibility—nondetachment; to become king presumably means that the ancestor must make an appearance. He not only wants to have certain things; he wants to be recognized as having them. So Glaucon has a peculiar understanding of soul; where did he get it?

Glaucon clearly loves justice. But, because he is so honest, he is bewildered. He does not know whether he is truly just or just only for its consequences. When he looks into himself, he finds secret longings for what is forbidden. He therefore focuses on what was downplayed in book 1 of the *Republic*—moral intention apart from consequences. Only if justice were its own reward could its reward never be attained by counterfeit means. To express this purity of intention, Glaucon is forced to make poetry. He has to find a way to express the supposedly internal and invisible in visible images. This, of course, means that, while Glaucon's poetic characters may not see

32 · See Benardete, *Socrates' Second Sailing*, 36–38.

the injustice of the unjust man, we see it, and his example would not work unless we could see it. Glaucon's longing for justice leads him first to understand the soul as something essentially hidden and permanent and then to attempt to make it manifest in its permanence and hiddenness. It leads him to understand soul as something wholly independent and detachable from body about which it makes sense to say that it can have a being apart from any seeming or coming to be, and then to be compelled to attempt to make it come to be visible. He could not say what he wanted to say except by making visible his "real self" as an invisible thing beyond the body. Now, it turns out that the so-called natural life of the perfectly unjust man is equally dependent on this understanding of soul, which originated in Glaucon's longing for justice. Glaucon's rejection of justice is rooted in justice.

In isolating the soul in this way, Glaucon simply does what the *polis* does and must do all the time. The *polis* assumes that, as responsible agents under the law, our souls are permanent, independent, and invisible; at the same time, as responsible agents under the law, our motives can be made visible and our souls altered by punishment. We are capable both of feeling guilty and of being found guilty in a court of law. Glaucon's tyrannical longing is simply the extension of this essentially political, but contradictory, understanding of the human soul. The tyrant, understanding himself as an absolutely free agent, profoundly resents all feelings of limitation. He therefore attempts to overcome these disproportions between himself and the world by annihilating any distinction between himself and the world. He seeks to remake the world as an outgrowth of his own will and so to eradicate the distinction between *nomos* and nature. Now, every political order must perforce expect its laws to be treated as though they were laws of nature. Glaucon's tyrannical longing is thus simply the natural extension of the political understanding of the human soul. Accordingly, its cure requires that Socrates provide a purification of the political so extreme as finally to imply a critique of the political altogether. What seems at first a mystifying, if monumental, move in the argument of book 2, the decision to look for justice first writ large in the city and only later as it appears in the soul, is in fact the only way Socrates could have proceeded, for Glaucon's demand that the just man be perfectly happy is only the claim that every city makes with respect to the justice of its own *nomoi*.[33]

33 · While the *Republic* does not explicitly acknowledge the tension between the city and time, Plato does provide an indirect account in his portrayal of the conditions making possible the coming to be of the conversation about the city—what has been called the dialogic city (Benardete, *Socrates' Second Sailing*, 47). For an apparent attempt at a direct account, one might turn to the *Timaeus*. Herodotus, of course, combines the timeless and the temporal in his *historiē*. This is the power of exemplary stories.

The problem of politics is the coincidence of the public and private goods—of duty and self-interest. If we identify the first with the beautiful or noble, *to kalon*, and the second with the good, *to agathon*, then perfect politics would require the conjunction of the two—*kalos k'agathos*, the Greek phrase for a complete gentleman. In terms of *nomos* and nature, this would mean the assertion that the *nomos*—what one ought to do—is by nature. This is justice. However, in Herodotus's Persia, as in Glaucon's soul, the attempt to bring this situation about leads to universal imperialism. In the *History*, as well as in the *Republic*, women are *the* obstacle to this ambitious undertaking. The Persians cannot acknowledge it, but Atossa has all the power, and it is no accident that the coming to be (*genesis*) of Socrates' best city should become problematic with the introduction of women in relation to birth (*genesis*) in book 5 of the *Republic*. In Persia, to be called worse than a woman is the worst insult there is (9.107), and, of course, Glaucon is said to be "most manly in everything" (357a). The Persians cannot acknowledge the fact that nature has a greater range than *nomos*; the standard sign of this is kinship—that is, the result of childbirth. They are a people who pride themselves on total truthfulness. But their overcoming of the split between being and seeming is possible only because they are sealed in the cave. For the Persians, there is no seeming because there is no being. *Nomos* is king of all. In the *History*, Herodotus uses the Greeks to point to various ways (none altogether successful) in which the necessary incompleteness of the political (the tension between public and private, *kalon* and *agathon*) can be acknowledged from within the political, thereby retarding its tendency to become unjust out of justice. The *Republic* is also such a critique of political life in which it is Socrates' intent not so much to respond to Glaucon's question at the beginning of book 2 as to show why he has asked it. In revealing the meaning of Glaucon's question and why it cannot be answered in the form it is asked, Socrates also reveals that while the soul is not what law must assume it to be, it nevertheless comes to light in the assumption.

CHAPTER 9

The Subject of Justice

On *Plato's* Cleitophon

Perhaps the one thing clear about the *Cleitophon* is that it belongs together with the *Republic*.[1] Plato has for some reason invited us to pair what is by far his shortest dialogue with his longest dialogue save one. Each is about justice, but in four pages, the one suggests that there may not be much to say about what the other discusses in some three hundred pages. Accordingly, while the fact that they belong together is clear, Plato's intention in pairing them is not. Socrates, who has only two speeches in the *Cleitophon*, begins the dialogue.

> Someone was describing Cleitophon, son of Aristonymos, to us just now, [saying] that conversing with Lysias, he blamed passing time [*diatribas*] with Socrates but overpraised intercourse [*sunousian*] with Thrasymachus. (408a1–4)

We need to notice the strangeness of this beginning.[2] Socrates is talking about someone presumably standing right next to him (in Greek, the first word of the dialogue is *Kleitophōnta*—"Cleitophon" in the accusative case) as though he were not there. He treats Cleitophon as an object to be discussed with an unnamed companion or companions. This is not uncon-

---

1 · There has long been a dispute about the authenticity of the *Cleitophon*. In a thorough review of the literature, David Roochnik has deftly shown how weak the case is for thinking it spurious and at the same time what the misunderstandings were that led to doubts about its authenticity (David Roochnik, "The Riddle of the *Cleitophon*," *Ancient Philosophy* 4 [1984]: 132–38). Along with most recent commentators, I have assumed the dialogue to be authentic.

2 · A number of suggestions have been made about this beginning; perhaps the most persuasive is that it takes the form of a charge in a court of law. See H. Brunnecke, "Kleitophon Wider Sokrates," *Archiv für Geschichte der Philosophie* 26 (1913): 453; Clifford Orwin, "On the *Cleitophon*," in *The Roots of Political Philosophy: Ten Forgotten Socratic Dialogues*, edited by Thomas L. Pangle (Ithaca, NY: Cornell University Press, 1987), 117–20; and Roochnik, "Riddle of the *Cleitophon*," 136.

nected to what may be at the core of Cleitophon's complaint—Socrates has favorites (408c4–d1 and 409a4), but Cleitophon is apparently not one of this inner circle. Socrates does not seem to give this man, who has a rather heady sense of his own dialectical abilities, the time of day.

Cleitophon proceeds to correct the hearsay account that Socrates has of his conversation with Lysias, claiming that, while he did indeed say some things critical of Socrates, he also praised him. In his second and final speech, Socrates says he is eager to learn these things from Cleitophon so that he may practice and pursue what is good about him and flee the bad with all his might. What follows is a long speech by Cleitophon (some 85 percent of the dialogue) in which he praises Socrates as a world-class exhorter to virtue, particularly to justice, but criticizes him severely for never really saying what justice is or how one gets it. The universally acknowledged problem of the *Cleitophon* is that Plato does not have Socrates respond. Mind you, these are not the high-level criticisms of the Eleatic Stranger or of "father" Parmenides, but of a minor Athenian politician who was something of a trimmer and supporter of the status quo whatever the status quo happened to be.[3] Why, then, is Cleitophon allowed this unprecedented opportunity to have the last word?

This problem is connected to another. Although the *Republic* and the *Cleitophon* are a pair, it is difficult to work out which precedes the other dramatically. In one way, it seems obvious that the *Cleitophon* comes before the *Republic*. It poses the question to which the *Republic* is the answer. Cleitophon first accuses Socrates of not delivering on the promise implied by his exhortation to justice; Socrates replies with a detailed analysis of what justice is and how one acquires it. On this account, Socrates would get the last word so long as one understands the two dialogues as one— not a dialogue in which one character speaks almost all the lines followed by a narration (a dialogue in which one character *does* speak all the lines) but an extended conversation, *Cleitophon-Republic*, of five speeches (Socrates1, Cleitophon1, Socrates2, Cleitophon2, and Socrates3 = the *Republic*).[4] Cleitophon would thus be the unnamed auditor to whom Socrates narrates the *Republic*, and, in an admittedly long speech beginning "I went down to the Piraeus," Socrates would give Cleitophon his due.

What makes this scenario difficult is that Cleitophon is one of the characters present in the *Republic*; it would, of course, be odd for Socrates to

3 · See Orwin, "On the *Cleitophon*," 119–20.
4 · If the *Cleitophon* represents the truth of the city's charges against Socrates (ibid., 120), then "the *Republic* is the true *Apology* of Socrates" (Allan Bloom, *The Republic of Plato* [New York: Basic Books, 1968], 307).

offer as new evidence a narration of a conversation in which Cleitophon was himself a participant. Isn't it more reasonable, then, to assume that the events *narrated* in the *Republic* come after the events of the *Cleitophon*? Socrates would then go to the house of Cephalus, see Cleitophon there among the others, and take the opportunity to respond to the unanswered charge of the *Cleitophon*. This is certainly possible, yet it is just as easy to reverse the order. At a crucial moment in the *Republic* (340a1–b9), Cleitophon speaks in defense of Thrasymachus's thesis that the just is whatever the rulers command. Now, while Socrates later claims to have become Thrasymachus's friend (498c9–d1), he says nothing of the sort about Cleitophon. Accordingly, it is perfectly possible that Cleitophon sat through the whole of the *Republic* unaffected by Socrates' arguments. His preference for Thrasymachus might even be a result of the conversation in the *Republic*, which far from being a reply to his charge against Socrates would then be an instance of precisely the sort of exhortative Socratic speech that has elicited from him a mixture of wonder and disappointment. It is even possible that the events in the house of Cephalus preceded the events of the *Cleitophon* and are subsequently followed by Socrates' narration of these same events to Cleitophon. Could there be something about narration that transforms an unpersuasive account of justice into one that Cleitophon might find persuasive? Be this as it may, the *Cleitophon* itself will prove to be about the relation between narration of dialogue—indirect discourse—and justice. As we do not seem to be able to answer the question of which dialogue comes first with the information we have, we are left to wonder about our ignorance. An answer would require that we know much more about what each of the characters intends by his speeches; lacking the hubris of Cleitophon, we will be reluctant to claim to see inside the souls of these characters. We can know only that we cannot know.

With this problem in mind, let's begin again at the beginning.

> Someone was describing Cleitophon, son of Aristonymos, to us just now, [saying] that conversing with Lysias, he blamed passing time [*diatribas*] with Socrates but overpraised intercourse [*sunousian*] with Thrasymachus. (408a1–4)

Again, the first word is *Cleitophon* in the accusative case. The vocative—the case used in addressing someone—would have been the more customary beginning (of the twenty-six nonnarrated Platonic dialogues, twenty-one have a vocative in the first sentence). Socrates is surely addressing Cleitophon, but, because of the way they ignore Cleitophon's presence, his words just as surely mean something more than is explicit. Socrates behaves rudely, and so it seems reasonable for Cleitophon to conclude that he is angry with him.[5] The source of this anger is what "someone" reported. Now, the Greek at the beginning has an interesting ambiguity. The accusative *Kleitophōnta* is followed by a subordinate clause in which the accusative becomes the nominative subject of the clause—"Someone described Cleitophon [accusative], that, conversing [nominative], he blamed . . . and he praised. . . ." Yet it is also grammatically possible that the one doing the nominative conversing and the subsequent blaming and praising was the nominative "someone." This ambiguity gets an odd resolution since, by describing Cleitophon, the someone who reported to Socrates certainly had to converse, to utter words, in a way that indicated blame and praise. Both Cleitophon and "someone" conversed, praised, and blamed. This is simply to say that a narration of a speech—that is, indirect discourse of the form "he said that . . ."—always involves unifying the perspectives of the narrator and speaker. At the same time, there is something illusory about such a unity. Here, our anonymous tattletale says that Cleitophon "overpraised" Thrasymachus. Now, the verb *huperphaineō* might mean either that Cleitophon praised Thrasymachus a lot or that he praised him excessively, but even supposing that Cleitophon praised him excessively, did he know he was overpraising, or did he believe he was only giving Thrasymachus his due? Is the "over" of "overpraised" the insertion of the narrator? Narration necessarily obscures this distinction and so misrepresents the extent to which it is possible to render another's meaning altogether in speech. Two souls are not so easily made one.

That the *Cleitophon* is intended to put us in mind of this difficulty is made clear at the beginning in several ways. Cleitophon is said to have blamed *diatribas* with Socrates (literally, the plural of something like "rubbing across" but also "passing time" and even "lecture"). He overpraises the *sunousia* of Thrasymachus (literally, "being with" but also "intercourse"—sexual and otherwise—and, again, "lecture"). So, for Cleitophon, the measure of the superiority of Thrasymachus to Socrates might be that it is really possible to "be with" the one but not the other. Later, when Cleitophon introduces his praise of Socrates, he speaks of how "coming to be with [Socrates] often he was amazed listening" (407a5–6). Between that time and this, his disappointment has left him less amazed and less inclined to describe himself as "being with" Socrates. What seems to be at stake is the possibility of a genuine sharing—a *koinōnia* or community (see 410c6)—of souls.

Cleitophon responds to Socrates' response to the report of his words

5 · In conversation, David O'Connor of Notre Dame University has proposed an alternative interpretation—that Socrates is being playful and teasing Cleitophon so as to defuse a potentially awkward situation. That both alternatives are arguable suggests that, at the very least, Socrates' intention is not altogether available to Cleitophon.

by saying that the reporter didn't get it right. It was not his intention to be insulting. Nevertheless,

> since you are manifest in finding fault with me, pretending to think nothing of it, I myself would be pleased to go through them [Cleitophon's speeches] with you since we also happen to be alone [*monō*]. (406a7–10)

A number of things are important here. Although Cleitophon begins by asserting that Socrates has not understood his intention, he assumes with increasing certitude that he knows Socrates' intentions perfectly. Whereas Socrates will say, "*It* is manifest that you know in what way I am worse and better" (407a2), Cleitophon uses another phrase that idiomatically means the same thing but literally means "*You* are manifest" (my emphasis). Furthermore, he claims to know not only that Socrates is upset with him but also that Socrates is attempting to conceal it. He professes to know that Socrates thinks poorly of him and that he thinks more harshly of him than he ought. There is apparently no limit to Cleitophon's insight into Socrates' soul. He sees not only Socrates' apparent intentions but the reality Socrates hides behind them and even the reality of *these* intentions that he presumes to be hidden from Socrates himself. All of this Cleitophon says they can now discuss because they are alone (*monō*). This last is especially striking. Earlier (406a1) Socrates had spoken of what someone had related "to us." Now, "us" cannot include Cleitophon, but *monō* implies that no one else is present. Is Socrates referring to himself in the plural? This would not be unusual in Greek and means the opposite of its English equivalent—it is not the royal but the humble "we." The plural would fit with Socrates' perennial claim not even to know himself; there are more of him than meet the eye. Cleitophon, on the other hand, says they are now *monō*. Greek has not only singular and plural numbers but also a dual used to refer to pairs of things. *Monō* is the dual form of a word that means "alone" or "solitary." Being alone means being separated from others, being a unit (*monas*). Cleitophon's language suggests that it is unproblematic for two to be one, to be together (*sunousia*) as one (*monas*) is what it means to be alone (*monō*) with Socrates. Cleitophon assumes he can know Socrates inside out—know his soul—even though he began by denying that *he* had been rightly understood. Indeed, the rest of the dialogue is a response to Socrates' ironic suggestion that Cleitophon knows him even better than he knows himself (407a2).

We are now in a better position to make a provisional speculation about the intention of the *Cleitophon*. It is paired with the *Republic* in being about justice. The interchange at the beginning suggests that it is also about the problem of narration. Underlying the problem of narration is the deeper problem of the extent to which it is ever possible to know another soul, be one with another, and so share with another. In addition, by referring to himself in the plural, Socrates forces us to wonder to what extent it is possible for us to know our own souls, be with ourselves, and so share with ourselves. The *Cleitophon*, in its language and in its story, raises the possibility that we are fundamentally alone. To be alone in this way would call into question the very possibility of a common good and, with it, of justice. This is the thematic connection to the *Republic*.

Cleitophon appears in the *Republic*, book 1, in a brief interchange with Polemarchus (340a1–b9). Socrates has just placed in peril Thrasymachus's first definition of justice (that it is the advantage of the stronger), for if the stronger are those who rule, and they sometimes make mistakes about what is to their own advantage, they will sometimes command others to do what is not really to their own advantage. The following is their interchange:

"Yes, by Zeus, Socrates," said Polemarchus, "most clearly."

"If you are to be witness for it/him," interrupted Cleitophon.

"And what requires a witness?" he said. "For Thrasymachus himself agrees that those ruling sometimes command what is bad for themselves, but that for the others to do these things is just."

"Because, Polemarchus, Thrasymachus set down to be just doing the things bid by the rulers."

"But also, Cleitophon, he set down to be just the advantage of the stronger. And setting down both these things, he agreed that sometimes the stronger bid the weaker and those ruled to do things disadvantageous for them. From these agreements, the advantage of the stronger would be no more just than what is not advantageous."

"But," said Cleitophon, "he said/meant [*legei*] to be just what the stronger considers advantageous for himself. This is to be done by the weaker, and this he set down to be just."

"But he did not say/mean it in this way," said Polemarchus.[6]

Cleitophon thinks that whatever the stronger think is to their advantage is just. In addition, his language (he uses the verb *legein*, which can mean either "to think" or "to say") suggests that he does not recognize the possibility that men can be unclear about their own intentions, either to themselves or to others. To be unclear about our own intentions is just another way of saying that it is possible for us not to know what the consequences of our intentions are so that is possible for us to make mistakes. It is thus a necessity

---

6 · Notice that, in this interchange, it has to be the action and not the *people* who are just, for the people experience opposite effects from the action.

of what Cleitophon intends here that we think without ambiguity. Because such thinking would be perfectly translatable into speech, Cleitophon can recognize no distinction between direct and indirect discourse. "Thrasymachus said" and "Thrasymachus meant" are the same in fact as they are in Greek. And yet Cleitophon had to intervene in order to clarify what Thrasymachus meant. Accordingly, because what Cleitophon does belies what he says, he cannot himself be altogether clear about what he means. This is especially funny in the context since Thrasymachus will immediately disavow Cleitophon's interpretation of what he intended.

From the *Republic*, we learn that, for Cleitophon, thinking and speaking must be one, and so we understand why he is so frustrated in the dialogue that bears his name. For Cleitophon, Socrates' behavior toward him can mean only one of two things. Either Socrates is unable to say what is just (because he does not know), or he is unwilling to say and therefore willingly deprives Cleitophon of the greatest of goods (410c5–6). Socrates is not the man Cleitophon thought him to be either because he is unwise or because he is unjust.

Let us return to the *Cleitophon.* In response to Socrates' expression of his resolve to practice and pursue what is good about himself and flee what is bad with all his might, Cleitophon provides a sketch of what is good and bad about Socrates. He finds most impressive the beauty of Socrates' speeches rebuking other human beings. Socrates, he says, sings like a deus ex machina, the god who sometimes appears miraculously at the end of a tragedy to give a final accounting and render justice because none of the characters in the play are aware of the truth of their situations. Without perhaps realizing it, Cleitophon has indicated the problem with what he will demand of Socrates. True justice would require the ability of a god to look within human beings and fully know their souls. Cleitophon attributes this ability to Socrates. Later when he reports having spoken "in the way of [Socrates]" (408d1), he will tacitly claim it for himself. Here, he "quotes" one of Socrates' beautiful exhortations. It is unprecedented among Socratic speeches in Plato for the range of its addressees—"O human beings."[7] Accordingly, one might wonder whether Socrates really said it. Has Cleitophon invented a Socratic speech and presented it to Socrates as his own? Earlier he had moved effortlessly from Socratic speeches to Socratic intentions; now he reverses the order. So well does Cleitophon think he knows the intention of Socrates that he has no qualms about inventing a speech to accompany this "obvious" intention.

Interpreting Cleitophon's Socratic speech involves the difficult task of separating what Cleitophon thinks he is saying from what he is really say-

7 · See Orwin, "On the *Cleitophon*," 113.

ing. In the speech, his "Socrates" first chides human beings generally for being so ignorant as to do nothing of what they ought. In particular, they are too zealous about acquiring money or goods (*khrēmata*) without worrying sufficiently about whether they or the sons who will be their heirs know how to use these goods justly. Human beings generally err, then, in thinking that things are themselves good when it is the use of these things that is really good. Not things themselves but the manner of their use is what is important, and this manner is here identified with justice. Cleitophon seems to think that the fathers are scolded because they are concerned solely with wealth—external goods. In fact, his own speech is unintelligible unless they are at least as much concerned with providing these goods for their sons. Money is for them really a means for demonstrating their goodwill toward those whom they love. Without this goodwill, the exhortation that follows would fall on deaf ears. In one way, then, these fathers already know that nothing is good apart from a state of soul, even though they seem to be able to show this goodness only by way of external goods.

Even Cleitophon must acknowledge that they do not simply leave it at handing over their coffers to their heirs. They have educated their children, albeit in the most conventional manner. Still, Cleitophon's Socrates censures them, for they do not recognize that despite all this education in "letters, music, and gymnastics," both they and their children remain *amousia*—unmusical.

> And yet on account of this false musical step and laxness, but not on account of lack of measure in keeping step with the lyre, both brother making war with brother, they do and suffer the most extreme things and cities with cities, attacking without measure and disharmoniously, they are internally at odds. (407c6–d1)

Translating the passage so that the masculine "brothers" match up with the masculine "warring" and the feminine "cities" match up with the feminine "attacking" suggests that, while Cleitophon believes that cities may suffer *internal* strife and disunity, inner disharmony is not a possibility for human beings. The closest Cleitophon comes is "brother against brother." Being out of step, for him, means being out of step with another and not with oneself. For Cleitophon, the internal harmony of the just is identical to the internal harmony of the tyrant; he understands neither as being at odds with himself.[8]

In the final section of the quoted speech, Cleitophon has Socrates reply to an imagined objection from those he is exhorting that injustice is not

---

8 · Both the perfectly just man and the perfectly unjust man are for him like statues. See Plato *Republic* 361d4–6.

finally a matter of education since it is voluntary. His "Socrates" replies that this is not possible since these men also agree that no one would choose something so bad. Even should the "choice" of injustice result from the power of pleasure over the unjust, no one would choose for pleasure to have such power over him. Accordingly, "the *logos* in every way chooses doing injustice to be involuntary" (407d7–8); injustice is a consequence of lack of education. We must take great care for justice, "both every man in private and at the same time cities altogether in public" (407e1–2); this is the goal of education.

On the face of it, this is simply a statement of the apparently Socratic view that virtue is knowledge. Cleitophon takes it seriously enough to believe that it means that true education would present to the soul an object so manifestly its appropriate goal that no inner disposition would be required to choose it. The soul would be attracted to it rather like a magnet to iron. Of course, if injustice is not voluntary because it springs from misunderstanding, then justice, which must come to be as a consequence of understanding, should not be voluntary either. Socrates' knowledge of the ways in which he is better and worse would differ not at all from his disposition to pursue and practice the one and flee the other with all his might. Indeed, his second speech would be a mere tautology, for to know what is better would mean to pursue it. Socrates' "might [*kratos*]" in pursuing the better and fleeing the worse would disappear, and he would be no different from anyone else. The *logos* might choose; we would not. Justice understood in this way begins to look rather mechanical and not altogether different from the way in which men can be controlled by pleasures. Cleitophon's Socrates has thus described the just soul as so harmonized that it mechanically pursues what is reasonable but with the consequence that justice would be completely divorced from any will to do good. Under these conditions, it might make sense to train, habituate, or program human beings, but what would be the sense of exhorting them? Vocative and accusative cases would be indistinguishable.

That this is indeed the problem becomes clearer in the sequel. Cleitophon continues his encomium of Socrates but stops quoting, indicating what he admires in the next step of the argument by way of indirect discourse. He praises Socrates for criticizing those who pay more attention to their bodies than their souls as caring more for the ruled part than the ruling part. One could almost say that they are more concerned with the effect than the cause. Socrates is always concerned with the hidden cause. Cleitophon extends this principle so that whatever "someone does not know how to use, it is better [*kreitton*] to let the use of it be" (407e8–9). This includes the parts of our body, our bodies as a whole, things external to us subject to various arts, and, finally, our very souls.

This speech [*logos*] of yours also ends beautifully, [saying] that whoever does not know how to use his soul, it is better [*kreitton*] for him to keep quiet regarding the soul and not to live than to live acting on his own. But if there should be some necessity to live, better [*ameinon*], then, to pass life as a slave than as a free man for such a one, giving over, as of a ship, the rudder of his thought to another, to one having learned the art of piloting human beings, which you, Socrates, often name *politikē*, saying that this is the same as the art of judging/punishment and justice. (408a4–b5)

The word *kreitton* means "better," but originally it meant "stronger" or "mightier"; it is the word that is central for Cleitophon's account of justice in *Republic*, book 1, and cognate with the word that Socrates uses to say that he pursues the better and flees the worse with all his might. To do the strong thing is to do the just thing. When we do not know what that is, we ought to kill ourselves. Failing that, we ought at least to give ourselves up to others and let them use us well (although here what we do is *ameinon* and not *kreitton*). Cleitophon presents Socrates as always aiming at the cause, the ruling part, of human beings. The part that uses everything else is the part that needs education; it is what Clifford Orwin calls the "unused user."[9] However, Cleitophon has no way of thinking about it except as the sort of thing that can itself be used. The soul is for him just another thing subject to manipulation, like the body or a lyre. Even though he says that it should choose to die or enslave itself if it does not know how to use itself, he does not seem to realize the significance of his own account, for a soul that gives up its exercise of authority over itself is no longer a soul. It cannot be used as a soul, for if it becomes an instrument, good or bad, it has ceased to be a soul. Its desire to be good precludes its voluntary enslavement. The art of politics is thus double. It involves justice, understood as knowing the best way to steer souls (408b2), but it also involves punishment (408b4), the presupposition of which is that souls are responsible for what they do.

Cleitophon praises the Socratic speeches of which he has just given an account for their beauty, by which he means that they are most protreptic or exhortative and most useful for simply (*atekhnōs*, which literally means "artlessly") awakening us. Cleitophon views speeches as tools that are meant to have results and are to be evaluated in terms of the results they have. On this scale, Socrates' speeches are pretty good, but they are only a beginning. They awaken us to the need to become just, but they do not make us just—Socrates' speeches awaken us artlessly. Because he wants to move on to the next step, to become virtuous, Cleitophon begins to ask what the art is that concerns the virtue of the soul.

9 · Orwin, "On the *Cleitophon*," 123.

His approach is curiously indirect, however. Cleitophon does not ask Socrates himself; instead, he approaches Socrates' contemporaries, those who share his desires, his comrades, or "however one ought to name such a thing in relation to you concerning them" (408c6–7). Cleitophon, the self-conscious outsider, doesn't know exactly what it means to be in with Socrates, but his suspicion is clearly that being a member of the club means sharing a doctrine or a teaching—a *didagma* (409b6). This makes it all the more exasperating for him that he has not received the teaching. Cleitophon wants to find out what it is, but at the same time, he wants to prove himself. Accordingly, he decides who the favored few are within the Socratic circle and then proceeds to enter the dialectical lists with them intent on showing that he is at least as worthy as they are. So proud is he of his victory over them that he quotes himself at length. But, once again, Cleitophon's action belies his conclusion, for if what were at stake were simply an art of justice embodied in a teaching, he would want the teaching at all costs but would feel no particular need to subject his "enemies" to a humiliating defeat. When Socrates later tells him that justice is harming enemies and doing good to friends (410a8–b1), perhaps he is not so much proclaiming a doctrine as scolding Cleitophon for unjust behavior to those whom he ought to have considered friends—partners in philosophical inquiry. Cleitophon does not acknowledge the extent to which justice must be a disposition in the soul to do what is good.

To Cleitophon's question about what sort of art it is that has to do with the virtue of the soul, "the one of them seeming/reputed to be most powerful regarding these things, answering me, said this art to be 'what,' he said, 'you hear Socrates saying, nothing other than justice'" (409a4–6). Cleitophon takes this to be a mere name, justice, but the Greek, *hēnper akoueis su legontos Sōkratous*, could also mean not the content of what Socrates says but something like "what, when Socrates is speaking, you hear." Justice would not then be what Socrates says one should pursue; it would be Socrates' speaking that one should pursue.[10]

Cleitophon is never utterly unaware of these possibilities; he knows that Socrates' activity is important, but he nevertheless thinks that it is possible to isolate something over and above this activity in which justice consists. Cleitophon makes an analogy to the art of medicine, which has a double result: it produces health and it produces doctors—a product and a teaching. So also must the art of justice have a double result; it produces just men,

---

10 · Cleitophon, as usual, treats speech as unambiguous and assumes he understands. Plato, however, lets us know that he intends the ambiguity by using the very same grammatical form (a genitive absolute) to introduce Cleitophon's next quotation of himself: *eipontos d'emou*—"and then, me speaking."

who are comparable to the doctors, but what is comparable to health? This is what Cleitophon demands of Socrates' followers. Now, had he been more careful, he would have seen that medicine yields healthy *human beings* and doctors and that the doctors it produces need not be healthy human beings. Then he would not have been able to say that the comparable doubleness of the art of justice yields just men and some unknown product, for surely just men would be the product analogous to healthy men, and teachers of justice would be analogous to doctors. Cleitophon would have had to ask whether it is in fact possible to be a teacher of justice and not be just in the same way it is possible to be a teacher of health and not be healthy. Once again, this has to do with the extent to which the soul can detach itself from itself and treat itself as an object without undermining its character as soul. Because the intent to be just is not separable from justice, Socrates' "artless" exhortations to justice cannot be understood as simply preliminary to the justice to which they exhort us.

Cleitophon quotes his own question—"what product the just man is able to make for us" (409b8–c1)—but the answers of Socrates' friends are given only in indirect discourse, thus revealing, at what ought to be the most important part of their dialogue, that they are simply straw men for him; his voice is sufficient. They reply with a series of answers: the advantageous, the needful, the beneficial, and the profitable.[11] To this, Cleitophon replies, again quoting himself (he is clearly more impressed with his questions than with their answers), that none of these are peculiar to justice—each in its way applying as well, for example, to carpentry. Finally, a Hektor appears to contest Cleitophon's Achilles, and the one reputed to be the most accomplished or refined of Socrates' companions offers the answer, again in indirect discourse, that the product peculiar to justice and none of the other arts is friendship within (or among) cities. Because there are many so-called friendships that are defective, Cleitophon presses the issue, and the core of friendship comes to be defined as like-mindedness—*homonoia*.

Only here in the dialogue does the theme that dominates the logic of the action intrude into the argument itself. We have been concerned from the outset with what it would mean for two to be one. Cleitophon now asks whether like-mindedness means likeness of opinion or likeness of knowledge, and his antagonist dismisses the former contemptuously. Many harmful, and hence unjust, things come to be among men owing to likeness of opinion (whether this is the opinion of his antagonist or of Cleitophon or belongs alike to both we cannot say owing to the indirect discourse). Accordingly, justice produces friendship, which is really like-mindedness,

---

11 · With one exception, the gainful, it is the list of answers that Thrasymachus prohibits Socrates from giving to the question of justice in *Republic*, book 1 (336c6–d3).

which, in turn, is likeness of knowledge. But all of the arts produce some likeness of knowledge in different human beings, as those present in their little group are quick to point out to the one who was formerly first among them. Cleitophon's report of their coming around to his side is beautifully reported. It is in direct discourse but with a wonderful ambiguity.

> Now, when we were at this point in the *logos*, being perplexed, those present were adequate to jump on him and to say that the *logos* had come round again to the same point as at the start, and they/I said [*elegon*] that "medicine was a like-mindedness as well as all the arts, and they are able to say what they are about. But with respect to the like-mindedness meant/said by you, wherever it's aiming, it has fled, and whatever its product is is unclear." (409e10–410a4)

The group has become absolutely like-minded in its contemptuous attitude toward its once most favored member. Cleitophon, who has won his victory, honors them by quoting them . . . , or does he? The verb he uses to introduce the quotation, *elegon*, can mean either "they said" or "I said." That they are indistinguishable from him is a consequence of their like-mindedness. If the just are to be defined by what is in their minds, and if what is in the mind of one is not distinguishable from what is in the mind of another because it is a species of knowledge, then the just will be indistinguishable from one another. They will thus not be personally responsible for what they choose to do, and so their justice will be not so much a virtue as a class characteristic that defines them as objects. Justice will have to do with a certain kind of behavior; it will have nothing to do with a will to do what is good.

Cleitophon reports the final stage of his inquiry, his two conversations with Socrates, in indirect discourse. We therefore do not know what Socrates said; we know only what Cleitophon took him to mean—first, that "it belongs to justice to harm enemies and to do well by friends" (410a8–b1) and after "that the just man never harms anyone" (410b1–2). This is especially puzzling since Socrates relates something very much like the first in *Republic*, book 1, as the view of Polemarchus (333d7–8, 334b8–9) but refutes it and proceeds to replace it with something like the second (335d11–12). Cleitophon seems to take each of the two as a *logos* applicable to all men at all times, and, therefore, Socrates must appear to him simply inconsistent. But the two may well be directed at him at particular times. Perhaps Socrates intended to take Cleitophon through the stages of the argument of the *Republic*, because the experience he would undergo would answer his question in a way that a simple *logos* could not. We cannot know, for Cleitophon grew impatient and gave up.

This issue may be put somewhat differently. Cleitophon longs to be like Socrates. His various attempts to be one or alone (*monō*) with Socrates range from making Socrates speak with his voice by quoting him at length in an imagined speech, attempting to usurp Socrates' position among his coterie of youths by aping his manner of questioning and defeating his favorites, and finally approaching Socrates himself—being with Socrates. But Cleitophon never truly understands his own desire and so never distinguishes between emulating Socrates as a character and appropriating Socratic teachings; for Cleitophon, "Socrates speaking" is the content of Socrates' speeches. Because Cleitophon does not understand the significance of the vocative case, he will end the dialogue just as Socrates had begun it—by talking about himself in the accusative (410d5). Cleitophon cannot preserve the dual number within *monō*; if Socrates recedes into the speeches of Socrates, by appropriating these speeches, Cleitophon would become Socrates and quotation would become a narration unaware that it was collapsing the voices of narrator and character. The unintended consequence of this way of understanding things is that, despite himself, Cleitophon too would recede into the speeches of Cleitophon; he would become an object correctly characterized in the accusative case. It is in anticipation of this problem that Plato has Socrates begin the dialogue as he does.

The *Cleitophon* presents what seems to be an insurmountable problem for the possibility of justice. Cleitophon at first seems to have a case against Socrates, who presents us with a glowing picture of justice and makes us long for it, but in the end, it is all a tease. Socrates can't deliver the good—in the *Republic*, he even admits as much (532a–534e). Cleitophon, who wants justice defined, takes his business elsewhere—to Thrasymachus and to Lysias (who, we know, wrote at least one speech praising mind and the nonlover that included no vocatives within it—see *Phaedrus* 230e–237a). In the course of his accusation against Socrates, we come to see that Cleitophon does not understand the inaccessibility of human intentions and its correlate, the inaccessibility of the human soul. At first glance, this looks devastating, for if we cannot know the intentions of another, a common good is impossible, and with it justice. The good is irrevocably private. Socrates didn't respond to Cleitophon because there is no response. Still, we ought to have second thoughts about this sad conclusion, for it is not just that the definition of justice is tragically unavailable to us so that what we need most is deprived us. Rather, the definition of justice would be its destruction. The will to do what is good cannot be reduced to the content of the good that is willed; to attempt to do so is to make goodness mechanical and so not really goodness. Justice is not so much the order willed by the soul as the soul's willing of an order. This order is, in turn, necessarily imperfect, so that we learn from the *Cleitophon* the curious fact that the very hiddenness of the soul that makes perfect justice impossible is at the same time the necessary condition for the possibility of any justice whatsoever.

A completely knowable, intelligible world—a world where the nature of everything is so nailed down that everything is knowable as an object in the accusative case—would be a world inhospitable to the human soul. Justice is a sign that there are such things as souls in the world—beings we address in the vocative and do not simply describe. The *Cleitophon* means to remind us of the value of this indeterminacy by showing us the mistake that underlies Cleitophon's blame of Socrates. As a result of his perfectly predictable longing for perfect justice, Cleitophon does not understand the sense in which virtue is the exhortation to virtue and the will to be just is justice.

CHAPTER 10

The Object of Tyranny

Plato's Hipparchus

Plato's *Hipparchus* is generally not taken particularly seriously; it is thought either spurious or negligible. Yet its theme, love of the good, places it at the summit of philosophy, at least as Socrates presents it in the *Republic*.[1] Why, then, is such a slight writing the locus of the discussion of so monumental a question? As is so often the case in Platonic dialogues, in the *Hipparchus*, we find our way to the deepest questions by way of reflecting on the puzzles revealed in apparently superficial particulars. The most obvious such puzzle in the *Hipparchus* is its title, for Hipparchus is not a participant in the dialogue but rather the famous, or perhaps infamous, character for whom it is named. Socrates does give an extended account of him, but it does not seem at first to exemplify the dialogue's theme, and so its relevance for the whole is hard to make out. This digression is merely the most extensive and striking of several instances in the dialogue where Socrates says things that seem to come out of nowhere and to involve gratuitous details of language, plot, or character. There is a prominent string of these passages in the first section of the dialogue. What follows is first an account of this section and then of its significance in light of the long digression on Hipparchus.

This chapter was initially written as a talk for a conference on the thought of Seth Benar-dete in the spring of 2005 at Howard University. When I turned to the Hipparchus *shortly after Benardete's death in 2001, I was struck by how its display of the relation between the superficial and profound, the playful and serious, reminded me of reading books with him. A Platonic dialogue is, of course, many things; in its way, the* Hipparchus *stands as a monument to Seth Benardete.*

1 · See *Republic* 502c–516c. Consider as well the following remark of Seth Benardete: "Only two dialogues begin without any preliminaries—they start straight off with the question, 'What is?'—and in both cases the interlocutor is anonymous. That the love of the good emerges as the theme of one (*Hipparchus*) and law is the theme of the other (*Minos*) seems not unrelated to their evidently philosophical character. . . ." (*Socrates and Plato: The Dialectics of Eros* [Munich: Carl Friedrich von Siemens Stiftun, 1999], 51; see also 53n29).

While every Platonic dialogue, whatever its subject seems to be, is ultimately about philosophy, Plato nevertheless always begins with the recognizable. Accordingly, if we wish to understand pleasure, love, friendship, or justice, we would do well to turn to dialogues that raise these issues directly—to the *Philebus*, *Symposium*, *Lysis*, and *Republic*, for example. Yet Platonic dialogues have a way of transfiguring the ordinary. The truth of pleasure, love, friendship, and justice emerges eventually as something less easily recognizable but still more worthy—philosophy. Remarkably, this is true even of the *Phaedo*, where our customary understanding of death is transformed into philosophy. We view death in a revealingly incoherent manner that displays the duplicitous longing of the human soul for its own permanence. When it finally understands itself, this longing is philosophy as the practice of dying and having died.

The obvious subject matter of Plato's *Hipparchus* is love of gain—*philokerdeia*. The word and its cognates are rare in the Greek texts we have; with astonishingly few exceptions, they occur solely in two brief passages in Plato. Of some forty instances, only four are post-Platonic and only two pre-Platonic. Six are found in Plato's contemporary, Xenophon. The remaining twenty-eight instances occur in Plato—nineteen in the six and a half Stephanus pages that constitute the *Hipparchus*, nine in four pages of book 9 of the *Republic* (eight in a single two-page argument), and one in the first book of the *Laws*.[2] In general, Plato, and in particular, the *Hipparchus*, may therefore be said to be *the* classical source for our understanding of love of gain.

In *Republic*, book 9, Socrates provides three arguments to prove that the life of the tyrant is the worst of lives. In the second of these, he argues that life constituted by the love of wisdom—philosophy—is highest because unlike the two other contenders for the title of best of lives (the love of gain and the love of honor), philosophy alone involves experience of the other two. In this argument (not particularly persuasive, by the way), love of gain seems to mean thoughtlessly wanting to fulfill whatever desires arise in us. The *Hipparchus* presents a similar picture but with somewhat different emphasis. In the view of Socrates' anonymous interlocutor, love of gain is contemptible—low-class (of course, it characterizes the lowest class in Socrates' city in speech in the *Republic*). Assuming that this non-Socratic

---

2 · See Theocritus *Idylls* Id, poem 16, line 60; Josephus *Antiquitates Judaicae* 2.201; Epictetus *Fragments: Appian Mithridatic Wars* 8.51; Pindar *Isthmian* 2, line 6; Aristophanes *Ploutos*, line 590; Xenophon *Anabasis* 1.9.16, *Kunegetikos* 13.12, *Kuropaideia* 1.6.32, and *Oikonomikos* 12.16, 14.7, and 14.10; Plato *Hipparchus* 225a1, 225a2, 225a7, 225b2, 225b4, 225b8, 225c2, 226d2, 226d6, 226d8, 226e2, 226e10, 227b1, 227b3, 227c7, 227c8, 227d1, 232c5, and 232c7, *Republic* 581a7, 581c4, 582a9, 582b3, 582b7, 582d8, 582e1, 583a10, 586d5, and *Laws* 649d5.

understanding of love of gain is the ordinary view from which Plato wishes to begin, Allan Bloom translates *philokerdēs* as "profiteer."[3] This seems to accord with the view of Xenophon, who, in four different books, repeatedly links *philokerdeia* to deception and injustice.[4] We may therefore reasonably call the *philokerdēs* a cheat. Thus, if every Platonic dialogue is ultimately about philosophy, we are naturally moved to wonder why Plato would write a dialogue in which he invites us to consider philosophy the highest kind of cheating.

The problem is still more complicated. *Philokerdeia* is a compound of the verb *philein* ("to love" or "to feel affection toward") and the noun *kerdos* ("gain" or "profit"). In the *Hipparchus*, Socrates gets his interlocutor—a young Athenian man—to admit two things. If the *philokerdeis* are those who wittingly think that they will gain from something worthless, then no one is a lover of gain, for to think that something is of no worth is precisely not to expect any benefit from it. We identify gain with benefit and so with the good, and we are all lovers of the good. On the other hand, if in loving gain, the *philokerdeis* love what is good, then, as all men must perforce love what is good for them, all men are *philokerdeis*. Either there are no lovers of gain, or all are lovers of gain, the principle of both arguments being the same—that all men love the good. Perhaps, then, the *Hipparchus* does not single out petty cheating as its theme, but rather, it displays the universal attribute of all human beings—love of the good. This would presumably link it to the *Republic*.

Is the *Hipparchus* about cheating, or is the *Hipparchus* about the good itself? Perhaps it is about both. The lover of gain is in his pettiness comic and in his grandness tragic. But how are we to think these two together? It may be worth mentioning another pair of claims here. On the one hand, philosophy is the highest and paradigmatic human activity; on the other hand, philosophy is ridiculous. Owing to his preoccupation with the heavens, Thales falls into a well, much to the amusement of the slave girl who is watching. The togetherness of this pair—the high and the ridiculous—is the underlying subject matter of Plato's *Hipparchus*.

The *Hipparchus* divides roughly into five sections. Its first attempt to answer the question of who the lovers of gain are leads to the conclusion that no one is a lover of gain (225a–226d); this is the section to which I will pay special attention. Its second section attempt leads to the conclusion that, since everyone loves the good, everyone is a lover of gain (226d–228a). In

---

3 · See Allan Bloom, "On the *Hipparchus*," in *The Roots of Political Philosophy*, edited by Thomas Pangle (Ithaca, NY: Cornell University Press, 1987), 35.

4 · See *Oikonomikos* 12.16, 14.7, and 14.10; *Anabasis* 1.9.16; *Kurou Paideia* 1.6.32; and *Kunēgetikos* 13.12.

response to the *aporia* constituted by pairing these two sections, Socrates playfully accuses his interlocutor of deception—of cheating—and, in frustration, his interlocutor, somewhat more seriously, returns the accusation. To this charge, Socrates responds with the third section, the long digression about Hipparchus from which the dialogue gets its title (228b–229d). Hipparchus was a former ruler of Athens, who, although generally thought to be a tyrant, was really, as Socrates assures his interlocutor, a good and wise man whose wisdom consists in part in saying things like "Do not deceive a friend." This seemingly thin device is used to connect the Hipparchus section (a quarter of the whole) to the rest of the dialogue. The digression is, of course, revisionist history, since the common view, as we know from Thucydides' own revision of it, was that Hipparchus was a tyrant whose assassination by Harmodius and Aristogeiton was a source of great civic pride in democratic Athens.[5] Following the pep talk of the Hipparchus section, Socrates pushes to continue the argument by offering to let his companion take back any of several premises that led to *aporia*. The comrade chooses to retract his claim that the gainful is always good, a claim that he had in fact attempted to retract earlier and that Socrates proceeds to prove anew in the next section (229d–232a). In the remainder (232a–c), Socrates recapitulates the previous arguments and draws the conclusion that since all are lovers of gain, the very man who contemptuously reproaches lovers of gain—this anonymous young Athenian, for example—is necessarily himself a lover of gain. We note that, if love of gain is the same as love of the good, presumably this very attempt to condemn love of gain is a manifestation of the comrade's love of gain.

The *Hipparchus* begins with Socrates asking not one but three questions:

> For what [is] the gain-loving? What ever is it, and who [are] the gain-loving ones? (225a1–2)[6]

We are plunged into the middle of a conversation of which we know neither the time, the place, nor the occasion. We know neither why Socrates raises these three questions nor why he thinks asking will be important to his young companion, although he does once remark that the companion seems to lash out randomly as though he has been recently cheated (225b10). At the beginning of a dialogue strikingly silent as to place and time, of the three questions Socrates asks, the first two go unanswered (one makes only the noun explicit—it is a nominal sentence; the other only the verb). The

5 · See Thucydides, *Historiae* (Oxford: Oxford Classical Texts, 1988), 1.20 and 6.54–59.
6 · All citations from the *Hipparchus* are from *Platonis Opera*, vol. 2, ed. John Burnet (Oxford: Oxford Classical Texts, 1988). Translations are my own.

question to which the companion replies, and that determines the subsequent course of the argument, restores the explicit subject, this time not in the abstract form of the gain-loving but rather by asking who those who love gain are; it once more suppresses the verb. The first formulation is the most abstract; the second places the question in time, for it contains what is literally a temporal indicator—"What *ever* [or at any *time*] is it?" This, in turn, gives way to the least abstract form of the question, where we ask not what "gain-loving" or even "the gain-lover" is but who the gain-lovers are. Is this the only form in which the question can really be addressed? Allan Bloom suggests that the unasked question of the dialogue—and the one requiring an answer for any adequate account of gain-loving—is "What is gain?"[7] I'm not so sure. Is gain ever intelligible apart from the one who gains? Suppose that the only way to understand gain is through the love of gain, and the only way to understand the love of gain is through the lover of gain. Suppose, in other words, that the good and gain are one— that, in Seth Benardete's words, "the good in the first place is the measure of other things in regard to their usefulness for someone or something."[8] Furthermore, if every *thing* for which something is useful is always in the end useful for some*one*, then all gain will ultimately be measured in terms of the one for whom it is a gain—a lover of gain.

That something like this is what Plato means us to see becomes clearer from the comrade's reply—his first attempt at defining the lover of gain. The term crucial to his definition is *worth*.[9]

> They [the *philokerdeis*] seem to me to be those who deem it worth it [or worthy] to gain from things worth [or worthy of] nothing. (225a3–4)

Worth might be said to be the companion's understanding of what it is one gains when one gains. For the comrade, because the lover of gain thinks it worth gaining from what is really of no worth, he is a cheater. He succeeds in milking some good for himself out of something that is really no good. And if what he is dealing with is really no good, then the good he derives from it must necessarily have its source elsewhere. Gaining this good for himself would involve cheating, however, only were it to entail another's loss, and, of course, this is the case only if the good, as always someone's good, when not for you, is for someone else. Without realizing, the companion has

7 · Bloom, "On the *Hipparchus*," 35–36.

8 · See Seth Benardete, *Socrates' Second Sailing: On Plato's* Republic (Chicago and London: University of Chicago Press, 1989), 155.

9 · This is the first appearance in the dialogue of the verb *axioō* and its cognate adjective *axios*. In the first two pages of this seven-and-a-half-page dialogue, they occur twenty-one times. Then they disappear for five pages and reappear six times in the final page.

pointed to the problem around which the *Hipparchus* is organized. *Axioun* means "to deem or think worthy," but this is a bit deceptive in its suggestion that the world contains objects that may be said to be of worth independent of their relation to anything else. While *axioun* ordinarily means "to deem worthy of reward," it may also mean "to deem worthy of punishment." One might fill out its meaning as follows: *axioun* means to deem something or someone worthy of, or fit for, something; it measures one thing against another. Its meaning quickly (perhaps even immediately) falls into a sort of shorthand in which this doubleness is suppressed and, according to which, because X is worthy of Y, X is worth something and so is of worth. But this slide obscures the fact that *worth* is always a relative term; "to be worthy" always means "to be worthy *of*." Furthermore, the first definition of the lover of gain suggests that "being worthy of" is a function of "being deemed of worth." There can be no gain without one to whom the gain will accrue. The word *psuche*, "soul," does not occur in the *Hipparchus*.[10] This is perhaps the cause of the difficulty Socrates and his companion have in defining love of gain, for "good" is unintelligible apart from "soul."[11]

Socrates' response to the first definition should therefore come as no surprise. If the good is always the good-for, and if good-for must ultimately mean good for someone, for a soul, then the question is whether the soul for which something is good must be aware of this goodness. Socrates asks if the lovers of gain knowingly deem worthy what is really of no worth, or, if they do it in ignorance, whether they aren't simply fools—thoughtless ones (*anoētoi*). But this is really to ask for the connection between the good and awareness of the good. For the companion to preserve his moral indignation at cheating, he must claim that lovers of gain know what they are doing. And, if there is anything to distinguish lovers of gain from the rest of mankind, we must agree. Lovers of gain are thus not fools but *panourgoi*—men so shameless as to dare to do absolutely anything for gain. So, presumably, lovers of gain first see that something is really worthless (and therefore, one would think, rather easy to acquire) and then cleverly devise a way to profit from it nevertheless. They are like alchemists or magicians. Or, like Rumpelstiltskin, they spin gold from straw. And yet, if the good is always the good-for, such a miraculous transformation would be possible

10 · There are four Platonic dialogues of which this is true; the others are *Theages*, *Euthyphro*, and *Crito*.

11 · That the good is always the good-for means that nothing would be good were there no souls in the world. A soul (and this does not mean only human soul), as that for which things are, is the ground of all worth (consider, for example, the first sentence of the first section of Kant's *Grundlegung zur Metaphysik der Sitten*). Without souls, such terms as *satisfaction*, *sufficiency*, and *perfection* would have no meaning. This is not to say that any soul can by itself determine precisely its own good.

only if what is ordinarily worth nothing suddenly, owing to the cleverness of a certain soul, comes to be a treasure trove. In assuming this godlike function, in making something from nothing by acknowledging no limits, the lover of gain reveals himself as the source of the worth of what was previously worthless. Love of gain understood in this way masks hyperbolic self-celebration. Yet, in its perversity, this way does reveal the truth about the soul as the origin of all worth.

To bring this point home, Socrates, as is his wont, introduces a homely example.

> Do you then say the lover of gain to be this sort—such as if a farming man [*geōrgos anēr*] should plant knowing that the plant is worth nothing, he would deem it worthy to gain from this rearing? (225b4–6)

Socrates' use of the phrase *geōrgos anēr* is the first of a series of instances in which he introduces something unexpected into the conversation—a gratuitous detail. The language is too elevated. Are farmers *andres*—he-men? Thucydides does have Pericles use the phrase when asking the Athenians whether they really think it will be so easy for the Spartans, who are *geōrgoi andres*, to learn the art of seamanship (I.142.7), but in a somewhat more appropriate way. Pericles is speaking of Spartans and in the context of their preparedness for war. Socrates' example is complicated. At first, it seems to mean that some farmers might knowingly plant worthless plants with the expectation of later passing them off as worth something. On second thought, we see that, whether he means the comrade to see it or no, what Socrates says is really true of all plants. At sowing time, a plant is only a seed—chicken feed. So, in a way, *all* farmers are cheats—seeking to profit from what is originally worth almost nothing. And if what is true of farming is true of all the arts, then, in working material into a new form for the sake of some use or advantage, all art would be a form of cheating. Now, Socrates is in his own way doing something similar. He makes an example of a class of men ordinarily taken quite for granted. These men of little worth are for the moment transformed and deemed worthy of all our attention. Is this why they are *geōrgoi andres*? Is to exemplify to make exemplary?

Socrates may make a big deal of the farmers, but his companion breezes right past them—replying curtly that the gain-lover "thinks he must profit from everything" (225b9–10). We notice in passing that he has substituted the phrase *oietai dein*—"he thinks he must"—for the verb *axioun*, thus tacitly claiming that to deem something worthy of doing is to think that one ought to do it. Socrates' response is unexpectedly harsh.

> Do not answer randomly [without plan or purpose—from *a/hekōn*, "not willfully"] in this way, as if having been done some injustice by

someone, but, paying attention to me, answer just as though I were asking again from the beginning. (225b10–c2)

Having barely digested the oxymoronic he-men farmers, we are now puzzled by another curiously gratuitous detail—Socrates' abrupt claim that the comrade is speaking at random when his reply seems fairly reasonable and in the spirit of a *ti esti* question. And what can Socrates mean by scolding him for harboring a grudge? How does he know this? To feel cheated, one must presume some knowledge of the world's moral landscape. Socrates seems somehow to discern that moralism is the cause of his companion's inability to apply his mind. Isn't it strange, though, that this is likened to answering at random or without purpose? One would think moralism would rather involve the sort of tunnel vision that occurs when one looks at the world not randomly but with a predetermined goal or end in mind. Still, if we approach the world with excessive moralism—with a grudge—we don't open our minds to it. To open your mind means to take what is before you seriously, to attend to it in all of its detail. To be interested in something is to take an interest in it, to elevate its worth relative to the rest of the world, which then appropriately recedes into the background. Socrates' young comrade levels the worth of everything by ignoring what is to be learned by attending to details. He is so confident that he too easily looks past the specifics of Socrates' example of the *geōrgos anēr*. The comrade dismisses farmers, whose worth Socrates' exemplification has inflated, in his rush to get on to bigger, more important, things. At the same time, Socrates suggests that in acting in this intellectually random fashion, the young man has not paid sufficient attention not only to his example but also to *him*.

And so Socrates must recall him to the details of farming. He does so in a strikingly peculiar way. This is the third gratuitous detail. The farmer, Socrates says, would know about the worth of plants—for example, at what sort of season/hour/time (*hōra*) and in what sort of place (*khōra*) they are to be planted in a way that is worthy. Details of time and place (we recall that they are obtrusively absent in the setting of this dialogue) are perhaps *the* conditions for specificity. They are what the expert in the worth of anything would have to know. Rules are easily learned; their effective application to specific situations is another matter. Yet Socrates announces the general necessity to attend to place and time in a pun—*hōra/khōra*—that would collapse the difference between them and then likens his pun to the practice of the wise who are so very adept at beautifying their speeches in the law courts. The worth or good of something depends on the details of particular circumstances. Farmers must know when and where to plant. But to announce that this is the case is only to generalize in a beautiful way; it is certainly not to reproduce the real knowledge of the farmer. It invokes particulars as "the particular." Yet, as Nietzsche remarks, "The individual is a conceit vulnerable to the utmost."[12] The poetry of the wise is thus the illusory rendering of the particularity of the particular. It wants to disclose what is, but it is a deception—a cheat—that emerges out of the necessity to deal with the particular in a general way.[13] It is particularly at home in the law courts.

This general account of particularity leads to a serious error. Noticing the comrade's earlier conflation of the two, Socrates asks him whether to think it worthy (*axioun*) to gain is the same as to believe that one must (*oiesthai dein*) gain. The comrade agrees too readily. The subject of the infinitive *dein* here is the same as the subject of *oiesthai*. Whoever is doing the believing thinks that he is the one who must gain. *Axioun* doesn't work this way. I may deem a book worth writing without feeling a necessity to write it. Every artisan knows that he will lose from the use of shoddy materials in the sense that the final product will be worse. He may, however, deem it worth using shoddy materials, at less cost and so at a gain to himself, if the loss is borne by someone else. By accepting the equation of *oiesthai dein* and *axioun*, Socrates treats my gain and one's gain as though they mean the same thing—as though I in particular and the particular in general were the same. He overlooks the difference between subjects—grammatical and otherwise.

This allows Socrates to accuse the now befuddled comrade of trying to cheat him by deceptively claiming what he does not even himself believe— that is, that a man with the art of farming (*geōrgikos anēr*) would knowingly try to gain from a bad plant. Here Socrates adds (we are at first unsure why) that the comrade, being young, should not try to deceive one who is old. This is the fourth gratuitous detail in the first argument. What does Socrates' age have to do with the alleged deception? Socrates literally scolds the comrade for not turning his mind to him. Socrates' good is idiosyncratic; it is, for example, relative to his age. This difference in goods accounts for the possibility of deception, and so of cheating. The comrade, in his enthusiasm, takes the independence of the good from soul for granted. We will see that it is precisely because he is such a Platonist that Socrates can cheat him.

Let us look at the way Socrates formulates this accusation.

Do not attempt to deceive me, one already an older man, you being so young, by answering just now what you yourself do not even think, but say truly, do you think any man [*andra*] becoming someone who has

12 · Friedrich Nietzsche, *Aus dem Nachlass der Achtziger jahre*, in *Werke in drei Bänden*, vol. 3, edited by Karl Schlechta (Munich: Carl Hanser Verlag, 1966), 474.
13 · Compare *Minos* 315a7–8.

the art of farming [*geōrgikon*] and recognizing that he plants a plant worth nothing thinks to gain from this? (225d5–226a4)

Socrates first seems to accuse a young man more mentally agile than he of taking advantage of his failing powers. Yet this is obviously deeply ironic, for it is precisely at this point in the dialogue that Socrates most takes advantage of the youthful enthusiasm of the comrade by encouraging him to equate deeming it worth gaining from something useless and thinking one will gain from it oneself. This emerges especially clearly from the double use of the verb *oiesthai*, "to think." By having Socrates ask whether the comrade *thinks* that the farmer *thinks* he will gain from something worthless knowing it to be worthless, Plato indicates to us that there is thinking going on both within the example and in the reception of the example. Accordingly, the awareness that one is cheating, the possibility of which Socrates denies in the content of his question, is at the very moment of the question making its existence manifest on the level of his act of questioning. Socrates accuses the comrade of cheating in an argument in which he is supposed to be denying the possibility of cheating because it is not possible to think that one can gain from something of no worth. In fact, the argument itself is not worth much. The comrade doesn't know what he is doing and so is not really cheating. As Socrates knows this, he himself *is* cheating the comrade into thinking the argument is adequate, but, since its conclusion will serve to call into question the comrade's moral smugness and intellectual inattentiveness, he is doing it for his own good.

The list of examples that follows confirms this difficulty. An expert in horses might not expect his horse to thrive on meal that is worth nothing, and so, being aware that his horse will be corrupted, he will not expect to gain from worthless meal—unless, of course, he wants to use worthless meal to feed a horse that will in turn be worthless but that our expert will knowingly sell to someone else at a profit inflated by the fact that he has not had to spend very much on food. So he won't gain a healthy horse, but he will gain money that he could, should he wish, spend on purchasing other healthy horses. To be of worth is to be worth something, and this something is variable. A pilot may gain when his ship goes down if, for example, he wishes to collect the insurance or if he has a mortal enemy among the crew and wishes him dead. Gain and loss are not as obviously fixed as the comrade seems to think and as Socrates makes them seem, for they are always relative to a soul, and the intention of a particular soul—the good it aims at—is neither simply transparent nor constant. A sergeant who provides his troops with faulty equipment does something shockingly immoral, but if he does so in boot camp to force them to learn to adapt to circumstances, his goal is their education.[14] While it may well be the case that we never expect to gain from what is utterly worthless, we may very well expect to gain from appearances—either what appears worthless and is not or what appears to be of worth and is not. Love of gain understood as cheating depends on these discrepancies in how things appear to us. And such discrepancies are the necessary consequence of the existence of different souls. When Socrates, therefore, finally asks whether any of the craftsmen or of the rest of those men who are intelligent thinks he will gain from instruments or from equipment that are worth nothing, the comrade responds by saying, "It appears not" (226d1). This is the first of his answers to express anything less than complete certainty. What the comrade really means is "It appears not to you, Socrates, and I must agree because I can't see any way around it, but it doesn't really appear so to me." In defeating the comrade with bad arguments, Socrates has thus introduced him to the nature of gain as dependent upon soul. His second definition, accordingly, has a different tone.

> But, Socrates, I wish to say the gain-lovers to be those who at all times out of insatiability long beyond what is natural both for things quite small and for things worth little or nothing, and they love gain.

This is the beginning of the second argument, and we will not pursue it here. Socrates will drive his companion to the conclusion that since these men cannot knowingly love what is worth nothing and so must think what they love to be worth something, in fact they are no different from the rest of men since all love what they think to be good. It is worth noting, however, that in this second definition, the companion emphasizes not so much the state of the object loved by the lover of gain but the state of his soul—a state at all times filled with insatiable longing beyond what is natural. The love of gain, present in us all, contains the seed of tyranny.

At the end of the second argument, Socrates renews his charge that the comrade is acting deceitfully, "purposely saying things opposite to those we just now agreed on" (228a6–7). They have just shown that whatever men do, they do for the good; this holds as well for thinking. To think is to think purposely—for the good. To answer at random is not to think well. To raise a question is to be interested in a piece of the world, to have an interest in it but not yet to understand what it is good for, what worth it has. To seek to answer this question is to attempt to transform something hitherto not worth very much into something of worth. If there are no limits on our questions—that is, if we long to understand everything and thereby philosophize—then we seek to see the good in everything. Naturally, to those not interested in the world in this way, philosophy will appear to be cheating—

14 · Compare *Republic* 467c–e.

sophistry. Since the good must always be understood as the good-for, the attempt to understand everything as good points in two directions. I may either seek to change myself so that I become a soul for whom everything is in some way good—to become someone who is interested in everything; or I may seek to change the world so that everything in it is in some way good for my soul—to be someone who is interested solely in himself. The two alternatives are philosophy and tyranny. The long digression on Hipparchus, for which this dialogue is named, is thus not as gratuitous as it at first seems, for in it Socrates engages in a bit of sophistry that would transform a tyrant into a philosopher.

Directly after he forces the comrade to conclude that everybody loves gain, Socrates accuses him of deception, of "intentionally saying things contrary to what [they] just agreed" (228a6–7). He implies that the comrade is concealing the truth for a hidden advantage or gain. So Socrates accuses him of cheating, and yet it seems quite obvious that the comrade has been unwillingly brought into *aporia*. When he responds by protesting that it is Socrates who deceives by somehow turning things upside down in speeches, Socrates hushes him with language that suggests he has uttered sacrilege. The sacrilege is supposed to consist in not obeying or being persuaded by a good and wise man, who turns out to be Hipparchus. By introducing Hipparchus as though he were a god, Socrates embarks on an unexpected rehabilitation of an Athenian villain. Having just demonstrated that everyone loves the good, and having just accused the comrade of harboring a hidden intent of which he is not even aware, Socrates proceeds to tell a story that seeks to understand the tyrant Hipparchus as one who sought the good. On the surface, this story will deny that Hipparchus was in fact a tyrant and liken his rule to that of Kronos (whose reputation was, of course, itself not entirely untarnished). Perhaps, then, Socrates means to follow his argument that all men love the good by examining the most difficult case—the good loved by the tyrant. To make Hipparchus a good guy is necessary therefore not so much to show that he was not a tyrant as simply to understand tyranny. We are confronted first with a surface phenomenon. Convention will have set its worth, but as soon as the phenomenon becomes a puzzle for us, this worth is called into question. In trying to make sense of it, we are forced to get beneath the conventional surface—to mine for its true significance. This mining for truth is experienced as a movement from the less to the more valuable. Now, the comrade thinks of no worth those who think it worth profiting from things of no worth. He holds cheaters in contempt. Socrates means to show him first that to understand what makes cheaters tick, you have to understand them in light of the good at which, perhaps without even realizing it, their activity aims. To bring his point home, Socrates, before our very eyes, transforms an infamous Athenian tyrant into a "good and wise man" (228b2), "the eldest and wisest of the sons of Peisistratus" (228b5–6). Moreover, the good at which the tyrant aims is especially revealing, for to love everything is to reveal that everything is in principle lovable. We experience the true good in mining for the hidden good understood to be present even in what at first seems worthless.

Socrates' purified version of Hipparchus first showed "beautiful deeds of wisdom" (228b6–7) by bringing the poems of Homer to Athens and compelling the rhapsodes to perform the various parts in sequence—thereby assuring Homer's original intent. After that, he patronized living poets, bringing Anacreon and Simonides to Athens, presumably so that they might make poems. The poems of the poets deal with particulars but make them grander than they seem in ordinary life. One cannot be certain of Hipparchus's intent, but it seems plausible that he wished to beautify his world in the manner of those adepts whose wise sayings make things beautiful in the law courts. Apparently, however, this does not suffice, for Hipparchus proceeds to try to educate the citizens of Athens, not so much for their sakes but so that he might rule the best of men—that is, to make himself more splendid. Hipparchus does not begrudge these men his wisdom, for he is himself *kalos te k'agathos*—beautiful and good. After the townsmen come to wonder at this wisdom, Hipparchus extends his generosity and spreads his seed to the countryside, giving of himself by setting up statues of the god Hermes throughout the town and the country, statues inscribed with Hipparchus's own wise sayings set to meter. These are meant to overshadow the traditional wise sayings inscribed at Delphi—"Know thyself" and "Nothing in excess." We will return in a moment to these statues. For now, it is important to see that everything Hipparchus does in Athens may be understood to have as its purpose the reforming of his world so as to make it altogether good. But Hipparchus does not proceed by teasing out the goodness latent in things otherwise worth little or nothing. He knows that the good is the good-for, but he understands himself to be the him for whom it is good. Hipparchus grasps, in his way, the dependence of the good on the soul but understands this to mean that his soul is the fixed measure of all goodness. The Athenians are called "his citizens" (228e2), and the wisdom to be memorialized is regularly "his wisdom" (228d3–4, 228e6)—as though wisdom were an object to be possessed and placed on a statue. For Hipparchus, Hipparchus is the good, and he knows just who this Hipparchus is. The disagreement of subsequent generations over the true identity of Hipparchus is surely a sign of how badly he fared in his attempt to pass this knowledge along. Socrates may rehabilitate Hipparchus in this dialogue, discovering the worth in one worth little or nothing—Hipparchus does display with a certain purity the fundamental feature of the human soul—but even this rehabilitated Hipparchus is a tyrant.

The goodness of the tyrant is that he understands better than most the dependence of the good on the soul. For him the question "What is love of gain?" would lead not to the question "What is gain?" but to the question "Who is the lover?" And yet, the tyrant is finally a fool—*anoētos*—because of the way he understands himself. This problem is revealed in Socrates' account of the Hermae erected by Hipparchus as monuments. Hipparchus wants to be like Homer, admired for his wisdom. At the same time, he is aware that poems once cut loose from the poet are objects that may be appropriated by others for their own purposes. Rhapsodes need not sing the whole of Homer's *Iliad*; nor need they sing the poem in the order in which it was meant to be heard. A poem may present wisdom but with the consequence that what is most important, the wise man, vanishes. Hipparchus began by buying poems but then moved on to buying poets.

In his own case, Hipparchus seeks to overcome the dilemma of the separation of the poet from his poem by finding a way to make himself present alongside his wisdom even when he is absent. He understands that the good as the good-for is always dependent upon some soul or self, but, by thinking the soul can be directly represented, he misunderstands its being. In making himself, as what the good is *for*, an object to be placed alongside other objects, Hipparchus unwittingly reverts to the view that the good exists in the manner of other beings. He poeticizes the good. Socrates describes his plan as follows:

> But, when those citizens around the town had been educated by him, and wondered at him for his wisdom, planning in turn to educate those in the country, he stood up Hermae for them along the roads in the middle of the town and of each of the demes. And then he selected from his own wisdom, which he both learned and which he himself discovered, those things he considered to be wisest, and having stretched these poems of his and examples of his wisdom into elegiac meter, he inscribed them on Hermae in order that, first, his citizens would not wonder at those wise writings at Delphi—both the "Know thyself" and the "Nothing in excess" and the rest of this sort—but rather that they would consider the utterances of Hipparchus wise, so that while going here and there, and reading, and getting a taste of his wisdom, they might continue going back and forth from the country and also be educated in the rest. And the inscriptions are twofold. On the one hand, on the places on the left of each Hermes, it has been inscribed, saying that the Hermes stands in the middle of the town and of the deme. On the other hand, on the places on the right, it [or he] says, "This is a memorial of Hipparchus; walk thinking just things." And there are many other beautiful poems inscribed on other Hermae. But, indeed,

this one is on the Steiria Road, on which it [he] says, "This is a memorial of Hipparchus; deceive not a friend." I, then, would not, I suppose, dare to deceive you who are a friend to me nor distrust him being such as he is. . . . (228d3–229b3)

There is a good deal to be investigated here. Socrates goes on to provide an alternate version of the story of the killing of Hipparchus by Harmodius and Aristogeiton. So, apparently, Hipparchus was not very successful in immortalizing himself—he is the Ozymandias of his day. It also is probably no accident that just after Thucydides' own revision of this story in the context of the erotic longing that overtakes the city of Athens in the Sicilian expedition, the moving force of that expedition, Alcibiades, is brought down having been accused of the mutilation of the Hermae. But let us restrict ourselves to the passage cited.

Hipparchus wishes to set up monuments that will stand not only for his wisdom but, more important, for himself.[15] What exactly is an Athenian wandering the roads meant to experience when coming upon one of these statues? Not simply the wisdom of the sayings. For this, neither statue nor proprietary claim would be necessary. Hipparchus wishes to reproduce by way of these surrogates the awe in which the Athenians hold his person. Accordingly, he attempts to find a way to reproduce in the Athenians the experience of being in the presence of someone uttering a uniquely wise saying. Now, the inscription on the left is given to us in indirect discourse, and so we do not know exactly what form it takes. We are told that it locates the Hermae by town and deme, but we do not know whether we alone are being told that it is a Hermes or whether this is part of what is inscribed. It could be in the first person or in the third—"I am a Hermes and stand here in Colonus," or "I stand in Colonus," or "This Hermes stands in Colonus," or "This stands in Colonus." And is the god speaking or the statue? In any case, on the left, either the god or the statue announces its location; this presumably distinguishes it from all the other statues. We are given examples of two of the right-side inscriptions. They are directly quoted, but they are introduced in such a way that, once again, we do not know who or what is meant to be speaking, since *phēsin* may be translated either "he said" or "it said." On the left side of the left side, both say, "This [right here] is a memorial [or memory] of Hipparchus." If it is the god who says that this is a memorial of Hipparchus, what follows immediately to the right will be

15 · According to Thucydides (6.27), the Hermae were blocklike statues commonly set up at the entrances to private homes and temples. The description here is not very elaborate, but in general one may say that each Hermes is a figure accompanied by a pair of inscriptions—one on the right and one on the left, although it is not altogether clear what this means. Perhaps the two are visible at the same time, perhaps not.

a quotation; the god will cite a wise saying of Hipparchus, but by lending its authority to the saying, it will diminish the authority of Hipparchus. *Phēsin*, of course, could simply mean "it says," in which case, perhaps Hipparchus is meant to be the speaker of the whole line. Or the statue could identify *itself* as a memorial, and Hipparchus would be left as the speaker of the wise saying to the right. Or is the *saying* and not the statue meant to be the memorial? Hipparchus attempts to make himself permanent in his wisdom, but his intention is repeatedly thwarted by the difficulty of locating the soul from which the *logos* issues. First, we do not understand what the relation is between the statue and what is written on the statue. If the writing on the left has the form "I stand in Colonus," then the speaker is either the statue, which is quite impossible, for stone does not speak, or it is the god, in which case, the saying is not really true, for the god only symbolically stands in Colonus. Nor do we understand how the writing on the left is to be combined with the writing on the right, where an undetermined speaker tells us that this is either a memory of or a memorial to Hipparchus. And this same sentence introduces to its immediate right the quite different Hipparchan bon mots inscribed on each statue, each meant to remind us of one man—Hipparchus. What is clear is that Hipparchus has not found a way to celebrate himself for his wisdom by placing himself alongside his wisdom.

Hipparchus's true motive is revealed in the conclusion of the digression—the revisionist story of his death. In the standard version, Hipparchus was a tyrant who snubbed the sister of Harmodius by refusing to allow her to participate in a religious festival. Harmodius and his lover, Aristogeiton, then kill Hipparchus in a celebrated act of tyrannicide. Thucydides revises this account, first by citing evidence (inscriptions written on an altar and a pillar) to show that Hippias and not Hipparchus was tyrant and by providing an additional motive for the insult of Harmodius's sister—that Harmodius had twice rebuffed Hipparchus's sexual advances.[16] In Thucydides, this account is surrounded by a larger story of a time in Athens in which "*erōs* fell upon all alike to sail away" to conquer Sicily, clearly suggesting a connection between erotic and political rivalry.[17] Here, in his own revision, Socrates changes the character of the erotic rivalry. Hipparchus steals one of the students of Harmodius and Aristogeiton (Socrates knew but no longer remembers his name). This youth, who was beautiful and well born, wondered at their wisdom, but after being with Hipparchus (a sexual double entendre), he came to despise them. Being thus dishonored, Harmodius and Aristogeiton kill Hipparchus. It is not the slight to Harmodius's sister,

16 · For this account, see Thucydides 1.20 and 6.54–59.
17 · Thucydides 6.24.3.

nor the love of Aristogeiton for Harmodius, nor their love for the beautiful youth that motivates the tyrannicide; it is jealously over a reputation for wisdom. But how much has Socrates really changed? The *erōs* of Harmodius and Aristogeiton is politicized. In seeking to make themselves objects of admiration, of wonder, they mirror Hipparchus's tyrannical desire to be the beloved of all mankind—to be the good.

In Socrates' famous account of logographic necessity in the *Phaedrus*, he tells Phaedrus that a perfect speech, like an animal, must be an organic whole, with each part in its proper place. Yet a corpse too has this organic structure. An animal must move; it must be animated—ensouled. Socrates says that a *logos*, like an animal, must have a head (264c2–5) only eleven lines after he has addressed Phaedrus as "dear head" (264a8). *Logos* requires an addressee if it is to be animated. In the immediate sequel, Socrates contrasts the perfect speech with what is written on the tomb of Midas. There are two parts to the tomb—a statue of a girl in bronze and the inscribed *logos*. We take the speech to come from the girl, but this is an illusion, for they are really quite separate. The sign that the two are not together is that the inscription is artfully designed so as to let you begin anywhere; the four lines can be read in any order. The following is Seth Benardete's commentary on this passage.

> A nonliving being speaks, shaped in the likeness of a living being; it utters a speech about a nonliving being as if he were not nonliving. The speech itself is without any temporal order; any line can be put before or after any other. Its indifference to temporal order seems to be at one with its speaking of eternity. . . . The speech of the girl is random; the image of the girl is lifeless. The juxtaposition of the two points to the difficulty of putting them together. No tinkering with the syntax, though it may impose a necessity on the sequence, would make the utterance whole. It cannot be a whole unless it can be the utterance of the girl, and it cannot be her utterance unless she is alive.[18]

What is missing from Midas's tomb is soul.

Plato writes a dialogue in which Socrates defends cheating by understanding it as love of the good. In its most memorable passage, Socrates defends a tyrant by calling him good and wise. The wisdom of Hipparchus consists of his awareness that he *is* in some sense the good. His foolishness consists in taking this too seriously, in so treasuring himself as good that he cannot let go of himself. In misunderstanding himself—his soul—as something that can be made a permanent object of adoration, Hipparchus turns himself to

18 · Seth Benardete, *The Rhetoric of Morality and Philosophy* (Chicago and London: University of Chicago Press, 1991), 177.

gold and therewith becomes something of little or no worth. This reversal is rather funny. The *Hipparchus* is generally thought to be a trifle—if genuine, something Plato perhaps invented in his idle hours. Nevertheless, it proves to raise the highest of questions—the nature of philosophy in its relation to the good. Accordingly, the *Hipparchus* may be said to imitate what it is about, and so to demonstrate the manner in which philosophy, in finding the good everywhere, makes something from what seems at first nothing. In this, it is not tyrannical. It is true that the soul is inseparable from the good. But the soul can celebrate itself unqualifiedly as the good only if it knows what it is celebrating—if it has self-knowledge. Failing this, it must give itself up to that activity in which it most experiences itself as good. In taking up the least of things, in understanding their true significance and elevating their worth, it makes them good and thereby indirectly experiences itself in its goodness. This serious playfulness, the signature feature of philosophy, accounts for why Plato can be at once so serious about what is ordinarily taken to be superficial while at the same time being so deeply funny.

CHAPTER II

Plato's *Phaedrus*

Erōs *and the Structure of Soul*

The myth of the soul in the *Phaedrus* seems the loftiest and the most beautiful moment in the Platonic dialogues. No wonder, then, that its apparent subject should be what seem the two pillars of Platonic metaphysics—the immortal soul and the eternal ideas.[1] A certain irreverence, however, may be necessary to unearth just how central it is to Platonic philosophy. The *Phaedrus* as a whole divides in two.[2] Its first part consists of three speeches on love: one supposedly written by the speechwriter Lysias, in which a non-lover speaking to a beloved praises the advantages for a youth of sexual arrangements with someone who does not love him; a second speech invented off the cuff by Socrates, in which a man concealing his love praises nonlove to his beloved; and finally a third speech, in which Socrates, recanting his previous speech, addresses a beloved and praises love as divine madness. The second part of the dialogue is a long analysis of rhetoric and especially of writing in which Socrates gives an account of the perfect writing as subject to what he calls logographic necessity. In a good writing, just as in an animal, every part of the whole is where it is for a reason. Nothing can be moved or altered without threatening the integrity of the whole. Since the relation between these two parts of the *Phaedrus* itself is very dark, the dialogue begs us to ask, What makes it, as a writing, a whole? How does the writing about what a writing ought to be conform to its own standard?

Roughly speaking, it is possible to say that the first part of the *Phaedrus* is about *erōs* as a species of madness (or, as the idiom in Greek has it, being "out of oneself") or irrationality, and its second part is about *logos*, speech or reason. The problematic togetherness of the parts is therefore the prob-

1 · See Ronna Burger, *The Phaedo: A Platonic Labyrinth* (New Haven, CT, and London: Yale University Press, 1984), 1–2.

2 · See Seth Benardete, *The Rhetoric of Morality and Philosophy* (Chicago and London: University of Chicago Press, 1991), 103; and Ronna Burger, *Plato's* Phaedrus: *A Defense of a Philosophical Art of Writing* (Birmingham: University of Alabama Press, 1980), 3–7.

lematic togetherness of the rational and the irrational. If the *Phaedrus* is an animal, it is a rational animal. The problem of its wholeness is therefore the same as the problem of the wholeness of the rational animal.[3] The question that unifies the *Phaedrus* is thus the question of the human soul. Logographic necessity does govern the *Phaedrus* insofar as it mirrors the problematic unity of a certain kind of being—the human soul. What is the being of something that is essentially connected to the eternal and unchanging things by its longing to come to "be with" them—that is, by its longing to change?

The *Phaedrus* opens with the following question: "Dear Phaedrus," asks Socrates, "to where and from where?" Now, Phaedrus's answer—that he is out walking for his health—turns out to be a lie. He has a written copy of Lysias's speech concealed under his cloak and has been trying to memorize it. Phaedrus therefore presents a sort of parody of the central question of the dialogue—the source of motion or change in the human soul. The dialogue begins with questions about the origin and the end of Phaedrus's motion. The true answers to these questions are peculiar because they are the same. Phaedrus has just come from Lysias, but because he has with him the written version of Lysias's speech, his present motion may be said to be toward Lysias. Its purpose is the incorporation of Lysias's speech. Self-motion—the puzzle of the dialogue—apparently has something to do with going to the place from which you have come. To see why, we need to return to the myth.

Socrates' second speech is a recantation (*palinōidia* may mean either "a taking back" or "a saying over"). He claims that his first speech (now attributed to Phaedrus) was shameful; it was an attack on *erōs*, who is, after all, a god, or at least divine. *Erōs* is a kind of madness, but Socrates had erred in thinking all madness to be bad. Some madness is divine.[4] This first part of the speech contains virtually no argument save some extremely questionable etymology that turns on the addition of a tau to transform *manikē* ("madness") into *mantikē* ("prophecy") and the lengthening of an omicron

---

3 · See Benardete, *Rhetoric of Morality and Philosophy*, 103–5.

4 · Socrates divides madness into four kinds—prophetic, purifying, poetic (or muse-inspired), and erotic. It is worth noting that Socrates makes this division having called on the Muses to assist him in his first speech and directly after refusing to complete that speech because, possessed by nymphs, he had begun to utter epic verse. He then claims that his soul is prophetic and has ordered him to recant so as to purify himself. Socrates is therefore so thoroughly divinely mad that the problem (the first speech), the awareness of it as a problem, and the solution to the problem are all forms of divine madness. So Socrates' mad praise of moderation (his first speech) is to be cured by a moderate praise of madness—moderate because it will turn out to be quite rational to be mad (244a).

to an omega to transform *oionoistikē*—a fanciful compound of *oiēsis* ("notion"), *nous* ("mind"), and *historia* ("inquiry")—into *oiōnistikē* ("augury"). This all seems quite bizarre until one reflects that the Homeric version of *erōs* has an omicron instead of an omega and its genitive form *erous* gets transformed by the addition of a tau in Attic Greek to *erotos*.[5] The playful etymologies thus hint at a real etymology. Now, in Homeric Greek, *erōs* may mean something as neutral as desire. Only later does it come to mean exclusively sexual love. The real etymology therefore points to a real transformation in the meaning of erotic love. Socrates had given as his reason for recanting that he was almost speaking epic verse and that he had forgotten that Eros was a god. The transformation of the meaning of *erōs* has something to do with its deification, which, in turn, has something to do with the impulse behind not only etymology but also behind personification (Socrates personifies madness as well as *erōs* in this section). The first two speeches were not true (*etumos*, which ordinarily in later writers means only the true sense of a word according to its origin). We discover this through etymology—an attempt to find significance where previously there seemed only to be arbitrary change. However, these etymologies are false. The truth behind them is *erōs* insofar as what distinguishes *erōs* from ordinary desire is its tendency to imbue everything with significance. Idealizing *erōs*, making it a god, is in fact an example of *erōs*. Socrates begins his second speech with an etymological account in order to induce us to do etymology. We are seduced etymologically while being shown that the true significance of etymology is erotic seduction. A recantation is necessary because the first two speeches ignored this idealizing character of *erōs*, treating it as though it simply meant the desire to copulate. But *erōs* is about something else altogether. You only think you want sex. Socrates therefore begins his second speech by announcing that *erōs* is a god and then distinguishes between divine and human madness in order to emphasize that the erotic cannot be understood apart from the divine. To see what he means, we will have to turn to the question of the soul.

In the second part of the speech,[6] Socrates introduces an account of "the truth of the nature of the soul concerning both the divine and the human" (245c2–3). The argument is designed to show that the soul is immortal and runs something like this. If life is a movement, and if whatever moves itself by its own nature could never stop moving itself, then whatever moves itself would be deathless. Now, if there is anything that moves itself, it is soul. But there must be something self-moving. If there is motion, it must have a

---

5 · For this observation, see Benardete, *Rhetoric of Morality and Philosophy*, 133–34.
6 · Benardete sees that the speech has nine parts (*Rhetoric of Morality and Philosophy*, 132–33).

beginning. A beginning cannot be moved by anything else, or it would not be a beginning. Since there is motion, there must be a beginning of motion, which is therefore self-moved. This is what we call soul. As its very nature is self-motion, it cannot cease moving or die; hence, it is immortal.

There are enormous difficulties with this proof, as there are with every proof for the immortality of the soul in Plato (difficulties of which he is perfectly aware).[7] Its first words, *pasa psuchē*, can mean either "all soul" or "every soul," and so even if the argument were sound, it would remain a question whether individual souls were proved immortal or only something like the nature of soul or world soul. Nor is it particularly clear that self-motion and life are the same, or that soul is simply a principle of life. As we have seen, Aristotle couples life and awareness as the twin meaning of soul. Socrates never explains how self-moving soul is supposed to move other things, and so all he succeeds in demonstrating is that if there is motion, there must be "something" that is not moved itself but moves everything else. Whatever that may be, it is not so clear that it has anything to do with my soul. This, however, is nothing but the ambiguity with which we began; *pasa psuchē* as *all* soul may be understood in some way as a self-moving cause of the motion of everything else, but that need not mean that *every* soul is such a cause.

The problem can be stated somewhat differently. To say that the soul moves itself is to say that there is nothing external to it that initiates its motion; soul is not derivative. But this means that soul has as its very being to undergo motion or change—it is always becoming what it is not yet. Accordingly, it is never anything stable. That Plato means to indicate something to this effect is made clear from the almost complete absence of the verb "to be" in this account.[8] From 245c to 246a, there is a string of about a dozen nominal sentences—sentences in which nouns are juxtaposed with the copula left implicit but not actually stated.[9] These nouns are put together only because we put them together, just as it is we who couple things or pair them by putting them together in thought. Venus and earth, although millions of miles apart, may be twin planets, while two cars parked next to each other are not a pair unless we think of them as a pair. Plato therefore calls our attention to the characteristic "movement" of soul.

7 · See my "Socrates' Pre-Socratism: Some Remarks on the Structure of Plato's *Phaedo*," in *Review of Metaphysics* 33, no. 3 (Mar. 1980): 559–77, as well as my *Ancient Tragedy and the Origins of Modern Science* (Carbondale: Southern Illinois University Press, 1988), 124–33.

8 · I owe this observation to Seth Benardete.

9 · There are only two sentences containing the verb "to be"—one (245d3–4) says that the soul is ungenerated, and one (245e7–246a2) says that if the argument is as has been said, then soul is ungenerated and immortal.

It "rules over" bodies insofar as it brings them together in thought; in this movement, it shows itself. It is therefore not in the content but in the form of Socrates' argument that soul makes its appearance. Soul appears as a result of what it does and is known only relative to this motion. It is therefore not a being like other beings.

At the same time, this account of the radical independence of soul from other "beings" is at odds with the account that follows it of the structure of soul as two horses and a driver.[10] According to that account, human beings move themselves insofar as they are lovers. The source of motion in the lover is a lack, which he recognizes by looking at the beloved as an object of desire. But if the soul were truly to be self-moving, it would have to contain this object within itself. And yet, were that the case, it would not move at all; having contained its desire, it would come to a rest. Thus, while eternal motion presupposes self-motion in Socrates' explicit account, it is also at odds with it. The self-motion of soul can be eternal only if the object of desire is simultaneously within itself and beyond reach. In a way, this is simply the problem of *pasa psuchē*. All soul has eternal motion, and so self-motion, as its nature. What it means to be a soul is to move. But any particular soul must be radically incomplete and "other-directed" if it is to move at all. It must take its bearings from what is external to itself.

Accordingly, in the next sections of the myth, when Socrates attempts to give an account of the structure or form (*idea*) of soul as the being whose being it is to be self-moving, he will describe it as a pair of horses and a driver. However, the soul will be moved not by itself as a whole but by a part of itself.[11] To give an account—a *logos*—of the motion of something always means to give an account of it as moved from without. Thus, to attempt to describe the structure of soul as self-moving is to turn it into a being like all other beings, and that is to put it at rest—to kill it. To give an account of

10 · What all of this means is that there will be no order common to soul and what it moves—the bodies under heaven and the superheavenly beings Socrates will shortly call "being [*ousia*] really / in being [*ontōs*] being [*ousa*]." So, for example, there will be no clear connection between what a soul sees beyond heaven and this soul being well ordered. There is no indication that when the driver sticks his head into the superheavenly space, what he looks at has any effect whatsoever on his ability to control his horses. This has something to do with the fact that what nourishes him (superheavenly sights) is quite different from what nourishes them (pasturage beneath heaven).

11 · The problem was in a way already indicated grammatically at 245c5–6, where the argument for the deathlessness of soul begins with the claim that "what moves another [*to kinoun*] [is] also by another being moved [*kinoumenon*]." Since *kinoumenon* is both the middle and passive participle of the verb *kinein*, there is an interesting ambiguity. Is what moves another also moved by another, or is it moving itself by another?

soul without doing this is the task of the rest of Socrates' speech—the myth of the soul as two horses and a driver.

Soul is like a winged pair and a driver. It is not at first clear what the pair is of, what the wings attach to, or whether this triad also involves a chariot. The pair turn out to be horses, it never comes to be clear what the wings attach to, and the chariot is left altogether out of the account. Accordingly, we never know what it is that holds the parts of soul together—although whatever the chariot is, it seems fair to say that the principle of the unity of the soul is at the same time the burden that retards its ascent.

Socrates begins with a comparison of our horses to those of the gods. Ours are mixed—one itself beautiful and good and born from the beautiful and good, and one the opposite and from the opposite. The horses of the gods are both good and from the good. So immortal souls—both ours and those of the gods—are made up of horses generated from other horses? And if our souls contain for all eternity a defective horse, then what does it mean that Socrates goes on to give an account of our fall? Our doom looks to be preordained. On one version of Socrates' account, our condition is permanent. We are not to blame, but neither can we hope. On the other version of Socrates' account, our condition is the result of our fall. There is hope, but also blame.

The account of the souls of the gods is similarly problematic (moreover, they are never explicitly said to have souls). Socrates says the power by nature of our wingedness is "to lead the weighty upward" (246d6), but then what would it mean for the soul of a god, to which there would be no resistance—no weight—to be winged? Just what do Socrates' gods do with themselves? As they are souls, they fly in Zeus's celestial army, taking excursions to hyperurania (the place above heaven) to take in the sights (*théai*). However, one of the goddesses (*theaí*), Hestia, stays at home. Apparently, she has no ear for the (as yet unpunctuated) accents of Greek and is content to look at herself. Now, while Zeus cares for everything, Hestia, as goddess of the hearth, looks after her own—the home. That it is possible for her to stay at home calls attention to the fact that the others need a reason to go out. Why do perfect gods (*theoí*) go elsewhere to look at sights (*théai*)? Why are not they themselves the sights to be looked at? Zeus leads a curious army—perfectly suited to the ascent beyond heaven but, for that very reason, with no motive to go. It is easy for the gods to move precisely because they do not long to move. Thus, among them there is no envy or jealousy (247a7) but also no *erōs*. Socrates gives a double account of the gods. Zeus points to the perfect power to move, Hestia to the utter lack of motive to do so. As *théai*, *theaí* have no need to go anywhere. The gods, then, are the problematic combination of perfection and self-motion. And they are precisely what we long to be. At the same time, by making them so problematic,

Socrates has tacitly called into question the possibility of being what they are said to be. Must souls be imperfect in order to be at all? Is this what it means to characterize them as erotic?

If the gods are problematic in their being, so is the superheavenly place that they visit. It is a place of colorless, shapeless, intangible "sights." When gods go there, what precisely do they see?

> And in the circuit it may look down on justice itself, and it may look down on moderation, and it may look down on knowledge—not to which a coming to be is attributed nor which is somewhere being otherwise / other things [*alla*] in another of those we now call beings, but being the knowledge in that which is really / in being being. And the rest similarly, beholding and feasting upon [*hestiatheisa*] those really / in being being, plunging again into the inside of heaven, it came home, and when returning, its driver, standing the horses at the manger, both pitched ambrosia [to them] and after gave them nectar to drink. (247d5–e6)

These beings are really real—really, really real—but it is all very atomistic. Like a nominal sentence, hyperurania is a collection of predicates put next to one another without any account of their connection. All of them really are, but none of them are any of the others—justice is, but justice is not knowledge. It is not clear whether the gods sitting on the back of heaven see only one being—that is, the being moves with the back of heaven—or a variety of beings. In either case, there is something arbitrary about what they see and the order in which they see it. Unlike the perfect writing, hyperurania is no *kosmos*. Each god puts together its vision in an idiosyncratic way. This is yet more true of human beings, whose drivers spend a good deal of time trying to control their horses so as to avoid being crushed by the competition. At the very best, then, human beings get a partial view of an already atomized spectacle.

Even were the accounts of the superheavenly and of the souls of the gods coherent, the account of our ascent is riddled with difficulties. One of the effects of erotic longing is that the lover forgets mothers—not merely his own but all mothers (252a3).[12] Somewhat later, when describing Hera, the only goddess save Hestia mentioned in the account, Socrates says that those following her seek a kingly beloved (253b1–2). The gender of the beloved is masculine. At 248d2, Socrates makes clear that the birth that follows the incarnation of soul is of an *anēr*—a he-man. And perhaps most puzzling,

---

12 · "But it counts as nothing that it has forgotten mothers and siblings and all comrades, and that property is destroyed through lack of care." The verb is singular, its object plural. Hence, one seems to forget all mothers or motherhood as such.

at 251a1, he refers to sex for the purpose of begetting children as "contrary to nature." All of this calls our attention to what is the most evident difficulty of the account thus far—that *erōs* has been understood solely as a species of homosexual *erōs*—that is, pederasty. Socrates gives an account of birth that altogether abstracts from sexual generation, so much so that instead of sex being the cause of birth, birth is the cause of sex. Mothers are pointedly omitted from the account—they must be forgotten—in order to leave behind the origin of human beings as a one coming from two. Siblings have to be forgotten because what ties them together is a common source of generation. All of this is not surprising given how the account began. Soul as self-moving would have to be responsible for itself, self-generated. This self-idealizing embodied in the speech is how we represent ourselves to ourselves and seems to be the necessary condition for understanding oneself as self-moved. However, as it is not simply true, it leads to a series of contradictions in the images used to account for the motion of soul that give the argument a certain circularity.

Souls need nourishment to grow wings, but what nourishes them is to be obtained only from a place where their wings alone can take them. They must therefore feed on false nourishment (*doxa*—"seeming" or "opinion"), but, of course, this will hold them back as well. Souls are not able to reach the superheavenly place because they struggle among themselves, and yet they struggle among themselves because they are not able to reach the superheavenly place. They therefore fall because they lose their wings, but they lose their wings because they are injured in their fall. The regaining of their wings is described with such ambiguity that it is not clear whether it is the cause of an ascent or because of an ascent (249d4–8). We see souls choosing new lives but only for their second incarnation. Because they choose on the basis of what they have been in their first lives, we have no idea what it might mean for a soul to be incarnated for a first time. Such a soul would have to choose itself without yet being anything. The account of the birth of the soul thus presupposes that the soul already exists. The soul that forgets mothers is the soul that thinks of itself as coming from itself alone. To understand itself as self-moving, it must understand itself as immortal. But it is difficult to understand how a soul that is forever changes at all. Self-motion seems to require both mortality and immortality. The self that moves itself must be the same as itself; at the same time, the self that moves itself must be other than itself. Socrates' account of *erōs* is meant to "satisfy" both demands. The linear version of this issue is the argument about recollection.

Only the souls with drivers who once got their heads outside of heaven are human. Every human soul is therefore defined by having previously seen something of the beings that it might in principle recollect. The stimulus for this recollection is the glimpse of some semblance of what was once seen in hyperurania. We know it to be a semblance because it is beautiful. Because the very being of beauty consists in appearing (an illusory good is not really good, but a beautiful illusion remains beautiful), of all the hyperuranian beings, the beautiful is the only one to be really real (*to on ontōs*) here below. As the other hyperuranian beings appear here as beautiful, beauty is our privileged access to what we have forgotten. Every soul will be moved by what it finds beautiful, but what it finds beautiful will depend on the character of its partial glimpse of the beings.

This seems a rather beautiful account both of how we learn and of how love can be universal in significance but still inevitably idiosyncratic. There is a hitch, however. In order to move ourselves back to where we came from, we need to see that what is beautiful to us here is only a namesake. We must be moved by what we see (and here—250e1–252a1—the language is extremely erotic), and at the same time, we must discover that what we see is not really what moves us. We have fallen in love with a beloved having the form of a god (251a2). Love is, after all, of a person—not of justice showing itself as beautiful. But this means that we do not fall in love with a namesake of the being or beings we once saw; we rather fall in love with an image (251a6) of the god whom we first followed in our ascent. We fall in love with a soul that saw the beings and not with the beings that it saw. *Erōs* is apparently never directly connected to the beings themselves. Consequently, what we are remembering when we look at a beloved is simply another version of our present experience.

This is confirmed by what happens when the beloved is absent. We react in the same way to the absence of the imitation that we do to the absence of the original (which, as a god and not a being, was also an imitation). In both cases, the absence leads to motion by stimulating memory to generate an image of the beloved. The image is present as being absent and so makes self-motion possible. The self-motion of soul is therefore only possible given the perpetual nonpresence of the beloved. This nonpresence is the truth of *erōs*. It is therefore only after the lover turns the beloved into an image of something else that erotic love begins.

How, then, does this perpetual nonpresence of the beloved work?[13] Every human being, as once a follower of some god, chooses his beloved accordingly—the beloved mirroring the nature of the god. But how do lovers discover which god it is that they once followed? "Tracking, they discover from themselves the nature of their god" (252e7–253a1). The lover, then, chooses the beloved as a mirror of the god, who is, in turn, a mirror of himself. In pursuing the beloved, he therefore unwittingly pursues himself. The

---

13 · For this argument, see Benardete, *Rhetoric of Morality and Philosophy*, 147–49; and Burger, *Plato's* Phaedrus, 62–64.

image the lover pursues, which he projects on the beloved thinking it to be of a god, is an idealized version of himself. It is himself and not himself. *Erōs* as the pursuit of the self by the self is therefore the self-motion of soul. It is possible only because the soul mistakes itself for another. The soul externalizes itself and in so doing idealizes itself—it makes itself beautiful.

What are the consequences of all this for our understanding of the threefold structure of soul? Socrates returns to the horses in our soul toward the end of the myth, where we get the following description:

> Accordingly, the one of the pair being in the more beautiful position—with regard to form [*eidos*] both upright and well-jointed, carrying its neck high, hook-nosed, white to see, black of eye, a lover of honor with both moderation and shame, and a comrade of true opinion—is driven without being struck, by command and speech alone. Then again, the other—crooked, great, having been put together at random, strongnecked, short of neck and throat, snub-nosed, black-skinned, gray-eyed and bloodshot, comrade of hubris and imposture, with regard to ears hairy and deaf—scarcely submits to a whip with goads. (253d3–e5)

While the white horse has the white hat, so to speak, it is rather curious that in the subsequent account, the black horse proves to be *the* moving force in the soul. There would be no pursuit of the beloved at all were it not for the insistent urging of the black horse, both physically and in speech. It is also rather striking that of the two horses, it is the black who insists on holding to agreements and who argues (254c5–d1). Among the unflattering descriptions of this horse we find "snub-nosed," Socrates' notoriously distinctive feature.[14] We also find hubris, the charge frequently leveled at Socrates.[15] Socrates thus seems to use a projection of himself as black horse to describe how *erōs* is a projection of the self.

All of this leads us to suspect that the easy distinction between a good and bad part of the soul, and so its tripartite division, is not so simple as it first appears. Socrates initially pairs the driver and the white horse in their opposition to the demands of the black horse (at 254b2, he pairs them in a dual participle). He then goes on to describe how the driver controls the pair of horses.

> And they [the three parts of the soul] came to be before him [the beloved] and saw the visage of the beloved flashing like lightning. Looking, the driver's memory was borne back toward the nature of beauty. And he saw it again, mounted with moderation on a hallowed pedestal. Having seen, he was afraid, and, being awed, he fell backward, and at

14 · See, for example, *Theaetetus* 143e8–9.
15 · See, for example, *Symposium* 216b7.

the same time, he was compelled to draw back the reins so excessively as to make both of the pair of horses sit on their haunches—the one willingly on account of not resisting, but the hubristic one very unwillingly. (254b3–c3)

The verb tense changes to aorist in the middle of the account, and so the whole experience is presented in past time. The driver's "decision" to fall back from the beloved is therefore presented as a memory—almost as a conditioned reflex. In projecting an image to rein himself, the driver's memory is suspiciously like the present-time experience of the black horse.

Yanking the bit with force from the teeth of the hubristic horse, he [the driver] bloodied the bad-mouthing tongue and jaws, and, pushing legs and haunches to the earth, he gave [it] pains. When suffering the same thing often, the base one may cease from hubris. Only then, being humbled, does he follow the foresight of the driver, and when he sees the beautiful one, he is destroyed by fear. (254e2–8)

The connection is confirmed by the fact that the driver's experience is described in terms of feeling goads—exactly what he is said to inflict on the black horse to control it (254a1). The driver seems to be simply a black horse tamed by the memory of past experience. It is worth noting that the driver, presumably a human being, must have a soul itself consisting of two horses and a driver, and so on.

What might the nonmetaphorical meaning be of this reduction of the driver to the black horse? Is it possible that this account of *erōs* in terms of recollection is meant to indicate that we never have an immediate experience of what we call love, that the experience we call love is always already constituted by a "previous experience"? To be human, then, would be always to be looking back. This is what *erōs* as love of an image implies. What is at first read as present is in fact in the past tense. The experience of the immediate is always a recollection of what one has experienced. In this way, what moves us—what we long for—also always restrains us; that is, it represents our present longing in light of an ideal.

The white horse and driver were previously paired as the black horse and driver have just been. What, then, of the relation between the two horses? For that, we need first to ask about the beloved in the love relation.[16] The lover thinks of the beloved as a god and uses this god as a model when addressing his beloved. The beloved is supposed to become inspired by this image created by the lover. For the lover, it may be love at first sight, but to get love in return, he must transform his experience into words. But

16 · The following argument owes a great deal to Seth Benardete. See, for example, *Rhetoric of Morality and Philosophy*, 148–51.

since the lover's image was in fact unwittingly fashioned with himself as the model, the beloved is attracted to what he thinks is an image of himself but is in reality an idealized version of the lover. The beloved is not aware of this; he begins to feel a longing but is not quite sure what it is for. This, the birth of a lover from a beloved, is called by the beloved *philia*, friendship, rather than *erōs*. So now we have a beloved (that is, someone who is not in love, a nonlover) who is in fact in love but doesn't know it, and who calls his experience *philia*. But this is simply a description of the speaker in the speech of Lysias—a supposed nonlover praising the advantages of *philia*.

What has all of this to do with the white horse? The *Phaedrus* begins with three speeches on love.[17] The first, Lysias's speech, claims that the lover has no claim on the beloved. It is a utilitarian praise of dispassion that culminates in a praise of mind. The relation between lover and beloved articulated by Lysias is like the relation of the mind to the superheavenly beings. You love them; they do not return the favor. Lysias's speech is like the driver of the soul. Socrates' first speech, as a praise of moderation, seems at first to agree with Lysias, but in fact, it is given by one who conceals his love. This is the speech that Socrates attributes to Phaedrus, saying it came out of his mouth only because he was drugged (242d11–e1). Socrates says he is forced to speak as he does for the sake of Phaedrus. That is, the lover conceals his love, representing himself as moderate, because he is forced to project an image pleasing to his beloved. This appearance of moderation is like the white horse—noble, to be sure, but still a horse. The white horse is a projection of nobility by the black horse—an idealized version of both lover and beloved that serves as a check on unrestrained, immoderate *erōs*, the madness of which is praised in Socrates' second speech. The white horse is therefore the idealized version of the self that is both in the self and yet experienced as always other than the self. Love, as always of another, looks as though it undermines the self-motion of soul. If one simply loved oneself, there would be no self-motion; one would, like Hestia, stay at home, not changing or moving or growing at all. On the other hand, the consequence of loving what is utterly other than oneself would be something like self-contempt, and, though love means acknowledging a lack, it would be foolish to deny that it is something we love. Love is therefore always of what one thinks to be other but is really an idealized version of oneself projected as other than oneself. Of course, as idealized, it is actually in some sense other.

What, then, has happened to the tension between the soul as self-moving and the soul as having a form or structure? The soul seems to be a triple thing that collapses into a one. This does not occur all at once but rather

17 · For the relation of the three speeches on love to the three parts of the soul, see Benardete, *Rhetoric of Morality and Philosophy*, 152–54.

through a series of pairings. The driver and white horse, at one in their moderation, oppose the black horse. The driver is reduced to the memory of the awful experience of the black horse of its own imperfection. Finally, the white horse is reduced to the idealized projection of the black horse. In principle, it is therefore possible to think through the oneness of the soul. Each of its parts collapses into another. Yet, as this process always requires that the two that are collapsed be defined in terms of the third that remains, the reduction will never be completed all at once. The wholeness of the soul is a motion, but a motion with a certain structure. The truth of the soul is *erōs*, its experience of humbling itself in the pursuit of its own perfection. It is therefore connected to the divine, for the gods of the myth of the soul in the *Phaedrus* are nothing other than the white horses peculiar to the various kinds of human beings.

CHAPTER 12

The Grammar of Soul

The Middle Voice in Plato's Euthyphro

The *Euthyphro* is the Platonic dialogue about the holy—our relation to the gods. Its setting suggests a certain urgency, for Socrates is about to enter the court where he will hear the charges for which he will later be tried, convicted, and executed. This is the Socrates whom Plato immortalizes in his writings as the paradigmatic philosopher. So, one might say that in the *Euthyphro*, the best of men holds a conversation about the best of beings. While this should suffice to indicate the importance of the dialogue, it is no doubt not perfectly obvious that the way to approach this importance is a discussion of Greek grammar. Nevertheless, that is where we need to begin.

The English verb has two voices—active and passive. Voice is a fundamental feature of any verb since variations in tense, mood, aspect, person, and number must all occur in a voice—"he saw," "we were seen," "she will be seeing," "they may be seen," "to see," "having been seen," and so forth. "Voice," according to Emile Benveniste, "denotes a certain attitude of the subject with relation to the process—by which the process receives its fundamental determination."[1] Now, the Indo-European verbal system (we'll pay special attention to Plato's language, Attic Greek, in a moment) has not only active and passive voices; it also has a middle. Active and passive seem simple enough; the one involves actions done, the other actions undergone—"I hit" on the one hand and "I am hit" on the other. But the middle voice is harder; as its name suggests, it seems at first to be a sort of fuzzy intermediate—derivative from the more fundamental two voices—that, according to one Greek grammar, "usually denotes that the subject acts *on himself* or *for himself*"[2] (emphasis in the original). But how is it possible

1 · *Problems in General Linguistics* (Coral Gables, FL: University of Miami Press, 1971), 146. Much of what follows simply summarizes Benveniste's elegant discussion of the middle voice in Indo-European languages.

2 · Herbert Weir Smyth, *Greek Grammar* (Cambridge, MA: Harvard University Press, 1980), 107.

for a subject to do anything other than act on or for himself? This question, altogether natural, indicates why the boundaries of the middle voice are notoriously difficult to make out.

It is almost irresistible to think of the middle as a hybrid. Its very name (by the second century BC, it is called the *mesotēs*) suggests that it is a mean between active and passive produced by splitting the difference. This is especially true in Greek, where, with a few exceptions, middle and passive verb forms are identical, and one can determine which is meant only by the context. A middle, then, would be an active verb in which I am something like the passive object of my own action. In this, it is like the reflexive verb in modern European languages, which may be translated either as passive, or as active and taking the reflexive pronoun as an object, or in which the reflexivity seems to disappear altogether from view. *Sich interressieren* means "to be interested" or "to interest oneself." *Je me trouve* means "I find myself" or "I am." Yet it is of some interest that even here the priority of the passive to the middle is not so clear; *aquí se habla español* is translated "Spanish is spoken here," but a more literal rendering would be "Spanish speaks itself here."[3] And, while *je me souviens*—"I remember"— has a reflexive form, it is difficult to translate the reflexivity. In fact, there is every indication that historically in Indo-European languages, the original dualism was not active/passive but active/middle. Benveniste describes the dualism this way:

> In the active, the verbs denote a process that is accomplished outside the subject. In the middle ... the verb indicates a process centering in the subject, the subject being inside the process. ... Here the subject is the seat of the process ...; the subject is the center as well as the agent of the process; he achieves something which is being achieved in him. ...[4]

One can thus speculate that in Greek, some verbs lack a middle-passive form because the action they signal is too other-directed to support one, and some (called deponent verbs) lack an active form because their action is so internalized that it cannot even be contemplated apart from a transformation in the agent. *Aisthanesthai*, "to perceive," is such a verb.

Keeping the middle voice in mind, let us turn to Plato's *Euthyphro*. Middle-passive verb forms occur 291 times in the thirteen Stephanus pages of the dialogue. Of these, 83 have passive meanings and 208 have middle

3 · I have borrowed this example from an Internet posting by Carl W. Conrad, "Observations on Ancient Greek Voice," B-Greek Archives, May 27, 1997.
4 · *Problems in General Linguistics*, 148–49.

meanings. This distribution, however, is a little deceiving since 52 of these passive meanings occur in a single argument that extends over only a page and a half (10a–11b)—an argument that itself turns on the distinction between active and passive verbs and that would therefore be impossible to articulate without an unusual incidence of passive forms. In the eight pages prior to this argument, of the middle-passive forms, 19 are passive and 126 middle; in the four pages after, of 79 middle-passive forms, 10 are passive and 69 middle. Now, verbs are words of action, and, according to Socrates in the *Euthyphro*, "If something comes to be or is affected, not because it is something coming to be does it come to be, but because it comes to be, it is something coming to be" (10c1–3). Someone is loved (passive) because someone loves (active); accordingly, being loved exists because there is loving. Isn't it rather peculiar, then, that in a dialogue where Socrates makes such a strong claim about the dependence of passivity on activity in everything that comes to be or is affected—a claim that presumably covers all verbs—there should appear so many verbs that do not fit the paradigm, so that apart from the atypical argument that requires passives, by a proportion of more than seven to one, verbs with "passive" forms do not have passive meanings? What does it mean that for the purpose of his argument, Socrates ignores the whole range of "activity" described by the middle voice?

This is especially odd given his primary example. Of 52 passives in the argument, 29 involve the verb *philein*—"to love." The general problem might be stated this way. For both Plato (*Phaedrus* 245c) and Aristotle (*De Anima* III.9), soul is self-moving. When we try to make this intelligible to ourselves, we find ourselves dividing soul into a part that moves, and so is active, and a part that is moved, and so is passive. This, of course, simply begins a regress, for now we find ourselves asking how the part that moves the other part first moves itself. The middle does not allow itself to be deconstructed into active and passive elements. In an attempt to avoid this regress, both Plato and Aristotle turn to love as a way of explaining the self-motion of soul.[5] We are drawn out of ourselves by ourselves.

The *Euthyphro* begins with the words *ti neōteron*—"What's new?" or, more literally, "What has come to be newer?" It is a common way of speaking of innovation, even revolutionary innovation. Euthyphro is a young man with an eccentric understanding of the divine things and an estimate of his own stature as a religious seer that is so overgenerous as to be comical (for example, he assures Socrates that nothing will come of Meletus's charges against him). Euthyphro is surprised to find Socrates hanging around the Porch of the King, the location for preliminary hearings in judicial cases.

5 · See chapter 11 above and Aristotle's *Metaphysics* 1072b4.

He is certain that Socrates must be under indictment, for surely he would not be indicting another. Euthyphro, on the other hand, is not only indicting another; he is indicting his own father, the very source of his being, and for murder at that (although the circumstances are arguably unusually extenuating). The dialogue thus begins with a contrast between Euthyphro the zealous agent and Socrates the perennial patient. Indeed, Euthyphro is so paradigmatically the agent that he makes Zeus's binding of Kronos his model (Oedipus, by the way, also lurks in the wings). Like Zeus (and, indeed, Kronos as well), Euthyphro assaults his own father. Now, the binding of Kronos (whose name is a pun on *khronos*—time) marks the beginning of the reign of the Olympian gods—gods whose names no longer double as common nouns like *Ouranos* ("heaven") and *Gaia* ("earth"). The Greek gods are peculiar beings; they are at once principles of intelligibility (as Ares is the god of war, his notorious affair with Aphrodite can be understood as an allegory for the complicated relation between love and war—the theme of the *Iliad*), and they are agents in their own right (Ares is a person capable of being attracted to and sleeping with Aphrodite; unlike love and war, Aphrodite and Ares can be painted by Botticelli). As principles, the gods point to an unchanging eternal order of things. To understand the variety of and relations among them, then, would mean to understand the world. Yet, as persons, the gods are agents of the new. While the names of the Olympians no longer point directly to cosmic phenomena, Plato, at least, makes use of the fact that the accusative of Zeus's name (*Dia*) may be interpreted as "cause."[6] If the replacement of Kronos by Zeus means the overthrow of time, then Olympian rule stands for what it means to introduce into the world the possibility of causes that are not simply rooted in the past out of which they grow—causes that are not simply effects. These gods, and this is particularly important for the *Euthyphro*, represent what it means that there are souls in the world. Not accidentally, the word *psuchē*, "soul," does not occur in the *Euthyphro*.[7] In a world without the agency of souls, everything would be rooted so firmly in its past that there would be nothing unpredictable—nothing new—and so Euthyphro's opening question would make no sense. The problem hinted at by the first words of the dialogue, then, is this: How could there be agency in a world so fully intelligible that everything falls into place, has a place, is rooted, and so, in which there is no real change? The gods, at once principles of intelligibility and initiating agents, are the way we human

6 · See *Cratylus* 396a–b.

7 · See Leo Strauss, "On the *Euthyphron*," in *The Rebirth of Classical Political Rationalism* (Chicago and London: University of Chicago Press, 1989), 205.

beings formulate this problem to ourselves. And by speaking of gods, without quite realizing it, we have raised for ourselves the problem of soul.[8] The gods are, in a way, mythic versions of the middle voice of the verb in which the subject "inside the process" "achieves something which is being achieved in him," and, when scrutinized, they are every bit as puzzling. As we have seen, although the middle is fundamental, it is deceptively easy to construe as deriving from the combination of active and passive.

Euthyphro acts so as to transcend the fact of his having a past; his goal is a sort of parricide, with all the attendant tragic implications. His first impulse is to affirm the purity of his own agency.

> It's laughable, Socrates, that you think it to make any difference whether the one who is dead is stranger or kin, rather than to be necessary only to watch out for this: whether the killer killed in justice or not. . . . (4b7–9)

And yet he goes on to say that he is charging his father with murder in order to root out the pollution in his household. So Euthyphro attacks the idiosyncrasy of the ancestral for the sake of purifying the ancestral; he wishes to cleanse the stain on his family. This seems to be the fundamental character of the experience of the holy—it is an experience of being unclean, of shame, of needing to cleanse oneself. But the principle according to which this cleansing is undertaken is only a purer version of one's idiosyncratic self. Put differently, Euthyphro senses that there is something wrong with an unexamined loyalty to his own—to the particular—simply because it happens

---

8 · There is a further question: Do the Greek gods have souls? It is, of course, not unusual to speak of the human soul in its connection to the gods. In the *Phaedrus* (246d–248e), for example, the types of soul seem to be defined in terms of the gods they follow. And in the *Laws* (899a), the Athenian Stranger says that every man must regard the soul as a god. But neither of these quite amounts to saying that Zeus has a soul. On the one hand, the very perfection of the gods suggests that they cannot have souls; a being without longing seems to lack the signal characteristic of soul. And do even the very poets, who present the gods as having psychic characteristics like longing, jealousy, and so forth, ever explicitly say that they are ensouled? On the other hand, in Plato, the question is more complicated. At *Timaeus* 34a, the cosmos is a god and ensouled. The most important passage is probably *Phaedrus* 246c–d, where Socrates says that "neither seeing nor sufficiently conceiving god, we mold a deathless animal, having on the one hand soul, and on the other body, these being by nature together for all time." This, of course, may simply mean that we put together what cannot really go together—that we invent the gods. But even should this be the case, the gods seem to stand as a paradigm for what it would mean to put together perfectly perfect intelligibility and intelligence—that is, to give soul an intelligible structure. They are our idea of that of which it is not so clear that we can have an idea.

to be his own. But his first reaction is to correct the situation on the basis of a piety that consists in a deeper version of an unexamined loyalty to the particular and idiosyncratic. In practice, this takes the form of going to the city to adjudicate the conflict. In taking his father to court, Euthyphro acts out the actual historical development from the gods of the hearth—ancestor worship—to the gods of the city. When Socrates confronts him with the prospect of losing his case in the city, Euthyphro restates the case in terms of justice—no longer mentioning pollution. But then Socrates calls the gods of the city into question by showing that they too contain within them the tension that is within Euthyphro—that is, the story of the binding of Kronos by Zeus is precisely a sort of cleansing of the divine by an attack on the divine. Father Zeus replaces father Kronos. Euthyphro's attempt to cast himself as a perfectly responsible agent is thus riven by self-contradiction.

So much for Euthyphro's case; Socrates describes his own case in the following way:

> For he [Meletus], as he says, knows what way the young are corrupted [*diaphtheirontai*—this is the first passive verb in the dialogue] and who are those corrupting them. And he runs the risk of being someone wise, and, gazing down at my ignorance, he comes before the city charging me, as though before his mother, for corrupting those of his age. And he alone of the political men appears to me to begin rightly; for it is right first to care for the young, so that they will be the best possible, just as a good farmer is likely first to care for the young plants, and after this also the rest. And, in fact, Meletus is perhaps first thoroughly cleansing us who corrupt the buds of the youth, as he says. Next, after this it is clear that having cared for the older ones, he will come to be the cause of the most and greatest goods for the city as is likely to happen for one beginning [middle] from such a beginning. (2c3–3a5)

What is so startling about this account is Socrates' presentation of Meletus's understanding of the young in the city as plants to be nurtured or corrupted.[9] Or, put somewhat differently, if the city is our mother, then aren't we perennial children, never passing through adolescence and coming into our own? And if those in the city are so infantilized as to be like plants, altogether affected by conditions that either nurture or corrupt them, how can Socrates, who is, after all, one of them, be a cause of their corruption, or, for that matter, how can Meletus be a cause of their salvation? The first middle-passive verb form with a passive meaning in the dialogue is *diaphtheirontai*—Me-

---

9 · According to the Eleatic Stranger, in the age of Kronos, human beings were like plants; see *Statesman* 271a ff.

letus claims to know in what way the young *are corrupted*. But is being corrupted ever simply passive? Shouldn't *diaphtheirontai* be a middle so that the young are, in part at least, responsible for "corrupting themselves"? If we are to judge by Meletus, Socrates is a subject of passionate discussion among young men he has never even met. Great teachers are often like that. Not unlike Aristotle's unmoved mover, they move what is apart from them by example, by way of attraction rather than compulsion, by what they are, not what they do. Those they influence are persuaded (*peithontai*); they do not simply obey (*peithontai*). Being final and not efficient causes, they presuppose some principle of motion in the things they move. When you find a movie moving, you are only metaphorically grabbed by it. Socrates, an object of intense admiration in Athens, outdoes his ancestor Daedalus—he animates the statues of others.

By modeling himself on Zeus, Euthyphro presents himself as pure agent; this is what he thinks his piety consists in. Meletus, on the other hand, attacks Socrates for undermining the passive acquiescence of young and old to the norms of civic life. For Meletus, piety is pure passivity. Strangely, only criminals are agents. Euthyphro is at odds with himself, for he is passive in his emulation of the action of Zeus. Meletus is at odds with himself, for in coming to the rescue of the passivity of civic virtue, he is an agent; his piety turns criminal. This tension between agency and passivity sets the stage for the series of arguments about the holy that make up the bulk of the *Euthyphro*.

Socrates playfully sets forth a plan to become Euthyphro's student so that he can arrange a sort of plea bargain. He'll give up Euthyphro to Meletus, the rationale being that Euthyphro, as *his* teacher, must be understood to have corrupted him. Turning Meletus's view on himself, Socrates, for purposes of his own, will take refuge in the claim to be a plant, an altogether passive being. Of course, this begs the question of who corrupted Euthyphro, but Euthyphro doesn't notice, for Socrates has turned his overconfidence against itself. Euthyphro also doesn't notice how absurd the sequence of events in this plea bargain is, for Socrates doesn't claim to have learned anything from Euthyphro prior to being charged, and yet he plans to place the blame on Euthyphro for his own corruption. There can therefore be no causal connection whatsoever between what Socrates is supposed to have done and what Euthyphro is about to say. What, then, is the meaning of Socrates' plan? And, since it is clearly ironic and playful anyway, is there a serious meaning behind appealing to the comical, overconfident Euthyphro for help?

Socrates must defend himself against the view of Meletus that time rules everything in the sense that what comes before altogether determines what will follow, the world of Kronos where everything is a plant, a world where the young or new is necessarily simply an outgrowth of the old, and so where it is quite impossible for anything to be new. The rule of time means the rule of necessity. In his defense, Socrates will appeal to the man who stands for the reversal of time. Euthyphro/Zeus is a tool for attacking Meletus/ Kronos. To the suggestion that he take Socrates' place, Euthyphro says,

> Yes, *by Zeus* [emphasis mine], Socrates, if he should try to indict me, I would, as I suppose, discover where he is unsound, and, to our advantage, a speech in the law court would have arisen about him much earlier than about me. (5b8–c3)

That Socrates, who just met Euthyphro, could not possibly have learned from him the vices for which he has been indicted is a joke designed to make us see that something like the suspension or reversal of time is necessary for corruption, for something new, to occur. What Meletus has not considered is how his own ultraorthodox view itself gives birth to an attack on itself. He has not understood how what he charges Socrates with is possible, how it is possible for Euthyphro to turn on his father in the name of the ancestral, how Zeus is possible. The tradition is much more complex than Meletus realizes. At the same time, Euthyphro's response here is interesting; he shifts tenses in the verb—imagining Meletus trying to indict him in the present and then placing the whole event in the past so that he can play out its necessary consequences in his mind. To imagine the triumph of his will, Euthyphro can only reinstate the necessity of the time over which he has triumphed. Euthyphro does not understand his dependence on the tradition.

Socrates' plan is either to learn from Euthyphro what he needs to defend himself or to use Euthyphro as an excuse for his own guilt. He begins his course of study with the crucial question.

> Now then, before Zeus [this is the only time Socrates swears by Zeus in the dialogue], tell me what you just now were so strongly claiming to know clearly—what sort of thing you claim the pious to be and the impious, both with respect to murder and with respect to everything else? Or is not the holy itself by itself the same in every action, and the unholy in turn the opposite of all the holy, and everything that is going to be unholy is itself like to itself and having some one idea in accordance with unholiness? (5c8–d5)

What follows is generally taken to be the real substance of the dialogue. Socrates elicits from Euthyphro a series of definitions of the holy. None is successful, but at the very least, the procedure of asking for the *idea* or *eidos* of something—what it is "itself by itself"—is held to be one of the earliest examples of Plato's legendary "theory of ideas" or "forms." Socrates' insistence on a definition of the holy, as we will see, threatens to subordinate the gods, who are active persons, to utterly unchanging and passive principles. But we are getting ahead of ourselves.

Euthyphro responds to Socrates' request by saying that the holy is

> just what I am doing now, to go after one doing injustice, whether concerning murders or temple robberies, or to go after one erring with respect to any other such thing, whether it happens to be father, mother, or whoever else, and not to go after him is unholy. (5d8–e2)

Now, Socrates rejects this account on formal grounds, claiming that Euthyphro has only given an example of the holy. Socrates asks for the "*eidos* by which all holy things are holy" (6d10–11), and then the "one *idea*" by which "the unholy things are unholy and the holy things holy" (6d11–e1). This may not seem unfair, but we need to notice that there is surely a definition implied by Euthyphro's example—his extended comparison of his own action to that of Zeus. As Leo Strauss has seen, the implicit definition with which Euthyphro begins is that the holy is imitating the gods—doing what they do.[10] This, the most active of Euthyphro's definitions, shows up only between the lines—indirectly. As it never becomes explicit, it is never refuted. Nevertheless, it affects all subsequent definitions.

When Socrates presses him for a definition in a more acceptable form, Euthyphro replies that the holy is what is loved by the gods, the unholy what is not loved (6e10–7a1). First Socrates changes this to what is god-loved and god-hated (the two formulations are interestingly different—the adjectival versions being equally possible to translate as "god-loving" and "god-hating"); then he refutes it by showing that by Euthyphro's own account, since there are many gods and they are frequently at odds with one another, the same things will be both god-loved and god-hated, and so holy and unholy.[11] To solve the difficulty of diversity among the gods with respect to what they love, Socrates helps Euthyphro reinterpret his first explicit definition. The holy now becomes what all the gods love and the unholy what all the gods hate (9e1–3). Socrates' refutation of this definition is the grammatical argument that we have been haltingly approaching for some time now.

10 · Strauss, "On the *Euthyphron*," 197–98.
11 · In the course of this refutation, Socrates introduces a second implicit understanding of the holy—what we dare not deny, in this case, that the unjust should be punished (8c–e). This is the first of the definitions that involves fear.

Socrates asks whether the holy is loved by the gods because it is holy or holy because it is loved by the gods. A lot is at stake. If it is loved because it is holy, there is a reason for loving it—a reason that, once known, would presumably be higher and more lovable than the gods themselves. Our piety might consist in imitating the gods who love the holy, but in loving something higher than themselves, they would have ceased to be the gods we hold high. If there are principles of order higher than the gods as persons, the gods are not gods. If, on the other hand, the holy is holy because the gods love it, then the "order" in the world is dependent upon their whim. We would have no recourse but to do what the gods say since their power would exceed ours and their reasons for loving what they love would be no more available to us than the new line of argument Socrates announces at 9c–d was available to Euthyphro prior to his having announced it. After all, until Socrates says, "This came to mind at the same time you were speaking" (9c1–2), Euthyphro must have thought Socrates was paying attention. It seems that if the gods are altogether active, then we must be altogether passive. And if the gods are passive, then we may be active.

The grammatical argument is rather complicated, but at the risk of oversimplifying, this seems to be its gist. Wherever there is an action, there is corresponding being acted upon. Socrates gives a series of examples. That there is something carrying is the cause of something's being carried. Leading is the cause of being led. Seeing is the cause of being seen. Similarly, loving would be the cause of being loved. Accordingly, the cause of something's being loved by the gods is that they love it. But the holy is surely loved by the gods because it is holy and not holy because it is loved. Being loved by the gods is passive in the sense that it does not so much refer to the nature of the thing loved as to the gods' act of loving. By itself, it tells us nothing about the holy; accordingly, it cannot be right to define the holy as what is loved by the gods. As beautiful as Euthyphro's definition is in its form, it isn't much good to us, for in not telling us why the gods love what they love, it leaves us altogether in the dark about how we should behave.

Now, the difficulty with this argument is that, while it makes sense grammatically, finally it doesn't really make sense at all. Socrates' three examples are rather peculiar. He first pairs two participles, *pheron* ("carrying") and *pheromenon* ("being carried"). But in the middle, *pheromenon* can mean "carrying off for oneself," and *pheron* by itself can mean "fate."[12] At the end of the argument, Socrates exhorts Euthyphro to find another definition, saying they will not "differ" about the fact that the holy is loved by the gods (11b4). This "differ" is the verb *diapheresthai*, compounded out of

12 · See, for example, Sophocles' *Oedipus at Colonus* 1694.

the middle-passive form of "to carry." But surely "to differ" is as active as it is passive.

Socrates' second example is no more appropriate. *Agomenon*, which here must mean "being led," has meanings as various as "leading for oneself," "taking," and "marrying." And even were this not the case, surely if to be led means to follow, then following is as much an action as leading. One need not be altogether Hegelian to notice that sometimes being followed depends on those who follow. Furthermore, the first part of the *Euthyphro* itself provides a striking example of just how active one can be in being led. While Socrates has been following Euthyphro's lead, there is little doubt about who is in control here. And the case is no better with the third example—"seeing" (*horōn*) and "being seen" (*horōmenon*)—for *horōmenon* can mean "to make an appearance," to make oneself seen. Furthermore, when Socrates asks Euthyphro at 11a3, "Do you see?" he is asking him if he gets the point. The verb "to see" is active, but in describing what we undergo, isn't it in some way passive in its meaning?

The crucial verb, *philein* ("to love"), is every bit as problematic. Ordinarily in Greek, *philein* is nonsexual love; it is used initially of kin and later of friends. The middle-passive participle, *philoumenon*, is nevertheless often used to designate the beloved in a love relation. Is a beloved ever altogether passive? Socrates of all people surely understands flirtation. And what about the active verb? When we fall in love, are we doing something or undergoing something, suffering something? Even if the verb means something like "to be a friend of," can one be a friend without at the same time having been befriended? Aristotle, at least, thinks not.[13]

As if the distinction between active and passive were not already sufficiently confused, Socrates deepens the puzzle. Previously we had a "thing leading" and its correlative "thing led"—the active and passive participles of the verb, respectively. Now Socrates asks whether something is a "thing led" (passive participle) because "it is led" (finite passive verb) or vice versa. In other words, now the participle is being treated as passive, and the activity it is passively undergoing is being treated as active. Put differently, the first stage of Socrates' argument is this: I hit you; therefore, you are hit. The second stage is this: You are hit; therefore, you are in a state of being hit. In the first stage, "You are hit" is taken as passive; in the second stage, as active.

This proliferation and relativizing of active and passive is brought to a head at 10c in Socrates' general formulation of the point he has been making.

> I wish [middle] to say this: that if something comes to be [*gignetai*] or suffers / is affected [*paschei*], not because it is something coming to be

13 · See *Nicomachean Ethics* 1155b–1156a.

does it come to be, but it is something coming to be because it comes to be; nor does it suffer because it is something suffering, but because it suffers, it is something suffering.

Once again, Socrates makes the active/passive distinction in terms of the difference between the finite verb (for example, "it suffers") and the participle (for example, "something suffering"). What is so curious about this summation is that in order to express the meaning of the active in general, Socrates uses a deponent verb that has an active meaning but only a middle-passive form (*gignesthai*). And in order to express the meaning of the passive in general, Socrates uses a verb with a passive meaning but an active form (*paschein*). We are thus led to draw the general conclusion that depending on the situation, virtually any verb can be understood to carry active or passive meaning. It all depends on the direction from which you see the action. Since the dismantling of Euthyphro's claim that the holy is what is loved by the gods depends on the rigid distinction between active and passive voices, Plato has gone out of his way to call Socrates' refutation into question. Why?

In its subtext, Socrates' argument forces us to ask whether all human action is not reaction, and so in some measure passive. This is a way of asking whether all living beings are not necessarily reactive. One cannot kill the father because to attempt to erase one's past is to reaffirm its hold. There is no such thing, then, as pure will in the world, and *nothing* is loved simply because someone loves it. Action is always reaction *to*. This is the importance of the distinction Socrates makes at 11a7–9.

> And you run the risk, Euthyphro, upon being asked whatever the holy is, not to wish to clarify the being of it for me but to speak of a *pathos*/affect belonging to it.

Socrates seems to say that to define something means not to describe what happens to it but to say what it is in its being or essence—its *ousia*. Euthyphro had tried to say that the holiness of something consisted in its happening to be loved by the gods. Still, couldn't there be something the being or *ousia* of which was to have a certain sort of *pathos*? Isn't this just what we mean by soul, which cannot be anything apart from a power or ability to suffer, or undergo, certain sorts of experiences? Soul is thus inseparable from its affects; its being *is* first to be affected. If we were to understand gods to be perfect souls, they would have to have the perfection of this suffering, undergoing, or being affected. Worshipping them would then amount to worshipping pure receptivity—the fact that there is such a thing in the world as "being affected."

Let us begin again. All doing is ultimately something done by a soul, but there is no soul without undergoing or suffering (the *philon*, the loving thing, is the soul, but loving is something that happens to us).[14] All doing is thus first and foremost something undergone, something done to one. Action is necessarily reaction, and so there is nothing new—there are always fathers. Therefore, the question "What's new?" amounts to asking for a doing that is not reactive—an uncaused cause. "What's new?" means "Show me the perfect soul that only acts and does not react." There seem to be three possible responses to this request: (1) There is nothing new; we are only plants or billiard balls, moments in the march of time. (2) There is something new, a soul so active as to be altogether outside of the ordinary temporal order. Or (3) there is something in between (the first words of the *Euthyphro*, after all, are not "What's new?" but, literally, "What has come to be newer?"); we undergo and react, but we react unpredictably. The first alternative describes a world in which nothing changes and which would be totally intelligible save for the fact that there is no being in it to whom anything could become intelligible.[15] The second alternative describes a world in which there are beings who affect the world, but in which, precisely because it is possible for the radically new to come to be at any time, there can be no intelligibility. Finally, the third alternative describes our world. We are generated out of a temporal sequence without being swallowed up by that sequence. We are neither willful gods who annihilate time nor plants. We are souls with the power to react. Perhaps one might call it a power of refusal, a "*little* god" within us that does not so much tell us what to do as tell us what not to do.

Euthyphro is frustrated with this refutation, although not altogether sure what exactly has happened to him. In response to Socrates' request that he try again, he replies,

> But, Socrates, I at least do not have a clue how I am to tell you what I have in mind. For whatever we put forward [middle] moves around [middle] and does not want to remain where we place [middle] it. (11b6–8)

To this, Socrates replies that the things said by Euthyphro are like the statues of his ancestor, Daedalus—so well wrought that they move of their own accord.[16] When Euthyphro accuses him of being the Daedalus, Soc-

14 · At 11b1, Socrates says to Euthyphro, "So if it pleases you [that is, if it is *philon* / dear to you], don't hide it, but once again from the beginning, tell me what is the holy."
15 · See Stanley Rosen, *Nihilism: A Philosophical Essay* (New Haven, CT, and London: Yale University Press, 1969), 162.
16 · That Daedalus is the mythic figure at the bottom of this interlude is clearly important. He was a man who fashioned statues of human bodies so "real" that they moved

rates expresses great surprise. He would like nothing better, he says, than
for the argument to stay put; if his cleverness moves them, it is an involuntary wisdom. This interlude is instructive, for it is a disagreement about
who is the cause of a movement—Socrates or Euthyphro. Euthyphro begins
by admitting that he cannot describe what is going on around him—what
he has just undergone. For that reason, he attributes a will of their own to
"our" speeches. Socrates then disavows any responsibility for the movement
and claims Euthyphro is its cause. Euthyphro then responds by accusing
Socrates; it is as though he says, "If you will not admit that they moved
themselves and insist on a cause, then *you* are the cause." Socrates does not
deny the charge but says instead that if it is true, he must be more uncanny
than even Daedalus since he makes the words of others move and he does
so without even knowing how he did it. So the alleged cause of the motion
of the speeches shifts from the speeches themselves to Euthyphro, to Socrates, to a hidden part of Socrates of which he himself is altogether unaware.
The significance of this movement becomes clear from the way Euthyphro
jumps to the conclusion that the speeches have a mind of their own. Animating the speeches is a way to escape blame for the embarrassing situation
he finds himself in. While Socrates refuses to let him flee in this way, it is
still true that they did not want the speeches to fail, or at least did not know
that they wanted them to do so. This suggests that underneath the appearance that these beings are separate from both Socrates and Euthyphro and
have a life of their own lurks a part of Socrates and Euthyphro that gives
the speeches life without knowing that it does so. It is not the speeches that
are uncanny, but the soul in its hidden depths. Euthyphro's animation of
the speeches is simply a way of explaining himself to himself by projecting
his own hidden power, his soul, onto an external being. In animating their
speeches, Euthyphro has revealed how and why we make gods. And by this
attempt to make sense of things, he has rendered invisible what is responsible for the attempt and is truly at issue here, the soul. Socrates' refusal to
follow him in this theogony signals his understanding that the only way to
make the soul visible is to work backward from the reified beings to which,
out of perplexity about itself, it gives rise.

Socrates begins the second half of the dialogue by asking Euthyphro
whether all the holy is just, and then whether all the just is holy (11e4–12a2).
Euthyphro doesn't understand, and so, after expressing surprise because "in-

---

themselves. He gives human bodies souls. He is also the man who contrived a way to
escape Crete by fashioning wings from wax and feathers; his son Icarus attempted to
fly to heaven to be like the gods, and when the sun melted the wax in his wings, he
perished. His father, more moderate, took the middle course and made it safely to
the Peloponnese.

deed younger [newer/*neōteros*] you are than I not less than to the degree you are wiser" (12a4–5), Socrates introduces two examples of what he means. Just as fear (*deos*) is a class of which awe (*aidōs*) is a subclass and number is a class of which odd is a subclass, so also justice is a class of which the holy is a subclass. There is too much here to treat adequately; it must suffice to say that just as imitation of god was the implicit definition that fueled the first part of the dialogue, fear of god is the implicit definition that fuels the second part. Euthyphro is then led to agree that the holy is that part of the just that has to do with tending the gods (12e). This is refuted because it implies that we make the gods better. In the definition that seeks to correct this one, we are demoted from shepherds of the gods to their thralls; piety becomes the art of slavery to the gods (13d). This fails because it presupposes that the gods need us to produce something for them. The next suggestion is that piety involves the knowledge of prayer and sacrifice (14b); notice that relative to each other, the one is passive and the other active—one requests action and the other acts. This, however, degenerates into a business relation between gods and men in which, since they do not need anything, we must perforce cheat them. At the end, Euthyphro comes almost full circle and claims once again that the holy is what is loved by the gods (15b).

Euthyphro began the dialogue in such a hyperactive, self-intoxicated imitation of Zeus that Socrates openly wondered that he was not afraid lest he be doing something unholy (4e4–8). After the Daedalus interlude, the dialogue shifts in a decisive way. Socrates becomes openly active, and the underlying issue becomes the connection between the holy and fear. The shift is not arbitrary. While the argument of the first part of the dialogue is altogether aporetic, the action of the dialogue consists in placing Euthyphro in a situation where, in the face of something he does not understand, his fear leads him to assume the existence of an animate being. He and Socrates together seek a fixed principle of the holy. When they cannot find it, Euthyphro's confidence fades; to protect himself, he animates the *logos*. Plato has thereby allowed us to witness the creation of a god—supposedly as an explanation but really out of fear. In the second part of the dialogue, we come to see the natural consequences of such animation. First, gods are generated as explanatory metaphors—say, the cosmos being formed by the coupling of Ouranos and Gaia—and are objects of wonder. We make them gods and not simply principles because as uncaused causes of motion, there is only one thing comparable to them in our experience—soul. We thus animate them so that our world will make sense—to gain control over it. But in so doing, we must make them far more powerful than the souls of which we have experience. However, in order to be souls, they must share the fundamental feature of all soul—opacity. They thus move from becoming objects of wonder to objects of fear. As Strauss and others suggest, Socrates does indeed intend to move Euthyphro back toward the orthodoxy that he too easily forsook.[17] He will chasten his arrogant soul by making him god-fearing. By the end of the dialogue, Euthyphro, who was about to enter the court to prosecute his father, will "go away" (*apienai*, 15e). However, this is not simply a moral lesson. The movement Euthyphro undergoes points to what one might call a natural history of religion. To understand ourselves, we generate gods for their explanatory power as models of perfect agency. But their very perfection as agents threatens to undermine the intelligibility of our world and make it inexplicable. Once this happens, we must understand ourselves to be under the control of the same very powerful agents we have generated as tools for our self-understanding. There is no alternative but slavery. Euthyphro's initial claim to be like Zeus leads willy-nilly to his becoming a slave to Zeus, a plant. The active voice generates the passive voice as its corollary; the two together obscure the middle voice, which is their common origin. Euthyphro is in a way an immature "young" Socrates who easily gives way to Meletus, a decayed "old" Socrates; Euthyphro is Zeus, and Meletus is Kronos. Euthyphro is an active verb and Meletus a passive. Socrates is in the middle voice—at once the only place to be and a very unstable place to be.

Precisely because the *Euthyphro* is about the soul, it does not mention the soul. Instead, it presents us with the characteristic motion of soul. It discloses the nature of our souls as simultaneously and necessarily both active and passive, or rather, as in the middle and tending to fall apart into active and passive. The dialogue everywhere shows signs of this indeterminate dualism. Definitions, explicit and implicit, of the holy move from imitation of the gods to slavelike obedience, but neither extreme proves stable, for each regenerates its opposite out of itself. The dialogue contains a similar, if less obvious, dualism connected to philosophy. On the one hand, this "early dialogue" seems to provide an immature version of the "theory of ideas," according to which philosophy consists in seeking the fixed principles that render the whole intelligible. Yet, the ideas are only half the Platonic formula for philosophy; the other half is a powerful presentation of the person of Socrates as a model for emulation. To be intelligible, the whole must contain intelligence; yet if it contains intelligence, the whole must be incompletely intelligible. The philosophic counterpart of the question "Why do men worship gods?" is the question "Why do men need living models in order to learn?" Socrates is on trial in Athens because he is followed by the young. Their ardor may have something to do with the theory of ideas, but its more obvious cause is the example Socrates provides of the living soul at work. The young look to Socrates in order to understand themselves. It is the way of the soul to seek itself in what is apart from itself. This is what leads it to resolve itself into active and passive parts, neither of which can really exist by itself, only to then attempt to restore its original unity.[18] One might call this the grammar of the soul.

18 · The *Euthyphro* therefore means to articulate how the core of Socratic philosophy, the quest for self-knowledge, is at the heart of the human soul, but for that very reason, also at the heart of what gives rise to the trial and execution of Socrates. Socrates' indictment by Athens was at the same time a self-indictment.

· CONCLUSION ·

The Soul of Socrates

We saw from the *Phaedrus* how *erōs* is in a way the soul of the soul and from the *Euthyphro* how Socrates, in his essential imperfection, becomes like a god to whom the young look as a model for how to live. In the last speech in the *Symposium*, Alcibiades, one of those who was drawn in his youth to Socrates, substitutes a praise of Socrates for a praise of *erōs*. In the *Symposium*, Socrates enunciates his idiosyncratic principle of praise: to tell only the truth—that is, to select the most beautiful parts of the truth and arrange them in the seemliest manner (198d). This is connected to what one might call the fundamental principle of Socratic philosophy, which can begin from opinion/seeming/*doxa* because no *doxa*, however foolish, is simply wrong but rather always in its way a reflection of the real—nothing comes from nothing. Philosophy thus involves teasing out the being always underlying the seeming of things. This is why it is possible, and even necessary, for philosophy to begin by inquiring into prevailing opinions and not possible to build a deductive system from ironclad first principles. That political philosophy is the "eccentric" core of philosophy means finally that souls are always willy-nilly in love with the world.

In the *Symposium*, this means that nothing said in praise of *erōs* by the five speakers prior to Socrates is simply wrong. Accordingly, we expect Socrates' own account to reflect this. For example, Phaedrus's praise of love as devotion to a *higher* beloved ends with his being so jealous of the selflessness of the lover that he cannot help attributing this selflessness to the beloved Achilles as well (179e1–180a7). It looks as though the highest object of love must be given the attributes of a soul as a subject—a self that manifests its psychic nature in its willingness to forsake it for something thought to be higher. It is a lover willing to die for its beloved. Initially at least, this seems to be the key to Socrates' speech, and to Socrates' soul.

On the surface, Socrates' Diotima gives an account of love in which love as "I love you" vanishes in favor of love of the beautiful in itself—*to kalon kath'auto*. This emerges in the playful way in which Socrates uses word forms that may be either neuter or masculine to let us see that he is suppressing the personhood of the lover and the beloved (198d4–6). His argument plays out in a problematic way, for if *erōs* is the desire to possess only what one lacks, but the object of love is never a "what" but a "whom," does a whom that is possessed still remain a whom? Does a subject, once had, remain a subject? This has something to do with Socrates' inability to tell Diotima what one gets when one possesses the beautiful (204d5–11).

To explain how we continue to desire what we seem already to have, Socrates introduces time (206a9). Desire always includes the desire that what is present now also be present in the future. But this must mean that every desire includes within it a desire for the continuation of the being that is desiring—the soul as a self. Accordingly, as Aristophanes had seen already (and as we have seen from the *Phaedrus*), there is a sense in which all love is self-love. But the desire for the continuation of the desiring subject is necessarily also a desire for the continued absence of the object of desire. Our longing for perfection conceals a deeper longing for our imperfection. It is no accident, then, that the lovers Hephaistos approaches cannot tell him what they long for (192d2–9). *Erōs* as desire for the beautiful is always somehow the present intimation of something that remains alluring in its absence. We love the presence of this absence.

Our experience of the beautiful is thus never simply of something we have in its completion or perfection. The beautiful is not so much the perfect instance of its class but rather something that seems to jump its class—to be more than it is. The being of the beautiful is to point beyond itself. Because it is never perceived simply as what it is, but always as somehow more, there is something unsettling, even disordered, about it.[1] One might say that we experience beautiful things as objects within the whole that point to the order of the whole. They are images of the perfection of the whole. But if the whole is a perfect order with its parts functioning so as each to fit perfectly into the whole and perform its function with no waste or excess, and if a part of the whole that images the whole can do so only by being apart from and not limited by the other parts of the whole, then this part of the whole can be beautiful only by being disruptive of the perfect order of the whole. This disruption of the wholeness of the whole is the same as the introduction of seeming, and so falsity, into the being of the whole. The beautiful is thus intimately connected with the part of the whole for which things seem—the soul. Apparently, love understood as love of the beautiful is much more complicated than it at first seems to be.

The beautiful-itself is literally impossible to imagine. It seems more than

---

1 · See my *Ancient Tragedy and the Origins of Modern Science* (Carbondale: Southern Illinois University Press, 1988), 115–16.

anything to describe a tendency within *erōs* to leave the particular behind and to wish to make clear that this also means leaving behind the possession of the good, happiness, and immortality. That is, Diotima's praise of the beautiful-itself is really an account of how *erōs* engenders a certain contempt for all that is human. In this sense, the pursuit of the beautiful-itself is simply the most extreme version of what every speaker in the *Symposium* has advocated. But the account is inadequate, for it does not explain to us how it is possible to live this purified version of the erotic life without self-contempt. The truth of *erōs* is not simply self-contempt (the one thing Alcibiades seems to share with Apollodorus). Plato, at least, seems to consider Diotima's speech incomplete, for he gives us Alcibiades.

The incompleteness of Diotima's account emerges when we consider three things. The first, already seen, is that our experience of beauty always points beyond itself to something more. For this reason, we find beauty not only satisfying but also disturbing, unsettling, and a source of wonder. Second, when Diotima places the beautiful-itself at the peak of the ascent of *erōs*, either she is wrong or she cannot mean what she seems to mean. The beautiful-itself cannot be perfect, *kath'auto*, for its very being is to be incomplete—relational. Diotima must then mean that the beautiful-itself is the perfect manifestation—the paradigm—for this imperfection. It is perfectly, ideally incomplete, or perhaps the form of incompleteness. Now, third, our experience of something as at once present and yet never really present—as present in its necessary apartness from us—is a fair description of our experience of another person, of a soul, which, as a soul, can never be altogether objectified, determined, or fixed without ceasing to be what it is.

Perhaps the single consistent feature of every speech in Plato's *Symposium* is that whatever it claims to praise, it is always a praise of self. Diotima brings this into the open when she makes the object of *erōs* immortality. But then immortality strangely drops out of the argument, and "love of making the good one's own forever" gets replaced by contemplating the beautiful-itself (*theōrein to kalon kath'auto*). Diotima sees that it is not so easy to love oneself, for to love yourself, you would need to know yourself, grasp yourself, and it is not so clear that this is possible. *Erōs* is necessarily connected to pregnancy, generation, and conception—to *poiein*, or making, insofar as self-love requires that we project something that we can love outside of ourselves. Because soul is what goes out of itself for the sake of itself (even, as we have seen, in eating), self-love can show up only as other-love. This, of course, means that it must always be partially mistaken in its object. Being mistaken is the engine that drives Diotima's ascent. We get what we longed for only to discover it is not what we longed for. The peak of the ascent—*to kalon kath'auto*—is the beloved as so altogether other as to draw us completely outside ourselves. In so doing, it provides us with the perfect projection of ourselves as what always goes outside of itself for the sake of itself. The beautiful-itself is thus something like pure soul.

Put a little perversely, one might say that *to kalon kath'auto* is *perfectly* unsatisfactory. *Erōs* thus turns out to be not a simple desire that we want to satisfy but rather the desire to have one's dissatisfaction guaranteed—to *secure* our incompletion.[2] This is what self-love requires. So the *kalon kath'auto*, the beloved as pure soul, pure otherness, would have to show no interest whatsoever in the one who loves it; of course, this is true in Diotima's speech.

All of this points ahead to Alcibiades' speech, where we learn that *erōs*, even as self-love, is always love of another soul—that loving what you cannot have is not an accidental feature of some love but a necessary feature of love as such. Contrary to what we think at first, once we have seen that Diotima has given us an idealized version, a projection, of an experience that we can never really have, we see that Alcibiades' experience of Socrates (not necessarily his understanding of it) is not at odds with her account but is rather the truth of it.

It is not altogether wrong to say that the *Symposium* is a dialogue about *thumos*—anger or spiritedness—masquerading as a dialogue about *erōs*. *Thumos* is the self-regarding passion. This is connected to the first words of the *Symposium*—"I seem to me" (*dokō moi*). In its doubling of the *I*, *dokō moi* is an especially subjective expression.[3] It is first uttered by the dialogue's narrator, the angry Apollodorus. *Thumos* is constituted by sense of one's own incompleteness without any sense of what it would mean to be complete. It is a powerful, but in some way hollow, self-affirmation. It is accompanied by a sense of having suffered injustice, and so wounded pride. *Thumos* is thus at the center of politics—the attempt of human beings to gain control over their lives. Not surprisingly, it is at the heart of the story of Achilles. *Erōs*, on the other hand, seems at first not to be self-regarding in this way, requiring instead an object to attract our attention. But then it turns out that *erōs* always mistakes its object of love. It ultimately loves the beautiful-itself, and the beautiful-itself is not really lovable or, for that matter, even available to the imagination. The beautiful-itself is nothing other than the indeterminate sense of what would be necessary to make us complete. Its indeterminacy is simply the flip side of the indeterminacy of *thumos*. Accordingly, the desire for the perfect beloved is rooted not in *erōs* but in *thumos*. The love that is apparently totally self-ignoring is in fact the highest manifestation of self-love—*thumos*. Love is finally self-love, which

2 · This formulation was suggested to me by Gwen Grewal.

3 · *Ancient Tragedy and the Origins of Modern Science*, 5–13. See also Leo Strauss, *On Plato's* Symposium (Chicago and London: University of Chicago Press, 2001), 19.

is itself finally *thumos*. The angry Apollodorus is thus the appropriate narrator for the *Symposium*, which therefore appropriately ends with Alcibiades' charge that Socrates is on the inside altogether unerotic and just wants to make everyone love him as a means to his own self-affirmation. The final problem of the *Symposium* is thus the possibility that there is no such thing as Socratic *erōs*. Socrates, whether, as Alcibiades thinks, for self-affirmation or for self-discovery, simply uses people. He is unerotic.

Or is this missing the point? If we begin with the three occurrences of *dokō moi* in the dialogue, we see that it is first spoken by the angry Apollodorus to introduce his narrative, then by Eryximachus as he is just about to extend the range of *erōs* to the entire cosmos, and finally by Zeus as he gets the brilliant idea to cut the original circle-men, who are guilty of an assault on heaven, in two and so both weaken them and double the number of his worshippers. The three uses thus join together puritanical moralism, anger, and self-contempt (Apollodorus) with the perspective of a god who wishes to increase the number of his adorers (Zeus), with the extension of the beloved to include the whole (Eryximachus). Put together in this way, we can see that these are the elements of Alcibiades' understanding of Socrates, who is like a god and wants all the beauties to adore him, in his inner core is perfectly moderate and holds everyone else in contempt for not being so, and is capable of getting lost indefinitely in contemplation of the heavens. But Alcibiades is wrong in this understanding of Socrates. Not surprisingly, he projects his own longings onto Socrates and renders him unerotic. What, then, is Plato's view?

Alcibiades understands Socrates to be fickle. Indeed, there is some indication in the dialogue that he is not simply wrong. One need only think of Socrates' relations with Apollodorus, Aristodemus, and Alcibiades, and his flirtation with Agathon—not to mention Plato. Socrates never seems infatuated with a particular beloved to the exclusion of all others and so seems to use people for his own purposes—for self-knowledge in particular. But perhaps this ought to make us wonder about the significance of the ordinary fixation on one beloved. Must it not mean that the lover claims a knowledge of his beloved? Yet, as we have seen, if the beloved is a soul, it is never clear that such knowledge is really possible. We have, for example, just witnessed Alcibiades mistake Socrates by reading himself into Socrates. Suppose, then, Socrates is set apart from others not by the calculating utilitarianism of his "*erōs*" but by somehow always allowing himself to be drawn in by the particular beloved yet without so reifying or idealizing the soul in question that he assumes he knows with what or whom he is in love. Socratic *erōs*, then, would be, on the one hand, always of a particular beloved but, on the other, never sufficiently determinate as to drive out the experience of all others. Socrates might say playfully, "When I'm not near the girl I love, I love the girl I'm near," but not quite, for, because Socrates is not wedded to a single beloved, there is for him no clear-cut lover/beloved distinction. For Socrates, love of himself means love of whoever draws him out of himself. He is therefore at once genuinely smitten and at the same time never altogether loyal. This identity in Socrates of utter openness to the other with self-love is the activity of philosophy. In ordinary love, the lover can't get the beloved out of his head. But this means he cannot get a certain vision of the beloved out of his head—a vision that of necessity distorts reality. Yet without any such vision or image, one would never get out of oneself at all. The trick is apparently to allow yourself to be drawn out of yourself but not hold on to the image that draws you and threatens to trap you in a new version of yourself. Alcibiades is wrong about Socrates because Socrates could not affirm himself by being loved by all without first understanding "Socrates" to be a fixed and altogether known being. This, the presupposition of the longing for fame—for *kleos*—is the perennial temptation of the erotic soul. It is the odyssey of Achilles with which we began. But this longing for fame is the truth not of the nontragic Socrates but of the tragic Achilles wannabe, Alcibiades, who, in falling for Socrates in a paradigmatically conventional way, has penetrated the layers of this silenus only to find, hidden at his core, himself.

Index

Freud, Sigmund: structure of soul as ego, id, and superego, 22; theory of internalization, anticipated by Aristotle, 58

Furies: and Orestes, 124, 128; called *potniai*, 125n7

Gaia, 208; cosmos formed by coupling of Ouranos with, 219

Glaucon. *See* Gyges story

gnōsis (recognition) of knowledge, in *De Anima*, 26

Gyges story: construction of soul in, 155–58; *erōs* as metaphor for tyranny in, 146–47, 155; function of *ta kala* in, 148–49; Glaucon's construction of, 141–42; Greeks as paradigm for the human, 152–53; grounded by the power of women, 151–52; in Herodotus (1.8–12), *eidos* in, 142, 147n18; impossibility of Persian dominion, 152; limiting *erōs* in the political, 153–54; mortality in, 155; nature and *nomos* in, 143, 149–50, 157–58; *nomos*, importance of sight for, 148–49; as paradigm for structure of *History*, 143; as paradigm for structure of *Republic* books 4–12, 142; in Plato, *Republic* 359c–360b; contradictions in, 156–57; as poem, 142, 155–57; versus myth of Er, 154–55; versus image of cave, 155; visibility as problem of, 147–48, 156

Hades, 8, 19; discovery by Achilles upon death of Patrocles, 17; as poetic version of morality, 71–72; in *Helen*, called *Ploutos*, 119–20; and Persephone myth, 121; in *Republic*, descent by Er into, 154–55

Harmodius and Aristigeiton: in Thucydides' account of death of Hipparchus, 177; politicized *erōs* of, 188–90

Hawking, Stephen, 81

hearth, 91; as domain of Hestia, 197; gods of (ancestor worship), 210. *See also* Hestia

Heidegger, Martin, 47n20

Helen: causality of gods in, 117; choral odes in, 121; *kalon* versus *philon* in, 122; mixed genre of, compared to *Magic Flute*, 105; recognition, defectiveness and divinity of, 118; role of sight, 109, 116–17; summary of, 106; symbolism of Helen as *eidōlon*, 116, 122; theme of duplicity of identity as revealing of *muthos*, 108. *See also* soul

Hephaestus, as creator of shield of Achilles, 16

Hera, 10; in Herodotus, in Greek version of myth of Io, 144; and "Judgment of Paris," 106, 115; in *Phaedrus*, followers of, seeking a kingly beloved, 198; well disposed to Menelaus in *Helen*, 118–19

Heracleitus, 6; mention of *psuchē* in *Fragments*, 19n2

Herakles, divinity of, for Egyptians, 85–86

Hermae, Socratic account of, 187–88

Hermes: delivering Helen to Egypt, 106–10, 121; statues erected by Hipparchus, 186–88

Herodotus: Greeks as first fully human people in, 101; using language of subjects, 80, 90; as overcoming human temporality, 143; as psychologist, 7; religiosity of, 79; as revealing intrinsic limits of soul, 76; versus Persian *logioi*, 144. *See also* Gyges story; *Helen*; *History* (Herodotus)

Hesiod, 5–6, 125n5; as exemplary of Greek poetry, 76; *Works and Days*, *psuchē* appearing once in, 19n1; quoted in *Ethics*, 66

Hestia, in *Phaedrus*, 197–98, 203. *See also* hearth

Hipparchus: compared to *Minos*, 174n1; love of gain (*philokerdeia*), as theme of, 175–76; love of the good, as theme of, 174; high and ridiculous, as pair in, 176; philosophy as cheating in, 175–76, 184–85; and *Re-*

polis (continued)
    as means of placing good outside
    activity of individual, 63–64; polit-
    ical but contradictory understand-
    ing of human soul, 157
Politics, as completing treatment of
    politikē begun in Ethics, 75
Polyphemus, 35n8
Poseidon, in Iliad, 13, 14
psuchē, 8, 9, 19, 21, 22, 34, 195, 196, 208
puns, 33, 35, 93, 181, 208

ritual, 103, 124, 128, 130, 131, 133–37, 149
Rosen, Stanley, 217n15
Rousseau, Jean-Jacques, 29n4
Russell, Bertrand, 81

Sappho, 6
Scythians, in History (Herodotus): com-
    pared to Egyptians (book 4), 95;
    contradictions of, 92; disputed ori-
    gins of, 91; as embodying principle
    of motion, 96; fluidity of, 90; as the
    poetic people, 96–99
sensation. See Aristotle: De Anima
Shakespeare, William, 108, 115
Sicilian Expedition, 188
silenus, 228
Simonides, and Hipparchus of Athens,
    186
slavery, 76, 92, 98, 219, 220
Socrates: Euripides' plays "patched up
    by," 105; soul of, 223–28
    in Cleitophon: Cleitophon's repre-
    sentation of, 166–67; compared by
    Cleitophon to deus ex machina, 165
    in Euthyphro: erōs of, 227; Euthyphro
    compared to, 217–19; Euthyphro
    outstripped by, 211; as a god, 223;
    indictment by Athens, as object of
    admiration in Athens, 211; indict-
    ment by Athens as self-indictment,
    221n18; as paradigmatic philoso-
    pher, 205; as "perennial patient,"
    208; recantation of attack on erōs
    by, 193; on trial, 220
Solon, 71
Sophist, 143

sophistry as cheating, philosophy ap-
    pearing to be, 185
Sophocles, 6, 93n5, 125n6, 134n17,
    151n27, 214n12. See also Antigone
soul: absent in Euthyphro, 140, 208;
    absent in Hipparchus, 179; alien-
    ated nature of, 3; archaeology of, 2;
    in Aristotle, De Anima, doubleness
    of, 21–27, 32; characteristic mo-
    tion of, 220; in Christian tradition,
    versus Greek, 1–2; connectedness
    to world, 3; existence of, 57; in Eu-
    ripides, Iphigeneia among the Tau-
    rians, potentially tragic character
    of, 133, 136–37; freedom of, 1–2;
    in the gods, 209n8; Greeks, reason
    for privileging, 1–2; in Herodotus,
    causality and, 101; in Hipparchus,
    necessity for self-knowledge of, 191;
    importance of, for philosophy, 139;
    inadequacy of English language to
    define, 2–3; illusive character of, 3;
    immortality of, 16, 195; nutritive,
    28–31; objective nature of, 75; as
    origin of all worth or goodness,
    179n11, 179–80; perfection of, in
    Helen, 119; in Phaedrus, as "other-
    directed," 196, 199; as question
    constituting unity of Phaedrus, 193;
    as psyche, 3; revealing problematic
    nature of political life, 117; "seeing
    double" as defining characteristic
    of, 129; versus "self," 3; sensing,
    31–34, 48; of Socrates, 223–28;
    source of change in, 193; stability
    of, 7, 103; thinking, 34–54; tragedy
    as restoration of reality underlying
    ritual, 135–37
Sparta: account of, in Herodotus, in
    relation to Persia, 79; depicted in
    Helen, 100, 114, 116; disorder of
    double kingship of Sparta, 152
Stesichorus, 106
Stevens, Wallace, 97
Strauss, Leo, 1–2, 208n7; the holy as
    imitating the gods, 213; on Socrates'
    intention to return Euthyphro to
    orthodoxy, 220, 226n3

Printed and bound by CPI Group (UK) Ltd, Croydon, CR0 4YY

09/06/2025